Getting Primaried

Each of the past few election cycles has featured at least one instance of what has come to be called "primarying," challenges to incumbents on the grounds that they are not sufficiently partisan. For many observers, these races signify an increasingly polarized electorate and an increasing threat to moderates of both parties. Robert G. Boatright shows that primary challenges are not becoming more frequent; they wax and wane according to partisan turnover in Congress.

Boatright demonstrates that the recent rise of primarying has corresponded to the rise of national fundraising bases and new types of organizations that provide political partisans with an opportunity to coalesce around candidates throughout the country. Primary challenges supported by interest groups have garnered media attention disproportionate to their success in winning elections. Such challenges can work only if groups focus on a small number of incumbents.

Boatright's study makes three key contributions. First, it presents a history of congressional primary challenges over the past forty years, a history that not only measures the frequency of competitive challenges but also seeks to distinguish among types of challenges. Second, it provides a correction to accounts of the link between primary competition and political polarization. Third, it provides a new theoretical lens for understanding the role of interest groups in congressional elections.

ROBERT G. BOATRIGHT is Associate Professor of Political Science at Clark University.

LEGISLATIVE POLITICS & POLICY MAKING

Series Editors

Janet M. Box-Steffensmeier, Vernal Riffe Professor of Political Science,
The Ohio State University

David Canon, Professor of Political Science, University of Wisconsin, Madison

Getting Primaried

The Changing Politics of
Congressional Primary Challenges

Robert G. Boatright

THE UNIVERSITY OF MICHIGAN PRESS

Ann Arbor

First paperback edition 2014
Copyright © by the University of Michigan 2013
All rights reserved

Published in the United States of America by
The University of Michigan Press
Printed and bound by CPI Group (UK) Ltd, Croydon, CR0 4YY

2017   2016   2015   2014   5   4   3   2

A CIP catalog record for this book is available from the British Library.

Library of Congress Cataloging-in-Publication Data

Boatright, Robert G.
    Getting primaried : the changing politics of congressional primary
challenges / Robert G. Boatright.
        pages cm
    Includes bibliographical references and index.
    ISBN 978-0-472-11870-0 (cloth : alk. paper) — ISBN 978-0-472-02904-4 (e-book)
    1. Political campaigns—United States.   2. United States. Congress—Elections.   I. Title.

JK1976.B573   2013
324.273'154—dc23

                                                              2012042611

ISBN 978-0-472-03585-4 (pbk. : alk. paper)

Contents

Acknowledgments

This book began as a paper prepared for a conference entitled "Going to Extremes: The Fate of the Political Center in American Politics," held at Dartmouth College's Rockefeller Center in June of 2008. It never would have become a book without the encouragement and enthusiasm of several people who listened to my presentations of the research, suggested new angles for looking at the subject, and convinced me that I was onto something interesting. First and foremost among these people was Jeff Berry, who provided feedback on several of the chapters and shared with me the work he and Sarah Sobieraj were doing on a similar subject. Jeff also graciously fielded one particularly panicked phone call I made when I realized that the 2010 election data were throwing a wrench into my argument. Along the way, I presented this work at the 2009 "State of the Parties" conference at the University of Akron's Ray C. Bliss Institute of Applied Politics and at meetings of the American, Midwest, and Western Political Science Associations. Several audience members, discussants, and panel participants also provided helpful comments. In particular, Seth Masket, Michael Heaney, David Magleby, Ron Shaiko, and Ron Hrebenar all provided valuable feedback.

One of the nice features of both the Dartmouth and Akron conferences was that the papers were made available on the Internet. Although I am rather hard on the media in this book, it is important to note that many journalists care deeply about getting the story on primaries right. Ezra Klein of the *Washington Post* and Greg Giroux of *Congressional Quarterly* and *Roll Call* both stumbled on the conference papers, contacted me for further details, and wrote about my work. Talking to both of them helped me to think about how to present the argument here to a wider audience and, perhaps just as important, convinced me that there was a wider audience for the book.

As will become apparent in the pages to follow, a lot of numbers were crunched in the writing of this book. I am grateful to Michael Malbin and Brendan Glavin at the Campaign Finance Institute for helping me to make sense of the campaign finance data on primary challengers. Two capable research assistants, Amanda Gregoire and Marc Kadushin, also helped with some of the data work here, and Clark University's Harrington Fund covered the expenses of their work. My colleague Mark Miller also generously shared with me his stash of materials on congressional elections. John Boatright helped me with the comparisons between interest groups and business firms in chapter 5, but he is not responsible for any problems in those comparisons.

One of the most frustrating things about writing about contemporary politics is the timing of it all. Just when one is wrapping up the book, another election comes along and requires yet more updating of the story. I owe a large debt to Melody Herr, my editor at the University of Michigan Press, for her enthusiasm about this project and for her efficiency in helping to get this book done promptly. I had the good fortune to work with Melody and her staff on my previous book, and once it became apparent that she was interested in this one too, I never had any inclination to take it anywhere else.

Writing a book can be a lonely, painful experience—or so I hear. This one wasn't, and for that (and so many other things), I owe thanks to my wife, Audrey, and my children, Jacob and Dara. This time, I'll let the three of you do more celebrating when the book is done.

Introduction: An Epidemic of "Primarying"?

During the 2004 and 2006 elections, a new word entered the American political lexicon: the verb "to primary," meaning to mount a primary campaign against an incumbent member of Congress. Conservative and liberal bloggers spent much time discussing incumbent members of Congress who, in their opinion, needed to be primaried. Calls for primarying reached a fever pitch during the 2008 election cycle; a quick search of blogs such as DailyKos, firedoglake, and Free Republic turns up numerous calls for politicians to be primaried, based on their overall record or on one or two high-profile votes. In a few cases, the bloggers took aim at incumbents who were ineffective or had been accused of corruption. More often, however, these incumbents were criticized for being insufficiently partisan. In 2008, candidates who were threatened with being primaried tended to be Democrats who had supported some of President Bush's priorities or Republicans who had not supported them. In 2010, liberal groups took aim at Democratic incumbents who had not supported President Obama's agenda, and conservative groups, most notably those associated with the Tea Party movement, took aim at Republican incumbents who had.

Primary challenges to incumbent members of Congress are hardly unheard of, but they have rarely been a subject of national discussion. Congressional primary elections have received little scholarly attention, and the literature on primaries has generally concluded that they are either a minor irritant to incumbents in lopsidedly partisan districts—a byproduct of districts in which winning the primary is tantamount to winning the general election—or the consequence of scandalous misbehavior on the part of incumbents. Until recently, congressional primaries were mostly treated as low-visibility affairs, elections that tell one next to nothing about national politics.

All of this has changed during the past decade. A casual perusal of political websites and of the major American newspapers provides much evidence that primarying (or at least the threat of primarying) has become widespread and is becoming a standard weapon for activists on both the political left and right. After organized labor and progressive groups combined to back primary challenger Donna Edwards in her 2008 defeat of Maryland incumbent Al Wynn, the *Baltimore Sun* quoted a spokesperson for one liberal think tank as speculating that "it is possible that this is part of a larger, anti-incumbent trend" (Olson and Brown 2008). Likewise, an article in *Politico* noted that Wynn's defeat "had nothing to do with the more customary reasons why incumbents fail to win nomination" (Kraushaar 2008)—that is, he was done in not by redistricting or scandal but by being insufficiently partisan. The *Politico* article went on to predict that 2008 would be "a rough election cycle for incumbents facing serious intraparty challenges." Similar predictions were made in 2010 following Senator Blanche Lambert Lincoln's narrow primary win over a challenger backed by the same liberal-labor coalition.

Despite the prominence of such challenges from the left, however, progressive groups have taken their cues from the Club for Growth's strategy of bundling contributions for primary challengers to "RINOs," or Republicans in Name Only. Since 2000, the Club for Growth, a conservative advocacy group, has raised money for and run television advertisements on behalf of several prominent primary challengers to moderate Republican incumbents, including challengers to New Jersey representative Marge Roukema, New York representative Sherwood Boehlert, Pennsylvania senator Arlen Specter, and Rhode Island senator Lincoln Chafee. The club did not succeed in defeating an incumbent until 2006, however, when a conservative challenger ousted moderate first-term Republican Joe Schwarz in Michigan, and it did not succeed in ousting an established Republican until Maryland representative Wayne Gilchrest was defeated in his 2008 primary.

Although the Club for Growth has, by its own admission, been most successful in helping candidates in open-seat primaries (Noah 2004), its campaigns against incumbent Republicans have attracted more attention than its open-seat campaigns. In a well-publicized interview with the *New York Times* in 2003, the club's founder, Stephen Moore, claimed that incumbents "start wetting their pants" when the Club for Growth threatens to run a candidate against them and that it planned to "scalp" Arlen Specter (Bai 2003). By 2006, many on the left openly admitted that the club had inspired them to mount similar challenges. *The Nation* called for challenges to pro-war Democrats (Nichols 2006), and MoveOn.org singled out prominent Democrats who it claimed were insufficiently liberal or were enabling President Bush's policies, particularly in Iraq. Among the most celebrated such challenges on the left was Ned Lamont's victory in the Connecticut Senate primary over incumbent senator Joseph Lieberman.

It is easy to see why primarying makes for an irresistible story line. In a pop culture sense, primarying resembles a common trope in the gangster movie genre—a prominent gang member is suspected of secretly consorting with a rival gang or with the police, and some within the gang seek to bump him off in order to weed out traitors and make an example of him, to keep others in line, and perhaps in order to strengthen their own position in the gang. In a game-theoretic sense, primarying is an example of the "grim trigger" strategy: in order to keep adversaries in line, one must be able not only to make threats but to demonstrate the ability to carry out threats, even when doing so is to one's own disadvantage. Primarying represents a threat not only to the incumbent who is primaried but to those who might support the primary challenge—there is always the danger that, for instance, a liberal challenger to a moderate Democrat will be a weaker candidate in the general election and that the primary challenge will result in the opposition party winning the seat because either the successful primary challenger loses the general election or the incumbent is sufficiently weakened in the primary that he cannot win the general election.

The story behind primary challenges thus requires that the challenger and his or her supporters take on an almost cartoonish quality, as exemplified by Moore's over-the-top claims, the delicious irony of former Democratic vice presidential candidate Lieberman being parodied in advertisements for literally embracing President Bush, or the allegations by the Club for Growth that moderate Republicans Olympia Snowe and George Voinovich were "Franco-Americans" for occasionally putting the brakes on Republican proposals (they were said to be such not on the basis of their ethnicity but on account of the club's equation of their suspect patriotism with the surrender by the French to the Germans in World War II). Such preposterous allegations are absolutely ideal for garnering media attention during the early months of an election year. When the general election is far off, stories such as these offer a better diet for political junkies seeking to gain insight into the fall's elections than does, say, parsing fundraising figures for candidates.

While the gangster analogy may explain the immediate appeal of candidates such as Ned Lamont or the success of groups like the Club for Growth, there is a more theoretically serious aspect to the story as well. An important paradigm in the comparative study of political party systems is the so-called cartel theory (Katz and Mair 1995); in this theory, opposing parties collude in order to minimize ideological conflict and thus to restrict competition between each other. One consequence of this sort of behavior is that parties can maintain some level of power and work toward their policy objectives even when they do not govern. The threat posed by intraparty conflict is a threat geared toward sharpening, not reducing, interparty conflict—toward weakening the cartel. American political parties are, because of the dynamics of the two-party system, unable to enforce ideological homogeneity. Their success depends on compromise. Yet much of the story about heightened ideological polarization during the 1990s and 2000s lies in the efforts by some party leaders to discipline members. While some within the party may seek such discipline, the parties themselves do not provide sufficient mechanisms for doing this. As Hacker and Pierson (2005) point out, the establishment of competition for committee chairmanships and other perks of office has become increasingly tied to partisanship, but these mechanisms are insufficient in that they do not actually threaten the election prospects of individual members of Congress.

Primary challenges, in comparison, have consequences not only for the career advancement of politicians but for their continued ability to serve in Congress. While the cartel theory is an argument about party strength, about the ideological compromises strong political parties will make to maintain power, the evolution of primary challenges and the role that primary challengers have played in diminishing the ability of the parties to keep their candidates in office speak to the weakness of American parties today. I will offer evidence of this later in this book—whereas primary challenges were once most common in states where the political parties were less organized, today's primary challenges can take place almost anywhere, from Western states where the parties have generally played less of a role in organizing voters' choices to states such as Joseph Lieberman's Connecticut, where the parties have historically been able to limit internal conflict and nominate their preferred candidates without difficulty.

Journalists, Political Scientists, and the Primarying Phenomenon

The gangster analogy makes for a good story line to hang on primary challenges. Yet if this was an apt metaphor to describe the isolated challenges of the elections of the early 2000s, it seems we have already begun to think about primaries in a larger sense. As the 2010 election season developed, the results of competitive primary elections were mined by political analysts for clues as to what they foretold about the November general election. Many commentators took note of the "sour mood" of the electorate. A *USA Today* article in May asserted that candidate filings had surged dramatically (Fritze 2010). Could public disaffection with politics, many wondered, lead to still more primary challenges? "Every incumbent is at least a bit endangered," proclaimed political analyst Charlie Cook (2010). The *New York Times* discussed a "wave of anti-incumbent sentiment" and, like Cook, proclaimed that primary challenges were surging (Zeleny and Hulse 2010). There was certainly evidence that this was indeed the case. During the month of May, one veteran House Democrat, West Virginia's Allan Mollohan, was defeated in his bid for renomination; a sitting Republican senator, Utah's Robert Bennett, was blocked from even appearing on the primary ballot; Arlen Specter, now a Democrat, was defeated by a primary challenger; and Arkansas Democrat Blanche Lambert Lincoln was forced into a runoff by a primary challenger. Several other members of Congress, Democrats and Republicans alike, fended off serious primary challenges. The moves of those who were not even challenged—or were not even up for reelection—were dissected with an eye toward what might prompt a future challenge. Several news articles mentioned potential primary opposition to Senate Finance Committee chairman Charles Grassley, who has served as part of Senator Max Baucus's bipartisan working group on health care reform (Brownstein 2009; Calmes 2009). Although Grassley ultimately won renomination without challenge, the threat of primarying was held by some pundits to be a cause of Grassley's reluctance to seek a bipartisan compromise with Baucus. When South Carolina senator Lindsey Graham provided the only Republican vote at the Judiciary Committee hearing for Senate nominee Elena Kagan, the *Washington Post* immediately forecast a 2012 primary challenge, going so far as to list potential challengers (Cillizza 2010b). Less specific threats abounded— the Club for Growth distributed lists of the biggest-spending Republicans, and RedState posted a list, replete with vague references to primary challenges, of Republicans who voted in favor of reprimanding Representative Joe Wilson following his outburst during President Obama's health care address. On the left, a new political action committee, Accountability Now, was launched in early 2009 by prominent left-leaning bloggers, with the same purpose in mind (see Rutenberg 2009).

These developments suggested that as of 2010, primary challenges were no longer isolated occurrences, and the alleged proliferation of serious challenges—a proliferation that coincided with the rise of the purportedly leaderless Tea Party movement—suggested that primarying had gone viral. Writing in the *National Journal*, Ronald Brownstein (2010a) referred to the candidates behind these sorts of challenges as "the candidates that nobody sent." "The base in both parties," argued Brownstein, "appears to have grown increasingly intolerant of defection and insistent on lockstep loyalty." Although Brownstein alluded to the Club for Growth and MoveOn.org in his article, the nature of his title suggested that primary challenges were now a serious threat to the parties, beyond the control of "establishment" politicians. Brownstein listed a number of incumbent senators who would go on to face serious challenges, and he concluded that these campaigns were "especially ominous for congressional compromisers" and that they threaten to "create a political world where no one is in charge."

Newspaper columnists are not, of course, in the business of providing history lessons every time they report on the previous day's election results. The cumulative impact of so many news stories about primaries, occasionally presented in hysterical tones, cannot but lead one to conclude that competitive primaries are not the norm and that we are witnessing something unprecedented. What is missing from these accounts, however, is systematic explanations of what is normal and of why (apart from the electorate's alleged sour mood) we might be witnessing something unprecedented. In every election cycle, it is observed that Americans do not like Congress very much, and in any election cycle, one might be able to put together a story about incumbents who are defeated by primary challengers. Four such defeats in one month could be part of a trend, or they could merely be coincidental.

One way to find out whether such defeats are coincidental is to consider the reasons for the challenges. Not all primary elections are the same, although they are often treated as such. The 2010 primary elections previously discussed, for instance, featured a variety of different types of challengers. Specter had recently switched parties and was regarded with suspicion by some Democrats, Mollohan was criticized by his Democratic opponent for being *too* partisan, and Lincoln was criticized for being insufficiently partisan. Mollohan had also had ethics charges lodged against him. Bennett was a victim of Utah's unorthodox ballot access laws. These are not, in other words, all clear examples of the sort of "primarying" called for by the political left or right, nor should we expect the lessons we draw from these elections to be the same. There is also reason to be dubious about whether ideological primary challenges are truly anything new or whether they are more common or more successful than they ever were. After all, Franklin Delano Roosevelt famously sought to unseat many New Deal opponents in the 1938 Democratic primaries. Perhaps what we are seeing is not anything dramatically new but simply the application of a new name to a recurring phenomenon. To understand whether anything has in fact changed or what these changes mean, we need to be clear about how often primaries happen and why they happen.

While political pundits may not have a responsibility to provide context in their discussions of primaries, political scientists do. Yet political scientists, as I shall argue shortly, have largely bought into the media story line about primaries, partly because there is no established literature within political science on congressional primaries. This may prove the point of many pundits: if political scientists have not devoted much effort to studying primaries, this must be an indication that primaries have not, in the past, been very important. There have been efforts to document the occurrence of congressional primaries, but there have been few systematic attempts to distinguish between the different rationales for primary challenges. Primaries have begun, however, to play a role in discussions among political scientists of what ails American politics today. Political scientists have generally dismissed the allegation that primaries are more frequent than they once were, but they often blame primaries for polarization in Congress. William Galston and Pietro Nivola (2006, 26), for instance, introduce an edited volume on political polarization by asserting that "the dreaded *chance* of being ousted in a primary, however long the odds, now chills would-be centrists in both parties." In the same volume, Brookings Institution scholar Thomas Mann (2006, 280) notes that few incumbents face serious primary challenges, but he alleges that "politicians are demonstrably risk-averse" and that "they might adjust their behavior—by moving to their party's ideological pole—to ward off primary threats that have ended the careers of some of their colleagues in the House." Mann singles out primaries, campaign financing patterns, and redistricting as three of the major sources of congressional partisan polarization.

Other political scientists have supplied similar claims. Hacker and Pierson (2005) make claims about the Republican Party that resemble those of Mann. Theriault (2008, 110) explicitly notes that political scientists' work linking primaries to polarization has been largely speculative, but he goes on to link this speculation, again, to the financing of campaigns and the drawing of lopsidedly partisan districts. Levendusky (2009, 135) links primary competition to the sorting of the parties ideologically, predicting increased primary opposition for moderates of both parties.[1]

Clearly, there is much that we need to know about congressional primaries. This book is an effort to provide some context for contemporary discussions of primarying. In doing so, I shall demonstrate that, for all but a very small number of unfortunate incumbents, the threat of primary competition is largely a paper tiger—though there is something different about contemporary primaries, what is different is not their frequency or their consequences but the fact that the organizations that bankroll these primaries and recruit primary challengers have effectively marketed these challenges to their supporters and the media. The story about primarying makes for compelling reading, but it is a good story only so long as politicians believe it—and there are compelling reasons not to believe it.

Three Claims About Congressional Primaries

Most analyses of the past decade's high-profile primary challenges, in the media and within the political science literature, have revolved around three basic claims, none of which have been conclusively tested. In this book, I seek to address these claims, partly as a means of clearing up misperceptions about today's primary elections and partly as a means of providing systematic evidence about what is unique in contemporary congressional elections.

Primary Challenges Are More Frequent Today Than in the Past

It would be natural to assume, given coverage of congressional primaries over the past few election cycles, that they are more frequent today than they once were. Few accounts of primary competition make the direct claim that there are more challenges today, but one is left with this impression. Consider, for instance, Rhodes Cook's claim in early 2010 that primary elections are "usually a low hurdle for House, Senate, and Gubernatorial incumbents" and his argument that "in historical terms, the number of memorable primary seasons has been limited." Cook cautiously predicted that 2010 would be different. Cook's main concern is with primary defeats of incumbents, but one can conclude that in years where more incumbents are defeated, there are more serious challenges to incumbents as well.

Other accounts of primary competition fail to provide the historical depth that Rhodes Cook provides, but it is often implied. Both Charlie Cook (2010) and Michael Barone (2010), writing on the 2010 elections, cataloged the number of incumbents who faced serious primary challengers in 2010, with Barone noting that 2010 was "a tough year for the over-dog." The implication here, of course, is that incumbents did not have such a difficult time in other years. Barone goes on to note that many of the incumbents who faced challengers were opposed for district-specific or incumbent-specific reasons—they were particularly old, they were embroiled in scandals, they had faced strong opposition in the past, they represented majority-minority districts, and so on. But despite these idiosyncrasies, at some point in Barone's analysis, a confluence of reasons becomes a trend.

The actual data on past primary elections are rarely summarized in any of these studies, and even if we were to ascertain that there are not more primary elections than in the past, this assertion only opens up a host of secondary questions. I will consider three major sets of such questions here. First, how do we define primary competition? Should we limit our consideration to races where the incumbent is defeated or to races where the incumbent is held below a certain percentage of the vote? How do we distinguish between the primary opponent who receives 5 percent of the vote and the opponent who receives 45 percent? Second, how do we distinguish between types of primary opponents? It may well be that the number of primaries has not changed dramatically, but perhaps the number of instances of "primarying" has changed. Some types of primary challenges, after all, ought to be independent of the political climate or resistant to any sort of temporal trend, while others ought to be predictable. We have no reason to expect that the number of incumbents who become enmeshed in scandals will vary in predictable ways across elections, but we are led to expect, from the coverage of ideological challenges, that there is a temporal trend at work in those cases. Third, how do we distinguish between types of incumbents? Perhaps some types of incumbents are more likely to face primary opponents than they were in the past. The story generally told about primarying is that there are fewer moderate Democrats and Republicans than there once were, but these few moderates face more primary challengers than did moderates in bygone eras. So we effectively have two different trends that may offset each other—a declining number of centrists and an increasing percentage of moderates who face primary opposition.

Ultimately, asking how many primary challenges take place in any given year is more difficult than it appears. This is so in part because one rarely sees statistics on primary competition, apart from simple tables of the number of incumbents defeated in their renomination bids each year. We have bits and pieces of the story, but we are far from having a compelling and comprehensive story about variations in primary competition across election cycles. Absent such a story, it is natural to assume that we are witnessing some sort of change in the importance of primary elections.

The Threat Posed by Primary Challenges Is Greater Today Than in the Past

Another way to look at the claims of Charlie Cook and others about primaries is to say not that incumbents face more opposition in primaries but that incumbents have reason to worry more about such challenges. Saying that incumbents have reason to worry says nothing about what incumbents do, only that there are legitimate reasons for them to do something differently in order to ward off opposition. If there is a threat involved in primaries and if that threat cannot simply be explained by cataloging the number of such challenges, we must look at the characteristics of the challenge itself.

The explanation of this threat is generally clear in the literature. When Hacker and Pierson (2005, 123) note, for instance, that "primary contests have become more important than they once were," they are speaking of the increasing power of the party base (in their account, the Republican base, but other accounts note the power of the Democratic base). What does this "power" mean? One can look at this power primarily in terms of vote share, but this is problematic in that it confuses the result of the challenge with the threat it poses. The obvious place to look, then, is at the financial threat posed by primary challengers. A 2001 study of campaign finance in congressional primaries (Goodliffe and Magleby 2001, 68)—one of very few such studies—noted that it is rare for ideological groups to put money into congressional primaries. This is so, the authors note, partly because there are so few competitive primaries and partly because groups that truly wish to make a difference in the composition of Congress prefer to wait until the general election. The study concludes that virtually all strong primary challengers rely on their own funds. Has something changed in the degree of threat posed by primary challengers, particularly by ideological challengers, in the past decade? Looking at the behavior of interest groups and at the manner in which primary challengers raise money can help us answer this question. It surely does not lead to the only answer to the question—there are many other characteristics of primary challenges that might vary across time—but these are arguably the most measurable changes.

To restate, speaking of the "threat" of a primary challenge is just as problematic as speaking of changes in the number of primary challenges, but for a different reason. We can look at the numbers of primary challengers across time, and we can do so with little reference to incumbent behavior. Measuring threat, however, is somewhat subjective. Is a primary challenger who holds the incumbent to less than 70 or 60 percent of the vote more of a threat today than in the past? One might argue that votes speak for themselves, but we cannot know whether the incumbent perceived the challenge to be a threat or did anything to respond to the challenge while the campaign was happening. Perhaps a challenger who captured 30 percent of the vote while spending little money merely tapped into resentment of the incumbent but had little ability to defeat the incumbent, while a challenger who received a similar vote share but raised a substantial amount of money forced the incumbent to aggressively campaign and to spend money. In this second instance, the ultimate vote share may be a consequence of the fact that the incumbent perceived the challenger to be a threat and responded. For one to argue that challengers pose more of a threat than they once did implies that more challengers have the ability to win, whether or not they actually do.

Primary Challenges Have More of an Impact on Members of Congress Than They Once Did

The most common assertion in the literature, both scholarly and journalistic, about primary challenges is that they have consequences for the behavior of members of Congress. While not all claims of this nature—witness Mann's and Galston and Nivola's assertions previously cited—make it explicit that we are talking about ideological challenges, the context of these writings generally assumes that these are the sorts of challenges that have consequences. If it is clear that an incumbent is being challenged based on his or her competence or on the grounds of some sort of ethics charge, the consequences may be quite simple and unremarkable. Just as is the case when such allegations are made in the general election, the incumbent would be expected to work to clear his or her name or to show a renewed vigor in representing the district. We cannot necessarily measure these sorts of responses, but they would seem like responses that members of Congress might make to criticisms in any political context. Again, there is no clear temporal element here.

However, if ideological challenges have more of an effect than they once did, we ought to see measurable responses on the part of incumbents. The problem, though, is that some incumbents may successfully preempt challenges by changing their behavior before actual opponents emerge. There is no way to measure whether incumbents change their behavior out of fear of being challenged. We can only measure whether incumbents are affected by the challenge after it has taken place. We can, however, measure responses to actual challenges in two ways.

First, we can measure whether primary challenges have an effect on incumbents in the general election. The existing literature on this subject is worth revisiting insofar as its findings have been mixed and because it has rarely distinguished between types of primary challenges. One enduring claim in the literature on polarization is that moderates are becoming fewer in number because moderate districts are becoming fewer in number—as Masket (2009, 49) puts matters, "In a 'safe' district, the median general election voter is a partisan rather than an unattached independent; the tension between pleasing both the primary and general median voters is largely alleviated." This means, then, that an incumbent who survives being primaried should feel few effects in the general election; conservatives have nowhere to turn in the general election if they are unhappy with a moderate Republican representative. Ideological primary challenges, according to the standard logic, should have no consequences in the general election. This is a claim, again, that should be reevaluated.

Second, we can at least begin to test the assertion that primaries (or the threat thereof) pull incumbents away from the political center. We must, again, distinguish between types of challenges, and we must limit our analysis to incumbents who survive primary challenges. Are they chastened by the challenge they have beaten back? Do they change their behavior in order to ward off a future challenge? In looking solely at incumbents who do face challengers, we may be looking at the most recalcitrant moderates—candidates who refuse to change their behavior even when confronting an actual intraparty challenge. However, these are the candidates who have the most to worry about from primaries—the threat for them is real and will likely continue to weigh more heavily on them in future elections than is the case for incumbents who have not actually faced a primary challenge.

We must, then, be cautious about declaring that we have the ability to answer the claim that primaries or the threat of them lead to polarization. It seems unacceptable, however, to allow this claim to linger within so much of the academic and journalistic literature as the default explanation for excessive partisanship in Congress. It is possible, I would argue, to bring more light to bear on this question than has traditionally been provided.

Explaining Primary Challenges to Incumbents

This book is an effort to test each of the preceding three claims. It is premised on the contention that the only way to understand changes in congressional primary competition is to understand the reasons for primary challenges. Accordingly, I have reviewed accounts of congressional primary challenges from 1970 to the present and categorized different types of challenges that were at least minimally competitive. I employ these categories to distinguish between different types of challenges in terms of their frequency, their characteristics, and their effects. Some will find these categorizations somewhat reductionist—no election truly features only one line of attack. This is, however, an attempt both to expand the palette of traditional studies of congressional primaries, which rarely take into account the actual issues raised by the candidates, and to bring some order to a rather chaotic aspect of American elections. Primary elections are regulated by the states; variations in state election laws ensure that many states have particularly idiosyncratic methods for choosing nominees, for choosing who can appear on the ballot, or for choosing who can vote in primaries. Assessing the reasons why challengers have emerged enables one to step away from state-specific, institutional arguments in order to look at what appears to be a national phenomenon—the rise of the ideological primary challenge—while still allowing that primary challenges sometimes arise not because of national trends but because one particular incumbent made a mistake or because one particular issue is of concern to voters in one particular congressional district.

I spend relatively little time reviewing literature on congressional primaries here, because there is very little written about primaries. As I shall recount in subsequent chapters, most of what we know about the dynamics of primary elections has come from analyses of presidential primaries, which have different historical origins and patterns of competition and have had, for their creators, different goals. Most of what we know about congressional primaries has come from studies of state primary laws or of primary elections for open seats. I shall note here where these literatures, as well as the literature on congressional general elections, are of relevance, but this book is largely an attempt to tell a story that has not before been told.

Chapter 1 briefly summarizes some of the noteworthy features in the history of primary challenges to incumbents since 1970, with an eye toward seeing whether differences in accounts of these can supply us with testable hypotheses about changes in congressional primary competition. The chapter then outlines a theory of congressional primary challenges that draws on three developments that have taken place over the past four decades: changes in the types of political candidates that emerge in congressional elections; changes in the nature of the two major parties' coalitions and electoral strategies; and changes in the types of interest groups involved in congressional elections. These developments, I contend, indicate that the number of primary challenges is of less importance than the nationalization of these primaries and the possibility that these challenges signify the rise of a new breed of ideological nonparty groups.

Chapter 2 provides a more systematic look at patterns in the occurrence of congressional primary challenges. There are, in fact, fewer primary challenges today than there were thirty years ago, although there are more than there were during the 1990s. This is the case for all types of primary challenges; despite the national attention to primaries, "primarying" is not at all a new phenomenon. There are, however, predictable patterns to primary challenges—it is not the case that there is any sort of secular trend among primary challenges. Primary challenges wax and wane according to partisan turnover in Congress; volatile election cycles, such as those of 1974, 1994, and the 2006–10 period correspond to increased competition in primaries. We cannot necessarily impute motives to challengers based on simply measuring the occurrence of primaries, but it would seem that heightened ideological conflict within Congress breeds ideological conflict in primary elections as well.

Chapter 3 is a consideration of one of the most easily identifiable and comparable characteristics of congressional primary challengers, the financing of their campaigns. As such, it takes on the claim that primary opposition poses a greater threat to incumbents today than it once did. While chapter 2 indicates that the likelihood of any incumbent actually being challenged has changed little over the past four decades, campaign finance data indicate that when incumbents are challenged, they face candidates who look quite different from challengers of years past. Primary challengers over the past four decades have consistently relied mainly on individual donors and on their own pocketbooks, receiving little help from interest groups, political action committees (PACs), or party committees. But today's primary challengers, particularly today's ideological challengers, raise far more from individual donors than was the case in the past. The rise in individual contributions to primary challengers is far more dramatic than the changes in financing for incumbents or for general election challengers. This increase speaks to an orchestration of individual contributions. If organized interests do not give PAC money to challengers in significant amounts, they do appear to be playing a role in promoting primary challengers to their members. Ideological primary challengers raise far more of their money from outside of their states than was once the case; this is, in fact, one easy way to distinguish ideological challengers from other types of primary challengers.

Chapter 4 addresses the consequences primary challenges have for the challenged incumbents, above and beyond the cases where incumbents lose. I will show that there is little evidence that primary challenges have an effect on Congress, save in the very rare instances where incumbents are defeated. It may well be that all incumbents are somewhat scared of primary challenges, but the incumbents who actually face challengers tend to win reelection anyway, and these incumbents do not behave differently in subsequent election cycles. Such incumbents may eventually be replaced by more ideological successors, but the evidence of this is mixed. There is little evidence that moderates are pushed toward retirement because of primary challenges. The only way that primary challenges may have consequences is if incumbents believe the rhetoric about primaries and change their behavior not in response to actual challenges but in response to the threat of being challenged.

Chapters 2–4 document that evidence that congressional primary challenges play the outsized role frequently attributed to them is at best murky. Like many political phenomena, however, the conventional wisdom about what primary challenges mean can and, to an extent, has become self-perpetuating; that is, if everyone believes the story to be true and acts accordingly, the story might as well be true. As I argued at the outset of this introduction, the notion that incumbents who seek to straddle the distance between the two parties are at risk of defeat from self-styled enforcers of party discipline is a compelling story. It is replete with larger-than-life characters and with intrigues within the Madisonian factions that are today's Democratic and Republican parties. Primary challengers are hardly the "candidates that nobody sent" that Ronald Brownstein described. Somebody did send them, and the story of how they were sent requires a retelling of the incentives for those other American factions, organized interests, and how these incentives have changed in the new era of American campaign finance. Political parties are generally considered to be, as Anthony Downs (1957, 25) has famously put matters, "teams of men seeking to control the governing apparatus by gaining office." Yet interest groups are not motivated by the pursuit of office. They seek to expand their resources, to garner public attention, and to corner a "niche"—to acquire market share—in the competitive world of interest group politics. Traditional theories of interest group behavior tend to define these niches as having to do with particular areas of public policy, but over the past decade, many groups have begun to identify functional niches, where what is most important is not what policy matters groups care about but what sorts of political activities they perform. Congressional primaries have become just such a niche, and groups—both formally organized ones, such as the Club for Growth and MoveOn.org, and informal groups, such as the Tea Party or aficionados of particular blogs—have sought to fill the niche of encouraging primary opposition. In chapter 5, I explain in greater detail how these changes have come about and how the nexus between political parties and groups has shifted over the past decade.

The focus of this book is limited to primary challenges to incumbent members of the House and the Senate. The book does not attempt to provide a complete account of congressional primaries; I say little in this book about primaries for open seats or for the right to challenge an incumbent in the general election, for instance, though ideological conflict in these types of primaries can be just as fierce and though some of the greatest successes for groups like the Club for Growth or MoveOn.org have taken place in primaries that do not feature an incumbent.

This book is also not an attempt to disprove anyone's account of primary competition, largely because there are no comprehensive accounts of primary competition. Many of the comments I have already made here about the claims of political pundits or political scientists are somewhat glancing blows—offhand remarks about primary competition in books or articles that address much broader issues. I contend that Americans have been left with the *impression* that primary elections are more frequent and more consequential today and that this impression is created by fleeting assertions, not by anyone's detailed argument. If nothing else, this book is an effort to supply data to a discussion that has too little data to fall back on. Statistics on primary competition are hard to come by, and categorizations of different kinds of primary candidates are nonexistent. This book does not aspire to be the last word on primaries, only a brake on extravagant claims about them and a resource for those who would make historical arguments about primary competition.

The Normative Consequences of Primary Challenges

There is certainly a tone of disapproval in many of the accounts of primaries I have already cited, and this is clearly a disapproval shared by many members of Congress. The day he announced his retirement from Congress, Representative Barney Frank (a fierce Democratic partisan) could not resist lamenting the decline of bipartisanship, describing the Republican Party as consisting "half of people who think like Michele Bachmann . . . and half of people who are afraid of losing a primary to people who think like Michele Bachmann" (Isenstadt and Tau 2011).[2] Frank's biases aside, one can imagine similar statements being made by Republicans about Democrats. What is noteworthy here is that no one would accuse Frank of being a centrist; his comments indicate that even veteran politicians at the extremes of the two parties are discomfited by primarying.

I have strived here to maintain an agnosticism, however, about the effects of primary competition. I have done so in part because I believe that claims about the effects of primaries are overstated. Yet even if the consequences attributed to them—most notably a heightening of polarization between the parties in Congress, a loss of bipartisanship, and a dearth of centrist representatives—were proven to be a result of heightened primary competition, we need to discuss whether this is a bad thing. There is substantial evidence that these are problems for the functioning of Congress, but primarying is not a powerful enough force to blame for these things. It may be a symptom of the problem, but for four reasons, I am skeptical that it is even that.

First, no one would deny that some level of competition or at least the potential for competition is a prerequisite for democratic government. If there are many districts in which winning the primary is tantamount to winning the general election, we might blame redistricting for this problem, but we ought not to blame primary elections for this. Again, the number of primaries has not demonstrably increased over the past four decades, even as congressional districts have been redrawn to be less competitive. Theriault (2008, 62–84) has shown that more congressional districts have become safe for one party or the other since the 1970s; given this, perhaps we ought to see more primary challenges to incumbents. The fact that we do not indicates that primary challenges are simply too idiosyncratic to blame for any movement away from the political center on the part of incumbents. Jacobson (2006) questions the linkage between district extremism and redistricting, noting that partisan sorting among voters during the 1990s—after the 1992 redistricting—matters far more than the drawing of districts, but again, this sorting bears no relationship to primary challenges (see also Levendusky 2009, 135–36; Fiorina 2009, 165–68). The number of primary challenges actually declined during the stretch of the 1990s that Jacobson discusses. So either way one approaches the matter, primary challenges seem unlikely to be a major culprit.

Second, whatever one's partisan inclinations, some incumbents clearly deserve to be primaried. If an incumbent is demonstrably out of step with his or her district, it seems reasonable to conclude that such an incumbent ought to be challenged. As I shall demonstrate in chapter 2, there is some evidence that this is the case, but the evidence is slight. Moderate members of Congress who represent moderate districts or states are not out of step with their districts, but these moderates are also rarely challenged. Conspicuously missing among the conservative targets of primary challenges during the past decade have been moderate Republicans such as Maine's two senators, moderates who represent an area of the country that is hardly friendly territory for the GOP. Chapter 2 provides some evidence that Republican targets of ideological primary challenges are less out of step with their districts than are Democratic targets, but the number of cases is small enough that we should not make too much of this partisan difference. Perhaps the most unseemly consequence of the primarying phenomenon might be instances where incumbents well within the mainstream of their parties are attacked for being insufficiently partisan. This does occasionally happen, but such challenges rarely succeed (just as most primary challenges rarely succeed). We might perceive some injustice to this or to the element of randomness to it, but this seems merely an inevitable consequence of democratic elections—challengers can say whatever they want, and it is up to the voters to sort out what is true and what is not.

Third, most incumbents do not get challenged in their primaries—in any given election cycle or at any time in their congressional careers. Let us consider the great unproven (and probably unprovable) claim about primaries—that even a small number of instances of primarying can have an impact on the members of Congress who are not being primaried. According to this claim, the situation of Joseph Lieberman will have influenced many other members of Congress, members who took from the Lieberman challenge the lesson that it could happen to them. Lieberman cast very few votes that marked him as a particularly ripe candidate for a challenge, so it is hard to say that he was uniquely deserving. If this is the case, however, the lesson may merely be reinforced—a challenge could happen to anyone who sought to even once engage in any sort of bipartisanship. Both the causal variables (what brought on the challenge) and the consequences (the alleged change in member behavior) are impossible to quantify. Because incumbents also cannot quantify these things, though, the story becomes self-reinforcing. If incumbents believe they have reason to be scared, they may adjust their behavior, but these adjustments are small enough that we ought not to make too much of them. In the 2010 elections, for instance, some members of Congress perhaps sought to distance themselves from Washington in order to avoid anti-incumbent sentiment. Members always do this to a degree. But, of course, they could do this for reasons that have nothing to do with primary challenges. Perhaps they think about primaries when they do it, but if we cannot find any measurable effects, it seems that we should temper our speculation about the role of primaries here. This is not to say that waves of anti-incumbent sentiment within the electorate are not real or that there is nothing to be learned from periods of volatility in congressional elections, but these are very small pieces of the puzzle, and most incumbents will win reelection in any given year without being noticeably touched by these things in their primary campaigns.

Finally, let us consider the party response to primary challenges. For some, primary challenges represent a takeover of the parties by the more ideological elements of their bases, a takeover that has been thoroughly documented in many states (see, e.g., Masket 2009). For others, primaries represent a rebuke of the parties in general, a claim often documented with data on citizens' affect toward the parties. The most measurable party response, however, is that of the national party organizations. The parties' House and Senate campaign committees, simply due to the fact that they are organs of Congress, have always maintained a stance of neutrality in primaries or have worked to support incumbents in the face of any sort of primary challenge. It is virtually unheard of for the party committees to support challenges to incumbents. Yet the differences between primary challenges present a mixed picture of how these challenges influence the health of the parties. In some instances, a primary challenger may help the party in the general election; in others, a successful challenge may jeopardize the ability of the party to hold the seat. Even an unsuccessful challenger can so damage the incumbent that the incumbent will go on to lose the general election. As recounted by one such challenger, Rhode Island Republican senatorial candidate Steve Laffey (2007, 11–33), the party committees make substantial efforts to ward off divisive primaries; one would expect that, although they were unsuccessful in Laffey's case, they frequently do succeed. There are some congressional districts that are so overwhelmingly partisan that the incumbent's party will hold it no matter who it nominates; in such districts, however, the incumbent is rarely a moderate.

As I shall demonstrate in this book, the haphazard nature of primary challenges indicates that there are few regions of the country today where party organizations are able to ward off primary challenges. This may be a symptom of the weakening of local party organizations, but it is a relatively small symptom—one that eludes quantification and speaks more to the fact that the groups behind the most high-profile primary challenges have paid little heed to the obstacles party organizations pose to their efforts. If the grasp of parties on congressional nomination politics has weakened, this shift is more representative of the institutional priorities of the party campaign committees than to any sort of grand shift in primary competition. Primaries could happen indiscriminately, anywhere and to anyone, but they rarely do.

Conclusions

It is probably more exciting to read about primary elections today than I suspect it was during the 1970s. The stories included in this book reflect this, especially when contrasted to the rather dry state-by-state analyses of laws governing primary elections that so dominate the scant literature on primary elections written in decades past. This may be somewhat due to the proliferation of political media sources—one can now read fresh accounts of campaign politics and engage in online speculation about upcoming elections at any point in the election cycle. The batch of congressional primaries held on June 8, 2010, was dubbed "another Super Tuesday" by sources as varied as *Congressional Quarterly, Politico,* National Public Radio, and *Time.* To my knowledge, this is the first time congressional primaries in a midterm election have received this appellation. Yet amid all of this hype, what has changed the most is the hype itself.

This book seeks, first, to provide evidence that places primary elections in perspective and, then, to explain why, if so little has changed, we now care so much more about congressional primaries. I take two approaches toward these goals. First, I seek to provide a dose of skepticism about whether primary elections have changed, and to the extent that they have, I seek explanations that actually address demonstrable facts about the differences, not in the number of primary challenges today or their effects on Congress, but in the nature of the support for primary challenges to incumbents. Second, I seek to provide historical data on congressional primaries over the past four decades, data that have rarely played a role in discussions of primaries. For those seeking an argument, my first approach may be more appealing, despite the fact that there is much I cannot explain. For those seeking a starting point for further analysis or merely seeking a resource for looking at congressional primaries, my second goal should, at a minimum, be of service even to those who reject my argument.

If nothing else, I hope that this book will help to rescue the study of congressional primary competition from its undeserved status as a minor area in political science. The media have already largely done this work for me, so I am seeking to help the discipline to catch up. Perhaps studies of primaries have been lacking because they have generally been seen as rather dull affairs. As the assorted bits of punditry I have already summarized should make clear, this is not the case today. My argument, however, is that it was never really the case. In some ways, primaries are more intriguing than general elections: there is little orchestration of the message of primary candidates, the way there is of strong general election candidates, and the fact that primary challengers must often scrape together coalitions with little help from established campaign strategists makes for an unpredictable and fascinating mix. Collectively, as I shall argue in this book, primaries do not necessarily "mean" anything, at least not all of the things that have been ascribed to them by those who would use them to explain contemporary American politics. But for incumbents who find themselves facing opposition from the same party activists who may once have been their strongest supporters or for challengers who are inspired to run for office due to unhappiness with their party's standard-bearer, they mean quite a bit.

1 | Congressional Primary Challenges: A Brief History and a Theoretical Explanation

Very few members of Congress get there by knocking off incumbents of their own party in primary elections. So high are the odds against beating an incumbent, in fact, that most ambitious politicians tend to wait their turn. A primary challenger will find little help from the party's established donors, who will tend to view an incumbent of their party as the most likely victor in the general election. Incumbents have at their disposal a lengthy list of individuals who have contributed in the past, the resources of their party campaign committees to draw on in raising funds, and established relationships with a variety of PACs and organized interests. An ambitious politician risks alienating party supporters and incurring the wrath of the incumbent he or she challenges. It is unlikely that an incumbent who wins the primary but loses the general election or who decides a few years down the road to step down will be a future supporter of someone who has run against him or her in the primary.

For the past four decades, the literature on congressional elections has gradually fleshed out the contours of how races are run in the "candidate-centered" system of elections that has developed since the 1960s. To the extent that this literature takes primaries into account, it has held that it takes extraordinary circumstances for an incumbent to find himself or herself in danger in the primary and that it often takes a political neophyte to instigate a primary challenge. In this chapter, I shall look at how primary elections fit into this literature, at whether the nature of primaries has changed, and at how our theoretical accounts of primaries merit updating. I shall seek to demonstrate that the candidate-centered paradigm does not adequately explain primary challenges; that at least as far as congressional primaries are concerned, we are entering an era where a select number of primaries have effectively been nationalized; and that the appropriate way to look at primary challenges is as a forum for outside groups and players within the extended party network to hash out their ideological disagreements. To do this, I begin with an illustrative story.

Consider the case of Blanche Lambert, the 1992 primary challenger to Representative Bill Alexander in Arkansas's first congressional district. Alexander had represented this overwhelmingly Democratic district since 1968. He was a member in good standing of the Democratic leadership, serving as a deputy whip and a member of the House Appropriations Committee. The first district, despite its heavily Democratic registration, was not a particularly liberal district, but Alexander was not a particularly liberal Democrat. He was liberal enough that he had at times faced primary challenges from the right, and he had survived close calls in the elections of 1986, 1988, and 1990, winning 52 percent of the vote in 1986, 66 percent in 1988, and 54 percent in 1990. Alexander's Achilles' heel was not his politics, however.

By all accounts, Alexander was not an aggressive campaigner, something that may have inspired primary opponents. Alexander had faced criticism in the 1980s for his frequent foreign travel; his 1986 opponent, state senator Bill Wood, claimed in his campaign that Alexander had taken nineteen taxpayer-financed trips. Although Wood did have prior political experience, he was heavily outspent by Alexander. Alexander's 1988 foe, who had served as Wood's campaign manager, lacked both experience and money. Alexander's 1990 opponent, Mike Gibson, had little political experience, but the growing perception that Alexander was vulnerable enabled Gibson to raise far more money than Wood had.

Alexander might have survived the 1992 election as well had it not been for the House banking scandal.[1] A record number of incumbents faced primary opponents in 1992, a consequence of congressional redistricting, the banking scandal, and a general anti-incumbent environment. Alexander did not draw a strong primary opponent: Blanche Lambert was only thirty-one years old; she had never held elective office; and, as was frequently noted in the media, her résumé included a two-year stint as Alexander's receptionist, following her graduation from college in 1983. Lambert was clearly a more personable candidate than Alexander—a *Roll Call* article the week before the election quoted Lambert's campaign manager as saying that "once [voters] talk to her, they walk away liking her" (Curran and Glasser 1992). A *Washington Times* article appearing in the same week, which described her as "attractive and articulate, but not well known" (Aynesworth 1992), contended that she would fall short eventually, because she did not have enough money. Alexander suffered not only because his check bouncing played into the narrative that Lambert (and the media) offered about Alexander's ongoing financial and ethical problems but also perhaps because he was frequently linked to another check-bouncing Arkansas incumbent, Representative Beryl Anthony. Ultimately, Lambert defeated Alexander in the primary, winning 61 percent of the vote. Anthony lost as well. Lambert went on to win the general election, garnering 70 percent of the vote, while Anthony's primary opponent lost to a Republican.

Although Lambert might argue that it was her campaign that made the difference, much of the coverage of her 1992 victory focused more on what Alexander had done to lose the seat than on what Lambert had done to win. What Alexander had done to lose the seat had little to do with national political trends; Lambert came into office promising to be a more vigorous, sympathetic member of Congress, but she said little about whether she would vote any differently than had Alexander.

When one reads accounts of primary election defeats, stories such as Lambert's are common. In 1992, the same year that Lambert won her congressional seat, veteran Chicago Democrat Charlie Hayes was ousted from his seat by Chicago alderman Bobby Rush, nine-term California Republican Robert Lagomarsino was beaten by political novice (and multimillionaire) Michael Huffington, Democrat Chester Atkins lost his seat in Massachusetts, and nine other congressional incumbents were successfully challenged.[2] In all of these cases, primary defeats were seen as instances where incumbents had lost touch with their districts, could not be bothered to campaign, or had made ethical or political mistakes. Defeats such as these may add vigor to Congress, but they do not necessarily change the priorities of Congress.

Blanche Lambert served only two terms in the House. In 1996, now married, going by the name of Blanche Lambert Lincoln, and pregnant, she stepped down. In 1998, however, she ran for the seat of retiring Senator Dale Bumpers, handily defeating the state's attorney general in the primary and winning the general election by a margin of 53 to 42 percent. She was reelected by a similar margin in 2004. One could argue that in her congressional career, Lincoln strived to be everything that Alexander was not. She had few ethical scrapes, and she carved out a role in the Senate as an expert on agricultural policy and other issues of particular concern to Arkansas.

In 2010, Lincoln herself narrowly survived a primary challenge. It was, however, a very different challenge from the one Lincoln had run in 1992.

During the years after Democrats regained control of the Senate in 2006, Lincoln, a senator from a state that gave John McCain 59 percent of its presidential votes in 2008, found herself positioned to the right of most Democrats on many issues, including climate change, labor policy, and financial reform. In the months leading up to the 1992 election, voters in Arkansas's first district might have sensed trouble for Bill Alexander, but in all likelihood, no one outside the district would have noticed or cared. In early 2010, however, liberal activists around the country were told by MoveOn.org that Blanche Lambert Lincoln was planning to vote against the Democratic health care bill, that she opposed expanding college scholarships, that she wished to gut the Clean Air Act, and that she opposed President Obama's foreclosure plan. MoveOn declared in an e-mail that Lincoln was "one of the very worst corporate Democrats in Congress" (Sherrard 2010). In another e-mail sent out during the campaign, MoveOn declared that if Lincoln were to be defeated in her primary, "Washington will never be the same again. Democrats will know their base won't put up with them cutting deals with corporate interests and undercutting the change that Americans demanded in 2006 and again in 2008" (Ruben 2010). MoveOn's fundraising pitch was tailored to the locale of the recipient; for instance, in its efforts to support Lincoln's opponent's campaign, MoveOn told residents of Worcester, Massachusetts (a city, to state the obvious, very far away from Arkansas), "We need 4 people in Worcester to donate to hit our goal of $200,000."[3]

Lincoln's 2010 opponent, Bill Halter, was hardly the sort of political neophyte that Lincoln was when she first ran for Congress. Halter was the Arkansas lieutenant governor, so he might have been a formidable candidate even absent the appeals from outside groups. Halter's criticisms of Lincoln were entirely political, not personal. Just as Lincoln's first campaign was more about the incumbent than about her, however, so Halter's campaign was more about Lincoln than about him. In January of 2010, the leaders of the American Federation of State, County, and Municipal Employees (AFSCME) and the United Steelworkers discussed challenges to centrist Democratic senators; Lincoln was the only senator considered who was up for reelection in 2010. In an article discussing the unions' plans, Halter's name was not even mentioned (Barnes 2010a). While some Democratic leaders privately noted that Halter might not be the liberal he was often made out to be—and that whoever won the race would have a difficult time holding the seat against a strong Republican opponent—the race was framed by the national media as a referendum on whether the

Democratic base in Arkansas would accept Lincoln's occasional devia-
tions from party orthodoxy.

The manner in which this race was framed may ultimately have been
Halter's undoing. On May 18, Lincoln defeated Halter in the Arkansas primary by a narrow margin of 44 to 42 percent. However, like several other
Southern states, Arkansas requires a runoff if no candidate receives 50
percent. In the weeks preceding the June 8 runoff between Lincoln and
Halter, Lincoln argued that the race was about who best represented the
people of Arkansas and that outside groups were attempting to determine
who should represent the state. Lincoln drew on the help of former president Bill Clinton in order to drive this message home. She prevailed in the
runoff by a margin of 52 to 48 percent.[4]

Lincoln's victory was not, however, the end of the jockeying over what
the race meant. Her 1992 race was about Bill Alexander; had she lost, perhaps Alexander would have gotten some sort of message from his victory—
given his prior primary challenges, he may have simply resigned himself
to having to face primary opposition. At any rate, it seems unlikely that
anyone else would have taken much from it. In contrast, in an interview
appearing in Time on May 14, 2010 Lincoln noted, "There's just a lot of
national groups that are using this race to make points" (Von Drehle
2010). Win or lose, observers would get these points. In a June 9 *Washington Post* article, former presidential candidate Howard Dean argued that
more centrist incumbents would face challenges like Lincoln's unless they
"act like real Democrats," a spokesperson for MoveOn agreed that Lincoln's narrow victory was a warning to other Democrats, and former AFL-
CIO political director Steve Rosenthal termed Halter's race a "phenomenal
victory" for the cause of holding wayward Democrats accountable (Rucker
and Slevin 2010). The political director of the Service Employees Interna-
tional Union (SEIU) speculated that the challenge would make Lincoln a
better senator in the future, and AFSCME president Gerald McEntee argued that labor had "put down a marker in the sand" in the Lincoln race
(Barnes 2010b).

Polling during the primary showed Lincoln losing the general election
by a hefty margin, and polls taken in the month after her runoff victory
placed her 20 to 30 percentage points behind her Republican opponent.
Lincoln eventually closed the gap slightly, but she never really made the
general election race competitive, losing to Republican John Boozman by
a margin of 58 to 37 percent. The *New York Times* reported in October that
Lincoln found little support from the national Democratic Party after the

primary—not because of her politics, but because of her double-digit deficit in the polls—and that despite being "well respected by her colleagues and well liked by many of her constituents," she ran the sort of race generally run by underfunded challengers (Leibovich 2010). Some disgruntled Halter supporters speculated that Halter might have done better in the general election (Barnes 2010b).

One might draw two lessons from Blanche Lambert Lincoln's career. The first is uncontroversial—primary elections can take a variety of shapes. Both elections may have been referenda on the incumbents, but beyond this, Lincoln's 1992 campaign had little in common with Bill Halter's 2010 campaign. One might also conclude, though, that the very nature of primary elections has changed. Perhaps we have moved from predominantly local affairs, in which the occasional incumbent simply loses touch with the voters, to national affairs, in which questions such as whether an Arkansas Democrat ought to be different from a Massachusetts Democrat are largely moot. However, this could all be coincidence. It could be that some incumbents in 1992 faced challenges like the one Bill Halter ran in 2010 and that some incumbents in 2010 faced challenges like the one Blanche Lambert ran in 1992.

A Brief History of Primary Challenges, 1970–2010

Blanche Lambert Lincoln's story bears a striking resemblance to those of several other moderate members of Congress who have recently faced strong primary challenges from the left (in the case of Democratic incumbents) or the right (in the case of Republican incumbents). To find out exactly what Lambert's story tells us, it is necessary to look more closely at the evolution of primary challenges over the past four decades.

Given the claims detailed in the introduction to this book about the development of congressional primary challenges, the 1970s make for a good place to start in looking at congressional primaries and, more specifically, at the role of ideology in primaries. Prompted by the Democratic Party's McGovern-Fraser reforms, more states had begun to use primaries to select nominees, and the Supreme Court's congressional redistricting decisions of the 1960s had compelled states to draw districts according to a set of federal standards regarding population size, contiguity, and so forth. The single-member, equal population districts and the two-step election process we take for granted today only truly came to exist in the

1970s. While some variations remained in states' election procedures, we can be more confident about attributing primary challenges to national trends over the past four decades than we can in discussing elections in earlier decades.

In presenting a history of primary challenges since 1970, I shall here seek to highlight the stories behind these challenges—the issues that prompted challenges, the incumbents who were defeated or nearly defeated, and the relationship between these challenges and the larger political picture in each election cycle. To some readers, this may seem a bewildering collection of anecdotes, and that is partly the point. As I emphasize throughout this book, some of the stories that get told about primary competition are at odds with the data or at least give rise to ideas that are not borne out by careful study of trends in primary competition. The stories presented in this chapter are an effort to lay out some of the more noteworthy instances of primary competition; they are an effort to place contemporary instances of primary challenges in historical context while maintaining a respect for the idiosyncratic forces that cause primary challenges.

As a road map for the discussion to follow, figure 1.1 shows the overall distribution of competitive House primary challenges by year; as this figure indicates, there is not necessarily a consistent trend in the number of primary challenges. The past four election years have seen an increase in primary competition compared with the 1998 and 2000 elections, but there are far fewer incumbents facing primaries in the 2000s than there were during the 1970s. With the exception of the 1992 election—which featured a combination of a scandal that affected many incumbents (the House banking scandal) and redistricting—and the 2010 election, the number of competitive primaries was remarkably consistent between 1982 and 2008, with a range of fifteen to thirty competitive primaries per year. Patterns in Senate competition are less clear; I present data on the Senate in chapter 2.

Let us briefly consider some of the stories behind the challenges summarized in this figure. In each of the first three elections of the 1970s, ten or more members of Congress lost their bids for reelection. The years 1970 and 1972 were relatively typical in terms of overall turnover in Congress: the Republican Party lost twelve seats in the House in 1970, a midterm election year under a Republican president, and gained twelve seats in 1972, a presidential election year in which the Republican incumbent, Richard Nixon, easily defeated Democratic challenger George McGovern. Fewer incumbents were defeated in 1976 (three) and 1978 (eight). The

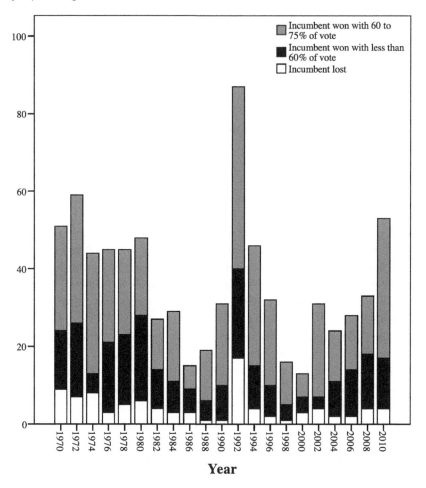

Fig. 1.1. Number of House primary challenges, by year

most atypical feature of elections in the 1970s was the Democratic land-slide in the 1974 election, held as the Watergate scandal was breaking. Democrats picked up forty-nine seats in the House and four seats in the Senate that year, and the incoming Democratic freshmen were markedly more liberal than the rest of their caucus.[5] Democrats may well have won almost all of the potentially competitive seats that year; they went on to win only one additional House seat and no Senate seats in 1976, and they lost fifteen House seats and three Senate seats in the 1978 midterm under Democratic president Jimmy Carter. In other words, with the exception of the 1974 gains, the 1970s followed typical trends in terms of general election results.

The 1970s featured a steady level of primary competition, a pattern that, at first glance, is not obviously related to larger political trends. Brady, Han, and Pope (2007) note that 1970 featured the largest number of defeated incumbents of any nonredistricting year, singling out Ronald Dellums's victory in the Berkeley area of California, Craig Barnes's defeat of twenty-year veteran Byron Rogers in Colorado, Paul Sarbanes's victory over thirteen-term representative George Fallon in Maryland, and Parren Mitchell's victory in the majority-minority Baltimore-area district in Maryland. All of these Democratic primary challengers ran with the support of liberal activist groups—civil rights groups, anti-war groups, or environmental groups. As Brady, Han, and Pope note, primary defeats accounted for 83 percent of all defeats of incumbents in that year—a high and highly unusual percentage. This surge in primary defeats was noted at the time; political scientist Jeff Fishel (1973), who remarked on the fact that six Democratic committee chairs lost to primary challengers in 1970 and 1972, speculated that this was the start of a trend toward greater primary competition.

The context of the 1970 elections, then, was conducive to issue-based challenges. Environmental activism had surged at the time, and anti-war activism was high. Subsequent elections followed a similar trend, albeit with the subtraction of Vietnam as a campaign issue. In 1972, a year complicated by redistricting, four Democrats faced strong challengers from the left. Most notably, Emmanuel Cellar, first elected in 1922, was narrowly defeated by thirty-year-old Elizabeth Holtzman.[6] Holtzman raised a variety of issues in her campaign, including Cellar's opposition to the Equal Rights Amendment and some questionable financial dealings on his part. As noted in that year's *Almanac of American Politics* (Barone et al. 1973, 686), however, the deciding factor in this race may simply have been that Holtzman ran an active campaign in a district that had not seen one for some time. Many other vulnerable incumbents—including Pennsylvania's Robert Nix, Texas's Wright Patman and William Poague, and Louisiana's Otto Passman—appear to have been vulnerable largely because they did little campaigning and represented districts where their party had an overwhelming advantage. Only one incumbent—Californian George P. Miller—was defeated or seriously challenged by a challenger who made Vietnam a focal point of his campaign. Busing, however, was a major issue in several campaigns, all of them Democratic districts. Michigan Democrat Lucien Nedzi, for instance, narrowly defeated an anti-busing candidate in a four-way primary, despite the fact that Nedzi also claimed to oppose busing (Barone et al. 1973, 500).

Through each of these elections, there was a steady stream of ideological campaigning in primaries, both from the left and the right, but it is not clear that either ideological or single-issue candidates had the sort of success that might stem from outside support in 1972 or 1974. We do not have campaign finance data to settle this issue, but in many instances, it seems plausible to assume that candidates were inspired by local conditions. In particular, the candidates who made busing an issue do not appear to have done so with support from national groups.

Competition in congressional primaries then declined and remained low for the next few elections, with the exception of 1980. Six incumbents lost to other incumbents in primaries following the 1982 redistricting, but only four other incumbents were defeated that year, and only twenty-seven incumbents faced credible challengers. Only one ideological challenge (in an overwhelmingly Democratic district in Florida) and one issue-based challenge (regarding social security, again in a heavily Democratic Florida district) took place. Only seven incumbents in the House were defeated in primaries from 1984 through 1990, and no Senate incumbents lost their renomination bids. The number of challenged incumbents declined, to twenty-nine in 1984 and to fewer than twenty in both 1986 and 1988. Ideological challenges were scarce as well—there were only six during this time, and there was no galvanizing national issue sparking primary challenges. The small number of ideologically tinged races that happened during the 1980s appear to have been primarily local affairs and not always instances of challenges from the margins. For instance, in both 1982 and 1984, Michigan Republican Mark Siljander faced primary challengers who argued that Siljander was too conservative for the district; he was defeated in the 1986 primary by Fred Upton, a Republican with somewhat more mainstream views. A similar fate befell California Republican Ernest Konnyu, who won a seat in the San Mateo area in 1986, was arguably too conservative for the district, and lost to moderate Republican Tom Campbell in 1988. Campbell, like Upton, appears simply to have been a better fit to the district and to have had no trouble winning without nationalizing the race.

One way in which 1980 was somewhat atypical, however, was in the level of competition in Senate primaries. There are generally so few Senate primary challenges that there is little to be gained from looking at a graph (akin to figure 1.1) of these challenges across different decades or different election years. During each of the four decades considered here, there were approximately fifteen competitive primary challenges. Seven Senate incumbents lost their seats during the 1970s, most for rather idiosyncratic reasons: they were appointees who had weak party support, they had become involved in scandals, or they simply faced another, more popular politician. In 1980 alone, however, eight Senators faced competitive primary challenges, and four of these senators were defeated. In chapter 2, I provide more analysis of these cases, but 1980 stands out as the only unusual year; beyond this, there is no clear trend.

There were a handful of high-profile challenges from the extremes in these election years, but they also show little national influence; they are largely instances, again, of incumbents who already had frequent troubles from the more partisan wings of their parties. Maryland Democrat Beverly Byron, who represented the somewhat conservative panhandle of Maryland, faced relatively competitive liberal challengers in 1988 and 1990. On Maryland's Eastern Shore, conservative Democrat Roy Dyson faced a liberal challenger in 1990; Dyson would go on to lose the seat to centrist Republican Wayne Gilchrest in the general election. Fred Upton, who had defeated Mark Siljander in 1986, faced a conservative challenger in 1990. All these challenges occurred in districts where moderate representatives have had trouble balancing the demands of the primary and general electorates, but the incumbents in these challenges had not raised the ire of partisan groups, and there is little evidence of national involvement in these primaries.

These primaries took place at a time of low turnover in Congress overall. One account of the 1988 election summed up the general election results by noting the unusual factors that contributed to general election defeats and noting that all of them "could be explained by factors that were idiosyncratic rather than structural" (Baker 1989, 169). On average, thirteen incumbents were defeated in each year from 1984 through 1990, and there was little change in the partisan balance of Congress.

Nineteen ninety-two, however, presented a major structural readjustment—the unusually disruptive 1992 redistricting—combined with scandal within Congress (the House banking scandal), a strong Democratic tide, and an even stronger anti-incumbent tide within the electorate. Including incumbent-versus-incumbent matchups brought about by redistricting, nineteen House members were defeated in their parties' primaries, and an astounding eighty-seven incumbents faced serious primary challengers. At least ten of the challenges, including six of the defeats, can be attributed primarily to redistricting, according to my reading of the summaries in the *Almanac of American Politics* (Barone et al.

1993). Scandals, primarily but not exclusively the House banking scandal, played a role in nineteen of these challenges and five other defeats. Only two of the defeated incumbents, however, lost to challengers who were primarily concerned with ideology.

The level of primary competition in 1994 and 1996 was nowhere near as high as it had been in 1992, but it was higher than it had been during the 1980s. Incumbent defeats in these years tell the traditional story—of the five House incumbents who lost in these two elections, three were African American Democrats who were challenged by younger African Americans, for reasons of competence, not ideology. Another losing incumbent, Greg Laughlin, had switched from the Democratic Party to the Republican Party. Although much of the media's attention in 1994 was on the Republican Party's gains in the general election, however, there were some signs that moderate Republicans were in trouble. California's Bill Thomas and Kansas's Jan Myers, for instance, both faced conservative challengers in their party's primaries in 1994; two Democrats also faced liberal primary challengers.

As the number of competitive general election races became fewer during the elections of 1996 through 2004, so the number of competitive primaries declined. This is not necessarily what one might expect. Many analysts noted that following the 2002 redistricting, the number of competitive districts had declined (Jacobson 2006; McDonald 2006). Having a greater number of lopsidedly partisan districts might indicate that primaries would become more important, not less. Only one incumbent lost his primary in 1998—California Republican Jay Kim, who had been plagued by scandal for most of his career. The three primary losers in 2000 included one incumbent who had switched parties (New York Republican turned Democrat Michael Forbes), another who had had difficulty throughout his career navigating the ethnic politics of his district (California Democrat Matthew Martinez), and Utah Republican Merrill Cook, who always kept his distance from the national Republican Party and ultimately lost his primary to a centrist challenger with stronger GOP ties. All but three of the ten incumbents defeated in primaries in 2002 and 2004 lost partly due to redistricting; the three exceptions were California Democrat Gary Condit, who was embroiled in a particularly high-profile scandal regarding the mysterious death of an intern from his office, and two African American Democrats who lost to more centrist African American challengers.

Only sixteen incumbents in 1998 and thirteen incumbents in 2000 were held to less than 75 percent of the primary vote—by far the lowest numbers in the past forty years. The number of challenges increased slightly in 2002, to thirty-one. One must keep in mind, however, that this was a redistricting year. There were still far fewer challenges in 2002 than there were in prior redistricting years. This decline in competition serves to highlight the number of instances of "primarying" in these years; that is, there were not more challenges to centrist representatives in these years than in prior elections, but the percentage of such challenges was higher. The Republican Party's capture of the House and Senate majorities in 1994 and its narrow majorities in the subsequent Congresses put pressure on moderate Republicans to support the party on major votes. The party's narrow majorities may also have shone a spotlight on wavering moderates. Almost all of the instances of primarying in these years took place on the Republican side. From 1996 through 2004, twenty-two Republicans were challenged from the right. Moreover, twenty of the twenty-two Republican challenges happened in just six states—Illinois, Maryland, New York, Pennsylvania, New Jersey, and Michigan. All of these are states where there has been a history of moderate Republican representatives.

From 1994 through 2004, only three Democrats faced primary challengers who were running from their left. As Republican primary challenges began to garner more attention, however, primarying appears to have become a more attractive option on the Democratic side. The 2006 challenge to Joseph Lieberman certainly contributed to this perception. There was not an atypically large number of primary challenges in 2006, but there were more than there had been in any nonredistricting year since 1996. Although some of the year's twenty-eight competitive primary challenges took place for the usual reasons, there were seven instances of primarying in 2006, five of which took place on the Democratic side. In contrast to Republican instances of primarying, many of which took place in states where the party had a tradition of moderation, four of these five Democratic challenges took place in traditionally Democratic areas— Rhode Island, the Chicago area, California, and Maryland. Many of the Republican moderates targeted in primaries in previous years had now retired, to be replaced by either Democrats or more conservative Republicans; the most consequential ideological primary challenge on the Republican side was to first-term incumbent Joe Schwarz, who had narrowly won an open seat in 2004 with help from some liberal groups. Schwarz lost his renomination bid in 2006 to conservative challenger Tim Walberg (Walberg, in turn, won the general election in 2006, lost his seat to a Democrat in the 2008 general election, and won it back in 2010).

With Democrats holding a comfortable advantage in the House going into the 2008 election, the parties were relatively evenly split in the number of ideological primary challenges. Four Democrats—in Georgia, Maryland, Iowa, and the Chicago area—faced challengers from the left. Three Republicans—in Maryland, South Carolina, and Utah—faced challengers from the right. The two Maryland races, in which Democratic incumbent Al Wynn and Republican incumbent Wayne Gilchrest were defeated, are among the purest cases of ideological challenges.

In the Wynn race, challenger Donna Edwards, who had narrowly lost to Wynn in 2006, received support from MoveOn.org and maintained an active presence on ActBlue, the online portal for campaign contributions. Although this is a majority-minority district, race appears to have played little role in the election (both candidates were African American), save perhaps for the fact that Edwards appears to have done better among white voters than among African American voters. Wynn's former district included sections of one almost entirely black county, Prince George's County, and parts of a more racially mixed neighboring county, Montgomery County. According to one analysis, Edwards received 67 percent of the vote in Montgomery County and 55 percent of the vote in Prince George's County (Fisher 2008). Edwards won the general election easily in this overwhelmingly Democratic district.

Gilchrest faced two credible opponents, state senator Andy Harris, who was backed by the Club for Growth, and former Senate candidate and self-financer E. J. Pipken. Gilchrest had faced ideological challengers in the past, including one in 2002 who had been backed by the Club for Growth. In past races, Gilchrest had been the recipient of support from the Republican Main Street Partnership, a group that had been formed to support moderate Republicans. Harris won the three-way primary with 43 percent of the vote, while Gilchrest and Pipken had 33 and 20 percent, respectively. Despite the Republican tilt of Gilchrest's former district, Harris was narrowly defeated in the general election by centrist Democrat Frank Kratovil (although Harris would handily defeat Kratovil in a 2010 rematch).

The sheer volume of money that went into these races—particularly into the Edwards race—is somewhat unusual. Shortly before the election, a *Washington Post* analysis noted that Edwards had raised $441,000 as of the last filing date before the primary and that 85 percent of her individual contributions had come from outside Maryland. Independent expenditures favoring Edwards totaled $1.2 million and included mailings and television advertisements by MoveOn.org, the SEIU, and the League of Conservation Voters (Helderman 2008). A MoveOn solicitation for donations to Edwards listed as her supporters the Sierra Club, EMILY's List, the United Food and Commercial Workers, ACORN, Democracy for America, and Women's Voices, Women Vote (Ruben 2008). This was indeed a large coalition for a primary challenger. Postelection commentary on the race speculated that the Edwards's victory may have partly stemmed from the aggressive campaign waged by Barack Obama in Maryland (Maryland is one of the few states where the presidential and congressional primaries are held on the same day) and that Edwards may have received support from newer voters organized by the Obama campaign (Fisher 2008). In the Gilchrest race, the Club for Growth spent an estimated six hundred thousand dollars on advertising; it had few other groups as allies, and Gilchrest had only a small independent campaign by the Main Street Partnership and the League of Conservation Voters (Kraushaar 2008).

There were signs in 2008 that, despite the success of Edwards and Harris, the push for ideological challenges to wayward incumbents was limited. Another high-profile race was the renomination bid of first-term Illinois Democrat Dan Lipinski, who was criticized by liberal challenger Mark Pera for being too frequent a supporter of Bush. Lipinski was likely seen as vulnerable partly because of his inexperience and his lack of political ties within the district—he is the son of the previous representative, William Lipinski, but had not resided in the district prior to winning the seat. The elder Lipinski unexpectedly withdrew from the 2004 race shortly before the filing deadline, leaving no time for anyone but his son to put together a campaign. Although Pera's campaign was also supported by MoveOn, Pera did rather poorly, finishing with 25 percent of the vote in a four-candidate race, while Lipinski received 54 percent. Although some of the other incumbents primaried in 2008 had long been discussed on liberal or conservative blogs—incumbents such as Iowa's Leonard Boswell and Georgia's David Scott—none of these candidates' opponents were the beneficiaries of national fundraising campaigns. This pattern held true in the Senate as well—of the four Senate incumbents with primary competition (Lindsay Graham, John Kerry, Frank Lautenberg, and Ted Stevens), only one (Kerry) faced an ideological challenger. Kerry's challenger ran poorly compared to the other three, Kerry paid little attention to him, and although the focus of the challenge was ideology, Kerry's unsuccessful presidential bid likely played a role in the challenge as well.[7]

The existence of primarying in both parties was evident in 2010 as well, but, despite the media attention lavished on the Arkansas Senate primary and the Alaska Senate primary, liberal and conservative activists alike were surely aware early in the election cycle that the election had the potential to yield substantial Republican gains. Many of the most visible battles between party insiders and insurgents took place not necessarily in challenger-versus-incumbent primaries but in open-seat primaries or out-party primaries where "establishment" candidates fought with outsiders. Such was the case in Republican Senate primaries in Colorado, California, Indiana, Nevada, Tennessee, and Delaware, as well as in open-seat House primaries in South Carolina, Idaho, and Florida. This dynamic was also evident in several gubernatorial races.

Despite this, the 2010 House of Representatives primaries still featured more challenges than in any year since 1992, and the challenges occurred in both parties and for a variety of reasons. I discuss several of these primaries at length elsewhere in this book, so I shall provide only a cursory summary here. Four House incumbents were defeated. Two of these four (Michigan Democrat Carolyn Cheeks Kilpatrick and West Virginia Democrat Alan Mollohan) had been accused of ethical misdeeds, and one of the two defeated Republicans (Mississippi's Parker Griffith) had first won his conservative district in 2008 as a Democrat and had switched parties in December of 2009. South Carolina Republican Bob Inglis was the fourth defeated incumbent. Inglis had been seriously challenged in 2008, and although he had a relatively conservative voting record, he had broken with the party on the Troubled Asset Relief Program and the Iraq War and had generally antagonized many South Carolina conservatives with his rhetoric. Inglis is the only House Republican who was clearly a victim of challenges inspired by the Tea Party, but these challenges should have come as no surprise to him. Ideological challengers had somewhat better luck in the Senate, where two Senators were defeated in their primaries, another was denied access to the party's ballot at all, and three others faced strong challengers.

One noteworthy feature of the 2010 election, however, was the number of new faces among those who faced ideological challengers. On the Democratic side, North Carolina's Heath Shuler, Utah's Jim Matheson, and Georgia's John Barrow—all indisputably among the more conservative members of the party—faced competitive liberal challengers for the first time in their careers, as did two Democrats closer to the party's ideological center, North Carolina's Larry Kissell and Massachusetts's Steven Lynch.[8] On the Republican side, Alabama's Jo Bonner, California's Mark Bono Mack, Texas's Kay Granger, and New Jersey's Leonard Lance all faced conservative challengers for the first time. None of these four were particularly liberal in their voting habits. With the exception of Lynch's challenger (discussed in chapter 5), none of the challengers to these representatives received very much media attention or raised very much money, but one could argue that the allegation that an incumbent has betrayed the party, has consorted too frequently with the opposition, or has simply spent too much time in Washington was a compelling enough claim to fuel at least a slightly competitive primary challenger, regardless of the truth behind that allegation. In May of 2010, the *Washington Post*'s Ezra Klein asked whether 2010 would be "the year of the primary challenge." That year did feature more challenges than previous years, but for almost all of the House challenges and at least some of the Senate challenges, the impetus for the challenges is beclouded with idiosyncrasies—most of the incumbents who lost or who nearly lost had problems other than a lack of fidelity to their party. Such is the case in most of the elections I have summarized here. The 2010 election, however, purportedly featured many challenges to moderates. It is therefore hard to know what to do with the fact that while we can find clear cases of primarying in the races where underfunded challengers held incumbents like Mary Bono Mack or Jo Bonner to 71 and 75 percent of the vote (respectively), we can identify only a small number of cases where a challenge that was indisputably based on ideology was more successful.

What are we to make of this summary of primary competition over the past forty years? At first glance, it is a bewildering array of names and anecdotes. Individual story lines may emerge, but it is difficult to place them into any sort of clear context. In any given year, there are few competitive primaries and even fewer primary upsets of incumbents, making it is easy to latch onto small trends that encompass only a handful of incumbents. Also, as we have seen in the case of Dan Lipinski, the actual reason for a primary challenge is not always clear. Challengers may talk about ideology or about alleged incompetence or scandal, but this talk may be a manifestation of what the challenger thinks the best strategy is, not necessarily a reflection of what the incumbent has actually done.

The point of this account, however, is that these sorts of anecdotes carry a substantial amount of weight within the political class. That one, two, or three incumbents are defeated in any given year by candidates who allege that the incumbent is insufficiently partisan may mean nothing, but it is natural to focus on these instances precisely because they are rare and unusual—and because, in instances such as Lieberman's, they have featured particularly well-known politicians. It is natural to assume that they mean something.

The Changing Significance of Primary Challenges

The preceding explanation of elections in the 2000s indicates that one can at least hypothesize about patterns within the two parties among the incumbents who are challenged. It is difficult to extract a pattern for this purpose from the elections of the 1970s, partly because there is simply so much else going on—there are more primary challenges, and it is difficult to claim any sort of meaning regarding the ideological challenges among them, because of the noise introduced by other sorts of primary challenges. It is clear from this explanation, however, that ideological primary challenges are nothing new; they arise periodically, and they appear to be more common in years when there is more general upheaval in congressional elections.

However, if we look at the relatively uncompetitive election years of the late 1990s and early 2000s, contemporary primary elections look more treacherous, at least for some incumbents. The vast majority of incumbents have little to worry about from primaries. The challengers who appear may be little different from primary candidates in previous years, but some of these challengers can draw on a base of support that is far different from the support available in the past.

This development should call our attention to three different types of literature on elections—the literatures on candidate emergence, on political parties, and on the role of interest groups in elections. None of these literatures do justice to today's primary challenges. In particular, changes in the composition of political parties and in the types of interest groups active in elections call for a reevaluation (or, given the scant literature on congressional primaries, an initial evaluation) of the meaning of congressional primary challenges. None of these changes are exclusively *about* primary challenges, but when put together, they show why we should think about Blanche Lambert Lincoln's near defeat in 2010 using a different theoretical lens than the one we use in assessing her 1992 victory. I seek to provide such a lens in the remainder of this chapter.

Changing Primary Challengers?

In any given congressional district, there is a large pool of potential congressional candidates. Numerous studies of congressional general elections have discussed the characteristics of congressional candidates, the strategic decision about whether or not to run, and the choice of what themes to raise in the campaign (see, e.g., Fowler and McClure 1989; Kazee

1994). Theories of political ambition emphasize the career ladder that most politicians seek to climb: a seat in Congress is a step up on that ladder, but not necessarily the final step; politicians do not want to harm their ability to continue to move up by running a long-shot race that will antagonize fellow partisans (see Schlesinger 1966, 1994). The literature on political ambition is of limited applicability to most challenger-versus-incumbent congressional primaries, simply because savvy politicians will surely understand that their best chance at winning a congressional seat lies not in challenging an incumbent of their own party but in waiting for that incumbent to retire or to seek higher office. This is the case even when the incumbent has obvious flaws (Layzell and Overby 1994). The literature does suggest that while primaries are often a referendum on the incumbent, those who challenge the incumbent do not do so solely because of any one shortcoming of the incumbent. They run because they want the seat. The reasons reported for the challenge, then, may simply be the challenger's assessment of what is most likely to work, not the actual reason for the run.

The extent to which this is the case may vary according to the level of political experience of the challenger. Some analyses of primary challenges have sought to distinguish between those that feature a politically experienced challenger and those that do not (Pearson and Lawless 2008). Experienced challengers are more likely to be running to win than are inexperienced challengers. In general elections, for instance, single-issue candidates have sometimes noted that they have run to raise the visibility of their issue, without actually expecting to win (Boatright 2004). For primary challengers, the same logic would seem to apply. The problem, however, is that while it is hard enough to distinguish between reported reasons for a challenge, it is even harder to distinguish between the *actual* motivations of challengers.

A primary challenger who values his or her stature within the party takes substantial risks in running against an incumbent. He or she cannot count on the support of traditional interest groups or party leaders, and as a result, a challenger who wishes to be politically competitive must create a network of donors and supporters from scratch. As the preceding history shows, there are exceptions to this rule—in the Gary Condit case, for instance, the incumbent was so weak that his opponent could essentially run the same sort of race he might run were he running in an open-seat primary. This means that although the 2008 Pearson and Lawless study shows that experienced challengers tend to outperform inexperienced challengers, there are so few experienced primary challengers that we must treat these results with care. Perhaps experienced challengers do better not because their experience translates into better campaigns but because they only select races where incumbency will not be a particularly great impediment. These races are rarely of the sort where ideological attacks on the incumbent will work; they are races where the incumbent has been implicated in a scandal or is otherwise weakened.

Gary Jacobson, creator of the standard measurement of candidate quality, shows, in his well-known textbook on congressional elections (2004, 166–69), that the appearance of a politically experienced challenger in the general election can be predicted by presidential popularity, trends in partisanship, and the state of the economy; that is, quality challengers emerge when the *party* holding a particular seat is struggling. For obvious reasons, it is problematic to use these variables to explain the emergence of primary challengers. The most we can say is that a quality challenger will outperform an inexperienced one, but this is largely because quality challengers will pick their battles and will defeat less-experienced candidates in races to face an incumbent. As I discovered in running many of the analyses in this book using Jacobson's measure, there is little that measurements of candidate quality can tell us about changes in primary competition across time.

There are, of course, exceptions to this rule, and these exceptions may provide some insight into changing levels of primary opposition to incumbents. David Canon's aptly titled book *Actors, Athletes, and Astronauts* chronicles the success of celebrities and other politically inexperienced candidates in congressional elections and in Congress. Canon (1990, 2) defines an amateur candidate as someone who has not held prior elective office. While it is true that everyone has to start somewhere, most treatments of political ambition assume that Congress is certainly not the first step on the political ladder; those who run for Congress in their initial bid for elective office will, according to Canon, have different goals than those who run for Congress only after gaining political experience at a lower level. Canon (1990, 24–31) distinguishes between three different types of amateur congressional candidates—the ambitious amateur, who runs for Congress because he or she is "in a hurry" and wishes to skip the first few steps on the ladder; the policy amateur, who runs because of a desire to raise particular issues; and the hopeless amateur, who runs for the thrill of running. In his discussion of primary challengers to incumbents, Canon contends that primary challengers are unlikely to be concerned with their prospects for general election success and are highly unlikely to have prior political experience. Given Canon's typology, it would seem that primary challengers are likely to be motivated either by a desire to do their democratic duty (i.e., to respond to appeals from others to run) or to wish to raise particular issues. Primaries are an excellent place to look for policy-oriented amateurs. The fact that Canon's study of amateurs provides such a nice typology of amateurs but does not dwell very much on primary elections is further indication that the sort of phenomena we see today represents somewhat of a change.

The unifying trait of Canon's political amateurs (think particularly of his book title here) is that some of the more successful among them can raise money and attract the attention of the voters based on their name recognition and nonpolitical appeal. For such candidates, perhaps a primary challenge makes sense; such candidates face less obvious risks if they lose, since they do not have established political careers anyway. The only problem, however, is that there are so few of them in Canon's data (which cover the period from 1972 to 1988), and there are no obvious instances of this in the recent primary challenges I have detailed in this chapter and the introduction. If we consider recent ideological challengers such as Andy Harris, Donna Edwards, Ned Lamont, and their ilk, there are no celebrities here, although some of these candidates arguably became celebrities because of their challenges.

I do not wish to belabor my dismissal of existing paradigms on candidate emergence here; I shall briefly return to this literature in the concluding chapter of this book. For now, it is sufficient for me to note that, with one qualification (or perhaps one and a half qualifications), I shall treat primary challengers in the manner that Jacobson treats experienced challengers—they are a symptom of the incumbent's problems, but we cannot necessarily get very much leverage on the situation by focusing on such hard-to-quantify factors as the challengers' skill at campaigning. I can and shall focus on primary challengers' line of attack in the campaign— that is, whether they choose to emphasize the incumbent's ideology, ethical misdeeds, or competence—but I shall treat these lines of attack as signs of potential vulnerabilities of the incumbent, not as a means of evaluating the challengers themselves. Presumably, an incumbent vulnerable on the basis of scandal or incompetence will face a challenger who talks about these things, but it is the incumbent's performance that has made this the logical choice for a challenger. The challenger's decision to focus on this theme is not easily amenable to analysis.

My qualification concerns fundraising. Canon's book, as the title suggests, is a description of congressional elections in an era where candidates essentially were on their own in raising money for their campaigns.

Without the resources of their party, amateur candidates needed personal wealth or name recognition in order to garner attention and money. The success of amateur candidates in a select number of recent primaries indicates that there are now nonparty networks that some primary challengers can tap into. This is a change of some consequence. There is, in effect, a pot of money for the candidate who steps forward to challenge a candidate who has strayed too far from party orthodoxy. Where this money came from, how much there is, and how candidates can find it are subjects I shall consider in the discussion of interest groups that shortly follows and in subsequent chapters.

As to my half qualification, the reader may notice that the story I have previously provided about candidate emergence does not quite capture what went on in the Blanche Lambert Lincoln story. Lincoln's 2010 opponent, Bill Halter, did, after all, hold statewide office, as have a few other Senate primary challengers who ran ideological campaigns. Perhaps this speaks to a different dynamic in Senate races. As much has been suggested by Jonathan Krasno (1994), who noted that experienced challengers appear in Senate general elections more frequently than in House general elections and who argued that this is a symptom of the lower reelection rate of Senate incumbents. It is certainly possible that the dynamics of Senate primary challenges are different than those of House primary challenges—again, I shall explore this in subsequent chapters. It is, however, hard to make a systematic argument that Halter's race was notably different from primarying instances in other Senate races over the past few election cycles, such as the challenges to moderates Joseph Lieberman, Lincoln Chafee, and Lisa Murkowski, where the challengers had little or no prior political experience. Experience may matter here, but as I will argue shortly, ideology seems likely to matter more.

Changing Political Parties

The literature on candidate emergence does not necessarily provide very much insight into why primary challenges might have changed, in their frequency or in their importance, over time. Apart from potentially illuminating the differences between parties, it cannot explain what is, in the end, conflict within the parties. Political parties have changed in consequential ways. To investigate this, we must look at the role primaries have played within the parties over time and at the ways in which parties and our theories about them have changed.

Treatments of primary elections at the presidential level have generally evaluated changes in procedures of candidate selection, with reference to what these changes can tell us about the strength or weakness of the political parties. Although the literature on congressional primaries is small enough that this is not necessarily a going concern in that literature, the same sort of reference point can help us understand how the role of parties in primary elections has changed. Prior to the late nineteenth century, it was standard practice for parties to choose their nominees according to whatever practices party leaders thought appropriate. State governments were reluctant to place restrictions on how nominees were to be chosen, partly because the states would then be expected to take the place of the parties in paying the costs of holding primary elections (Ezra 2005). Charles Edward Merriam, a professor of political science at the University of Chicago, published the first book-length study of congressional primaries in 1908. Merriam's account vividly describes the Progressive Era's concern with weakening the grip of party machines on nominations at all levels, and it links the establishment of primaries to the introduction of the Australian ballot during the 1890s. For Merriam, primaries were a means of opening up the political process, but they were controversial, partly because their establishment depended on judicial acknowledgment that parties are not necessarily private organizations—that there are some circumstances in which their internal affairs must be regulated by the state. Merriam also details the differences between northern primaries, in which parties had reason to be concerned that they might lose in the general election if they did not choose their strongest candidate, and southern primaries, in which winning the Democratic primary was tantamount to winning the general election.

The direct primary was one of the great achievements of the Progressive Era. Robert LaFollete's "Wisconsin idea" of direct primaries took hold during the 1890s in states such as Minnesota, Wisconsin, North Dakota, and California, where parties were traditionally less well organized, and it spread quickly throughout many northern states (see Ansolabehere, Hansen, et al. 2006, 2010; Merriam and Overacker 1928; Galderisi and Ezra 2001). By 1915, all but three states had adopted direct primary laws (Ware 2002, 15).[9] Southern states, which had traditionally employed primaries for a different reason—for the purpose of disenfranchising African American voters—used primaries that were nominally open but that actually restricted voting to those with a history within the party (see Key 1949, 406–516). As Ansolabehere, Hansen, et al. note (2006, 2010), the number of competitive primaries in the North surged during the 1920s and 1930s but steadily declined thereafter; in the South, competitive primaries declined after the Supreme Court's 1944 *Smith v. Allwright* decision ended the white primary. Ansolabehere, Hansen, et al. (2006, 2010) provide data on the percentage of incumbent-versus-challenger primaries where the incumbent was held to less than 60 percent of the vote; in both the North and the South, over 20 percent of incumbents faced competitive primary challengers during the 1920s, and over 30 percent of incumbents faced competitive primary challengers in the 1930s. By the 1960s, however, fewer than 10 percent of incumbents were facing competitive primary challengers.

The adoption of the direct primary was a change that Austin Ranney (1975, 121) considered to be among the most radical of the party reforms of the Progressive Era; reformers hoped—and party regulars feared—that primaries would lead to enduring challenges to the parties' favored candidates. Ranney's study, however, found little evidence of such conflict during the 1960s. In a more comprehensive, later analysis, Alan Ware (2002, 146–48) concluded that despite the debate between party regulars and outsiders, primary elections did not bring about dramatically different results than had the convention system or any other system by which party leaders had free rein in choosing their nominees. From the early twentieth century to the 1960s, according to Ware, there were very few primaries that clearly pitted party insiders against insurgents. The rise of so-called candidate-centered elections in the 1960s was not a direct cause of the establishment of primaries, but the technological and social changes that brought about a more candidate-centered system meant that it was not until the 1970s that primaries actually began to exhibit some of the "insider-versus-outsider" characteristics that were expected by Merriam and others.

How do we reconcile the claims of Ranney and Ware with the data of Ansolabehere, Hansen, et al. (2006, 2010), which show that there were far fewer competitive congressional primaries in the latter half of the twentieth century than there were in the first half? If Ware is correct (he does not provide any evidence to support his point), it must be the case that primaries in the first half of the twentieth century were of a different sort—they were a consequence of party factionalism or were contests of personality, not ideology. This is certainly the case for the South; as Key (1949, 410) notes, primary competition could often be merely the presentation of a limited set of alternatives by the party organization. It is hard to test such claims, but such a claim does correspond with what we know about changes in the value of congressional seats. Incumbents had begun to serve for longer by the mid-twentieth century (Brady, Buckley, and Rivers 1999) and to accrue political bases independent of their party organizations; the incumbency advantage, so pronounced in general elections by the 1960s and 1970s, may have been in evidence in primary elections by this time as well. Because so few incumbents are challenged, it is difficult to measure the incumbency advantage in primaries; standard textbook treatments of incumbents' advantages in the general election make no reference to primaries (see., e.g., Jacobson 2004, 26–28), but there is an obvious correlation between the increase in the incumbency advantage and the decline in primary challenges to incumbents. The lone study that seeks to measure the incumbency advantage in primaries, that of Ansolabehere, Hansen, et al. (2007), contends that incumbents' primary election advantage began to increase in the 1940s and 1950s—following the direct primary reforms but before the rise of the incumbency advantage in general elections—and that it was as high as 15 percent by the 1990s.

This shift also squares with a couple well-known features of some primary years during this time. First, consider what is perhaps the best-known story about primary competition during the first half of the twentieth century, Franklin Delano Roosevelt's explicit challenge to Southern Democrats who were not wholehearted supporters of his New Deal legislation. As recounted by Patterson (1967, 263–77; see also Dunn 2010), the 1938 election featured ten Democrats who were not reliable supporters of the Roosevelt administration—and who, in fact, had engaged in open talks about forming a coalition with conservative Republicans. Roosevelt campaigned against five of these ten, in some instances taking care to exclude them from speaking roles during presidential visits to their states, steering patronage positions away from their supporters, or openly campaigning for their opponents. These are ideological challenges, but as conflicts between a national party leader and state-level parties, they are also indicative of party factionalism. They are not evidently part of a movement. Roosevelt's role was unusual for the time: no president had played such a public role in primaries before, and it is almost unthinkable today to imagine a president openly supporting primary challenges to members of his own party.[10]

Second, one of the most striking features of congressional primary competition during the late 1960s and early 1970s was the increasing role of interest groups. Most accounts of the rise of candidate-centered campaigning note a few basic trends: a declining role for parties in selecting nominees, an increasing incumbency advantage, and an increase in the political power of "postmaterialist" interest groups—citizen groups with explicitly ideological ends but no direct ties to the parties (see., e.g., Menefee-Libey 2000). Brady, Han, and Pope (2007) note that several incumbents were defeated in the 1970 and 1972 primaries partly because of interest group campaigns against them. Although subsequent election years had fewer such cases, these elections coincide with the institutional-ization of many activist movements of the 1960s (see, e.g., Berry 1999) and immediately precede the explosion of political action committees in the 1970s. They indicate that one can combine Ware's claims and the data of Ansolabehere, Hansen, et al. into a coherent statement about the *possibility* of ideological primary challenges: they were expected by some in the early part of the twentieth century, but the political and technological ability for candidates and groups to wage effective primary challenges was not necessarily present until the 1970s. This does not mean that ideological challenges have flourished since this time but that they have sometimes been a possibility and have arguably been more of a possibility during the past four decades than they were before. The predicament in which Blanche Lambert Lincoln found herself in 2010 was, then, something that would have been highly unlikely before the 1970s, but it is not quite a novel feature of the 2000s. Moreover, one could argue that it is a logical and perhaps inevitable consequence of forces that have been in motion for over a century.

The past two decades have seen a substantial rethinking not only of how we measure the strength of the parties but of our basic definition of what a political party is. The dominant view of political parties through-out much of the 1970s and 1980s was encapsulated in V. O. Key's (1958) distinction between the party in government, the party organization, and the party in the electorate. The links between these three components of the party were tenuous, by design. Organizational strength had little to do with programmatic strength; that is, political parties sought to win elec-tions, but policy coherence or party unity had little to do with this pursuit and could actually harm the party at the ballot box. The decline of parties posited by many scholars of the 1970s was a decline in the parties' ability to select successful candidates and to control activists on the parties' ideo-logical extremes, and it was a decline in the parties' ability to ensure that voters would think about partisanship rather than the personal appeal of individual candidates. Primaries, as an outgrowth of the antipartyism of the Progressive Era, represented a threat to the parties, but the threat was far more worrisome at the presidential level than at the congressional level.

Literature of the 1990s and 2000s has stressed the organizational resur-gence of the party committees, as measured in terms of the financial re-sources available to the parties. It has also emphasized the changing fundraising role of the party in government—the success of congressional leaders in coupling advancement within the party with fidelity to the party's legislative goals and, perhaps more important, with raising money for the party committees and for needy candidates (see Currinder 2008). In 2002, the Bipartisan Campaign Reform Act prohibited what had come to be called "soft money," contributions that individuals, labor unions, and corporations made in unlimited amounts to the parties. The resilience of the parties in 2004 and beyond in creating networks of individual donors meant that the parties had come to rely more on smaller donors—the party in the electorate—to remain financially competitive (Corrado 2006; Dwyre and Kolodny 2006). The parties competed for money on an almost equal footing with candidates and interest groups. The distinction between Key's three components of the party had begun to break down, as had the distinction between organizational and programmatic strength.

Given these changes, one of the most intriguing new paradigms in analyzing parties is the notion of the party as a network, a multifaceted organization comprised of elected leaders, party activists, and leaders of interest groups allied with the parties (see, e.g., Skinner, Masket, and Dulio 2012; Bedlington and Malbin 2003; Heaney 2012; Herrnson 2009; Koger, Masket, and Noel 2009). In this conception of parties, disagreements between prominent individuals or groups within this network are hammered out in a less contained manner than were disagreements among old-style party bosses. These disagreements can be reflected in policy advocacy outside of the electoral arena, but they can also be worked out in elections themselves, as may be the case in contemporary primaries. At the presidential level, it was long held that changes in delegate selection procedures and campaign finance law meant that insurgent candidates could not actually win their party's nomination; the string of outsider candidates who came close but failed to win their party's nomination in the 1980s and 1990s included Democrats Edward Kennedy, Jesse Jackson Jr., Gary Hart, and Bill Bradley.[11] Howard Dean's brief ascension to front-runner status in the 2004 Democratic primaries and Barack Obama's victory in the 2008 primaries were both built on a network of small donors and grassroots activists with no history as party power brokers. Dean and Obama's successes in fundraising speak not only to a withering of the traditional party organization but to a triumph of particular pieces of the party network and to an expanding conception of how malleable the party is.

This does not mean that the parties *became* networks or that the traditional distinctions between the parties are no longer useful analytic tools. It does show, however, that Key's three wings of the party interact much more today than was once the case. Geographic constraints on the parties have attenuated. A party's leaders in Arkansas, for instance, no longer hold as much power over elections in Arkansas as they once did. If a race in Arkansas matters in terms of the party's legislative goals or in a battle over what it means to be a Democrat, it will draw attention from outside the state, and there will be support waiting for a primary challenger ready to step into the battle. It is hard to imagine such conflicts happening in more than a small number of places in any given year. Yet if the possibility that primaries could matter existed in the 1970s, it seemed likely by 2010 that a primary or two somewhere would matter, though the possibility that any one primary would be the one that mattered was still small.

As a final comment on the role of parties, it should be noted that the preceding summary of insurgent Democratic presidential candidates is just that—a list of Democrats. While Key's distinctions imply a relatively standardized, ideology-free conception of the party components—that is, both major parties are constituted similarly in terms of their official national organizations, and elected officials perform similar functions regardless of their party—party networks are fluid and ever evolving. There is a long history of literature on party culture (e.g., Freeman 1986; Reichley 2000), which has called attention to the more hierarchical nature of the Republican Party and the more group-oriented nature of the Democratic Party. In addition, party goals are dependent on the parties' short-term historical fortunes. As Philip Klinkner (1995) recounts, innovations in party strategy have generally been pioneered by the party out of power, the party that needed to do something different in order to win power. I shall defer (to a later chapter) speculation about how the Democratic and Republican party networks have treated primaries, but it is important to note here that we should be sensitive to differences between Democratic and Republican primary challenges. At a minimum, the unusual circumstances of the past two decades—in any given election, either party had a real chance of winning or losing at least one chamber of Congress, and narrow majorities of power prevailed in many of these years—should caution us that the salience of primary challenges is different today than it was during the era of Democratic congressional dominance in the 1970s and 1980s.

Changing Interest Groups

Just as our theoretical accounts of political parties are ripe for change, so our accounts of interest groups are due for reevaluation. As the preceding account of evolving party networks indicates, many, though certainly not all, interest groups are rightly considered to be part of the respective political parties' extended networks. In all of the more recent accounts, party networks include various types of groups and group leaders. Interest groups, however, have different goals and different membership constraints than political parties, and these differences are particularly pronounced in the case of congressional primaries. As we shall see, changes in the types of groups that are prominent in electoral politics and changes in interest group strategies have led to a greater role for groups in the past decade's most notorious primary challenges.

Conventional theories of interest group behavior have tended to rely on classifications of different group types. Some classifications emphasize group goals—for instance, there has long been a distinction between relatively nonpartisan groups that primarily seek access to lawmakers and more partisan—or at least more politically aggressive—groups that seek to influence election results (see, e.g., Wright 1996). This is a convenient means of distinguishing between established lobbying organizations, such as the National Association of Homebuilders, and organizations that engage in substantial independent spending during elections, such as the League of Conservation Voters. Other classifications emphasize the benefits groups provide to members (Olson 1971; Salisbury 1969). These classifications distinguish between groups that provide tangible, material benefits to members (e.g., labor unions), groups that provide solidary (or social) benefits to members (e.g., various local chambers of commerce), and groups that provide expressive benefits to members (e.g., groups that use a strong ideological or issue position to make members feel like they are making a difference or standing up for their beliefs). Still other theories use more easily measurable characteristics of groups to explain different motivations; they may, for instance, distinguish between liberal and conservative groups, between business and labor organizations, or between groups with different Federal Election Commission statuses or tax statuses—for instance, based on whether groups are registered as political action committees, whether their tax status permits them to engage in direct political advocacy, and so forth (Boatright et al. 2006).

Such classifications allow one to compare groups according to their outputs (what they do in the political arena) or their inputs (how they recruit members and raise money). Many such theories have always made a great deal of sense if one wishes to understand lobbying or issue advocacy. Underpinning these theories is a lengthy body of work on group entrepreneurs—on the people who create political organizations and endeavor to make them influential (Salisbury 1969; Walker 1983). For the purposes of this study, however, it is important to note that groups compete in a wide-open marketplace—more open, arguably, than is the market for political parties. Groups must worry more than political parties about their own survival. Interest groups that seek to influence elections must demonstrate results to their members—they must show either that they made a difference in advancing their issues of concern or that they helped to elect politicians who share their views. There are no unimpeachable metrics for this, but a group must at least have a story to tell to members or potential members about why citizens should contribute to that group and not others. In this regard, the sales pitches that groups present are like those presented by businesses (expressing why someone should purchase their product or buy their stock), philanthropic organizations, college alumni associations, or any other organization, political or not, that is competing with other organizations for the scarce resources of potential customers, contributors, or members.

Not all interest groups and not even all of those active in elections need to rely exclusively on such pitches. Business organizations or labor unions, for instance, provide enough nonpolitical benefits to members that their financial stability may not be entirely dependent on their successes in elections. Yet one of the most noteworthy changes in American electoral politics over the past decade has been the rise of groups that seek what I shall refer to as a "functional niche." If one peruses the list of the interest groups most active in elections during the 1990s,[12] one will see a large number of groups that sought an issue niche—that is, they sought to create a reputation as the dominant group in a particular policy domain. Organizations such as the Sierra Club, National Right to Life, the National Rifle Association, or the Human Rights Campaign have sought to appeal to members on the basis of their advocacy on behalf of one narrowly defined issue. Electoral work that seeks to advance this issue does not require that a group only support one party, and while such groups may have supported primary challengers at times, this support in itself is not a selling point for donors. While groups such as these would wish to emphasize their success in helping to elect pro-environment or anti-abortion candidates, they would not necessarily want to emphasize anything novel about their tactics in doing this. Such groups also have tended to be active both in elections and in lobbying.

At about the time of the 2004 election, however, a number of new organizations without obvious issue niches came to prominence (Weissman and Hassan 2006; Weissman and Ryan 2006, 2007). Many of the so-called

527 groups, so named because their tax status enabled them to raise unlimited donations but did not permit lobbying or direct contributions to legislators, advertised themselves to potential donors based not on what they stood for, apart from their partisan orientation, but on what they would do with their money. America Votes, the largest such group, raised just under eighty million dollars[13] to fund a sophisticated get-out-the-vote effort on behalf of presidential candidate John Kerry and Democratic candidates more generally. America Votes was very transparent about what it sought to do. In fact, its explanation of its function (and why it was doing something other organizations could not do) was part of its pitch to donors. Other groups promoted themselves on the basis of their effectiveness in airing advertisements. Many scholars attributed the formation of such groups to the recent prohibition on soft money contributions to the parties, but many of the organizations active in this election and beyond had existed for several years already. Two groups I shall discuss at length in this book, MoveOn.org and the Club for Growth, were formed in the late 1990s and rose to prominence on the basis of their effectiveness in using the Internet to raise small contributions (MoveOn) or in bundling contributions (the Club for Growth). Neither group limited itself to any one issue domain, but MoveOn exclusively supported liberal candidates, and the Club for Growth exclusively supported conservatives. Because these are not lobbying organizations, they can function within the broader party network and yet take an adversarial stance against the parties or prominent lawmakers within the parties and face few repercussions.

Groups with similar approaches have existed in the past. On the Republican side, the National Conservative PAC (NCPAC) in the 1980s and even the John Birch Society or the American Conservative Union (if one wishes to go further back) championed conservative candidates, and organizations such as Americans for Democratic Action or People for the American Way supported liberals without restricting themselves to any particular issue (see Sabato 1984). These organizations have not traditionally been major players in elections, however, restricting their activities to a small volume of PAC contributions or to providing their members with scorecards on where politicians stand. None of these groups were successful in both raising money and recruiting members; in some instances, these types of groups were dependent on a single wealthy patron. Certainly none of these groups competed directly with the party organizations for money. By the 2010 election, however, MoveOn presented an alternative to the Democratic Party for liberal donors (just as the 527 organizations may have done in 2004), and there was a proliferation of conservative groups—not only the Club for Growth, but new "Super PACs,"[14] such as Americans for Prosperity, American Crossroads, and the various Tea Party groups—that could recruit contributors based on their fidelity to ideological principles and their effectiveness in advancing these principles; they could appeal to donors on the grounds that they are more ideologically pure and more reliable than their favored party. Groups could recruit members based on their functional niche—what they would do to advance these ideological principles and why their political acumen was different from or better than that of other organizations or the parties.

The passage of the Bipartisan Campaign Reform Act (BCRA) may have hastened the formation of these groups (see La Raja 2008, 218–24). At least in the short term, the highest-spending Democratic groups in 2004 were clearly formed in anticipation of helping the Democratic nominee (who presumably would have exhausted his own funds after the Democratic primary) remain competitive with the incumbent George W. Bush (Boatright et al. 2006). BCRA prohibited large unregulated contributions to the parties, thus giving an advantage to groups that could accept such large individual contributions. It raised individual contribution limits and indexed them to inflation, thus increasing the importance of groups that could bundle individual contributions. BCRA also restricted the ability of established corporate, labor, or issue advocacy groups to advertise on television during the last months of the election, thus providing an opening for newly formed organizations that did not rely on corporate or labor money.

The increased financial clout for groups with a functional niche and the increased interest of these groups in their own parties' primaries cannot be attributed solely (or perhaps even primarily) to changes in campaign finance law. A more likely explanation is the development of Internet fundraising. The cost of soliciting donations via the Internet is a fraction of the cost of direct mail, and once an organization has a lengthy list of potential donors, it can solicit contributions from them again and again. Small contributions take on greater value than they did in the past—a small contributor can be solicited repeatedly, using different sales pitches, and that person may eventually contribute a substantial amount of money. Internet fundraising also requires that some contacts *not* be just requests for money. As the Howard Dean campaign learned, donors respond favorably to short-term incentives or markers of progress—a good fundraising quarter, success in a debate, and so forth (Teachout 2006; Biddle 2008). For groups that are seeking to cultivate small donors, "membership" entails no money at all, only the willingness to be on the group's e-mail list. For groups such as this to survive without membership dues, they need to provide frequent incentives for members to give. A primary campaign can be such an inducement—primaries occur at frequent intervals throughout the year preceding the general election and can serve as opportunities for groups to demonstrate their prowess to members. In comparison, a group concerned only about the general election gets only one chance to show its members that it is effective, and even then, given the volume of money that goes into a general election, the election of a preferred candidate in November does not necessarily show that any one group made any difference.

Thus the dynamics of Internet fundraising make primaries attractive, and the functional niche of these groups—their ability to show not only that their hearts are in the right place but that their strategy works—may well require that these groups take on candidates of their own party. Precisely because congressional primaries are often low-visibility, low-spending affairs, the activities of one group can make far more of a difference than is the case in a general election. As we saw earlier, political parties have also discovered how to use the Internet effectively and how to cultivate a base of smaller, more ideological donors. Relative to groups, however, parties are at a disadvantage in that they cannot take well-defined stands on policy, concentrate their efforts on a small number of elections, or provide donors with easily measurable indicators of progress prior to the general election. After all, someone will always win the party's primary election, and parties cannot effectively trumpet primary results as indicators of the party's strength or political acumen. Political parties have, of course, a well-established "brand" as far as voters are concerned, while interest groups must use their activities throughout the year as a means of creating a brand. In market terms, it is as if interest groups are akin to high-end restaurants—because there are many such restaurants, the risk of going out of business is high, so they seek to promote themselves based on the skill of their chefs, their reputation, or merely their trendiness. Parties, in comparison, are more akin to chain restaurants—such restaurants have been around for a while, and patrons know roughly what they will get or what their options will be, from one visit to the next and from one location to the next. The marketplace for interest groups is far more open than the market for parties, and this openness may well have driven some interest groups into congressional primaries.

These are broad claims to make about organized interest groups, and it must be emphasized that they apply to only a small fraction of the groups involved in politics. Established theories of group entrepreneurship, of

groups' electoral strategies, and of groups' lobbying activities are not necessarily invalid today. They do not, however, adequately capture the motivations of the groups that have become involved in primaries. Given that
the small number of groups active in primaries are among the biggest
spenders in elections today more broadly and that groups of their type are
relatively new to the political arena, it makes sense to conclude that interest groups are more responsible for primary challenges than are candidates or parties. As we shall see, nothing in the data I have assembled here
shows that the candidates who run against incumbents have changed.
There is some evidence that parties are less capable of warding off primary
challenges. What is most evident in the data, however, is that there has
been a change in the donor pool for primary challengers. These are developments consistent with the account of candidates, parties, and interest
groups that I have provided here.

A Brief Detour: Differences among the States in
Primary Laws

In sum, there are broader changes afoot that have influenced congressional primaries, even while some of the basic empirical facts about primary
challenges have changed little. I would be remiss, however, to proceed in
analyzing primaries further without including in this chapter a brief summary of some of the salient differences in state primary laws. I provide this
partly because these differences have been used in the past to explain primary competition, partly because I shall seek to demonstrate that these
differences do not do a very good job of explaining contemporary cases of
ideological primary challenges, and partly because there are a few instances in recent years where national groups have sought to exploit obscure state laws during the primary process. Collectively, these differences
show that there are some impediments, but not insurmountable ones, to
applying a one-size-fits-all approach to primaries over the time period I
consider here.

The Progressive movement's uneven success across the country can be
seen today when one compares state primary systems. Because laws relat-
ing to congressional primaries are set by the states, there is a wide range of
primary types. First, ballot access laws vary across states. As recounted by
Ansolabehere and Gerber (1996) and Hamm and Hogan (2008), filing fees
have an influence on whether elections are contested at all. Filing fees for
candidates range from no fee at all, as is the case in Indiana, to over one

thousand dollars, as is the case in Florida. States also vary in the number of signatures candidates must acquire on their petitions to run, ranging from no signatures to over one thousand. One would expect that a serious primary challenger would have little difficulty meeting these requirements. However, one might expect high fees or petition requirements to insulate incumbents from nuisance challengers, and one might imagine circumstances where an initially weak challenger gains strength because of problems that arise for the incumbent once the campaign is under way. In other words, these fees and requirements reduce the possibility of relatively unknown challengers simply being in the right place at the right time.

A small number of states have particularly idiosyncratic ballot rules (see Galderisi and Ezra 2001). In Virginia, for instance, the party can choose its nominee through a convention rather than through a primary, thus forestalling any challenges at all. In Utah, the party must endorse candidates in order for them to appear on the ballot, and it can endorse no more than two candidates. This can lead—as was the case for Senator Robert Bennett in 2010—to having the incumbent prevented from running in the primary at all. Eight states (Colorado, Connecticut, Massachusetts, New Mexico, New York, North Dakota, Rhode Island, and Utah) set a threshold—generally 20 to 30 percent of convention delegates' votes—for candidates to appear on the ballot (see Galderisi and Ezra 2001, 19).

Second, states vary in their requirements for voting in primaries. Kanthak and Morton (2001) distinguish between open primaries—where any registered voter can vote in a primary, whether that voter was previously registered as a member of that party or not—and closed primaries, in which voting is limited to those who are already registered party members.[15] Open primaries, they argue, provide an advantage to extreme candidates—candidates running on single issues, such as abortion, or candidates espousing views at odds with those of mainstream party members and moderate candidates.[16] They argue that semi-closed primaries (in which previously unaffiliated voters may vote) and semi-open primaries (in which voters can change their registration at the polls) provide an advantage to centrist candidates. Open and semi-open primaries introduce the possibility that some voters may vote in the opposing party's primary for a nominee they think would be weak in the general election; evidence is mixed, however, on whether a significant amount of such voting takes place (McGhee et al. 2011).

A small number of states have employed the "jungle" or "blanket" primary to choose candidates. In a blanket primary, candidates of all parties run in the same primary; if no candidate receives a majority of the votes in the primary, the top two vote getters, whether they are of opposing parties or of the same party, run against each other in the general election. Louisiana and Washington both have used this method in the past, and California adopted this system in 2010, but not before the state's 2010 primaries.[17] Nine states, all in the South, employ a runoff system for primaries; if no primary candidate receives a majority of the votes, the top two finishers face each other in a runoff (see Ezra 2005). Kanthak and Morton (2001; see also Gerber and Morton 1998) conclude that blanket primaries, like open primaries, can provide an advantage to moderate candidates. More recent studies, however, have found no noticeable differences in the types of candidates who emerge from these primaries (McGhee et al. 2011).

Third, the timing of congressional primaries can influence the appearance of primary challengers on the ballot or their success. This is the case for two reasons. First, in presidential election years, not all states hold their congressional primaries on the same date as their presidential primaries. It is difficult to systematically measure what sort of advantage might be conferred on congressional primary candidates who appear on the same ballot as presidential primary candidates; there is higher turnout in presidential primaries, and this turnout would be expected to include many voters who are less involved in politics in general than are those who would vote in a congressional primary. Whether this provides an advantage to particular types of primary candidates, however, is unclear. Second, states vary in the timing of their primaries; the earliest take place in March, the latest in September. In an analysis of general election challenges, Taylor and Boatright (2005) contend that early primaries provide an advantage to candidates with established fundraising operations. For primaries, this would mean that incumbents and those challengers who have an established political base will be stronger. Early primaries also simply mean that the incumbent has less time to do anything that would prompt a primary challenge and that the sorts of political trends that may manifest themselves in a general election will be less evident at the time of early primaries.

Cumulatively, these differences mean that it would be problematic to come up with a systematic analysis of changes in primary competition over time. One might look at variations by state, but these variations have little to do with the narrative about primaries that has taken hold in American political discourse of late. One might argue that when primarying occurs, it will be more frequent or more successful in some states than in others. Because congressional primary challenges are such a rare occurrence, however, any such claim would have few cases with which to substantiate it. This is one reason why analyses of the effects of ballot access laws, primary dates, and so forth have often focused on state legislatures, where there are more cases for each given primary type. As I shall note in the next chapter, few of the conventional measures of party strength—which has much to do with the nature of the primary system—seem to relate to the frequency of primary challenges today. There are state-level patterns in congressional primaries, and these patterns are useful in understanding particular cases of primary challenges. The highest-profile primary challenges of the past decade—to list just a few, challenges that have taken place in Arkansas, Connecticut, Illinois, Maryland, Michigan, New Jersey, Pennsylvania, Rhode Island, South Carolina, and Utah—are not easily reconciled with distinctions among states in terms of their ballot access laws, primary rules, or primary timing.

I do not mean, however, to deny the salience of differences in state laws regarding primaries. Yes, it appears from the record of the past several years that the sponsors of primary challenges are not deterred by the obstacles to a candidacy that exist in any given state. As some who read earlier drafts of this book remarked, however, many primary challenges have been made easier because of quirks in state primary laws. The ease with which groups like the Tea Party and the Club for Growth were able not just to defeat incumbent Utah Republican William Bennett in 2010 but to knock him entirely off the Republican ballot was a function of Utah's unusual primary procedure. This is best seen as an indication not that primary challenges or defeats are easier in Utah—the record of the past four decades provides little evidence that this has been the case—but that nonparty groups outside of Utah have had the resources and political acumen to notice this quirk and use it to their advantage. The Bennett defeat is best seen in the company of recent efforts by organizations outside of Wisconsin to exploit the state's recall laws to bring about the recall of many Wisconsin state legislators, of MoveOn.org's seamless transition from working against Blanche Lambert Lincoln in the Arkansas primary to working against her in the subsequent runoff election, of the increasing preparedness of outside groups as well as party organizations to litigate election recounts, and of the emphasis on the details of state caucuses and delegate selection that enabled Barack Obama to outmaneuver Hillary Clinton for the 2008 Democratic nomination.

In these instances, the actors that took advantage of obscure state laws were sometimes candidate or party organizations and sometimes outside groups. In all of these cases, organizations outside of the states in question used state provisions to achieve their ends. This is something that seems hard to reconcile with the focus in past literature on state differences. In the cases where nonparty groups are involved, the organizations with the resources to do this are organizations that have the resources to focus their attention on learning the ins and outs of state election law. Traditional access-oriented and policy-oriented groups seem unlikely to have such resources. The common thread here is that differences in state election laws appear to be more an opportunity than an impediment. In the case of primaries, they look more like a tool for nationalizing the process than like a bulwark that preserves states' distinctive political cultures.

Conclusions

In this chapter, I have sought to do two things. First, my historical account is an effort to provide the sort of narrative regarding primary competition that is so lacking in contemporary discussions of primaries. Few contemporary accounts reach as far back in history as I have here, but the easiest way to tell the story is to highlight previous primary challenges. As I have sought to show in the account of Blanche Lambert Lincoln's primary challenges, one can develop a compelling story line that seems to show that the nature of primaries has changed, so that we now see moderate incumbents threatened for straying from party orthodoxy. There are, however, two problems with this approach. First, not all primary challenges are the same, and we lose a lot of valuable information if we equate races such as Lambert Lincoln's two campaigns. Second, focusing on primary challenges cannot help us to find out why some incumbents are challenged and some are not.

Congressional primaries have received scant attention for the past several decades. It is possible to reach back to the development of primaries in order to discuss the impact of primary laws upon challengers. There is some merit to doing this, but as I shall show in the subsequent chapters of this book, laws regulating who can run and when candidates must file do not necessarily explain the emergence of strong primary challengers, nor do they tell us anything about differences in the reasons why challengers emerge and in what challengers talk about in their campaigns. "Nuisance" candidates may be more frequent in states where it is easier to challenge an incumbent, but strong challengers are unlikely to be deterred by obstacles to appearing on the ballot. The frequency of competitive challenges and the alleged increase in ideological challenges cannot be explained on a state-by-state basis.

Second, I have sought to provide a theoretical framework to explain what, in fact, might explain the changed role primaries play in contemporary political discourse. Clearly something has changed, if only because primaries have become a standard piece of contemporary debates on political polarization. If it is not the frequency of primaries, the likelihood of primary defeats, or the consequences of primaries, then perhaps what has changed is the way we talk about primaries. We speak differently about primaries today, I have argued, because the incentives for primary challengers have changed, the nature of the parties has changed, and (perhaps most important) the role of nonparty organizations has changed, such that groups with a functional niche—an ability to sell themselves to prospective members based on their unorthodox election strategies—have prospered. Forty years ago, one would have been hard pressed to find anyone outside of Alaska or Arkansas who cared about those states' primary elections. Today, thanks to the nationalization of congressional primaries, such elections are believed by many to matter quite a bit.

The narrative I have provided in this chapter is deliberately messy. Every challenge has a unique story, and many aspects of those stories evade quantification. At some point, however, stories that play on the unique circumstances that brought about the downfall of one or two scandal-prone, lazy, or simply unlucky members of Congress metastasize into broader claims about changes in American electoral politics. This is precisely where we find ourselves today. The paradox presented by the research of Ansolabehere, Hansen, et al. remains with us—there are fewer competitive primaries today than there were in earlier decades, yet the attention given to such challenges gives the appearance that they are more of a threat to incumbents than they once were. The only way to resolve this paradox is to move away from anecdotes, to look at the reasons for challenges over time and to identify characteristics of primary challenges that are measurable across time. In the next chapter, I take up this task.

2 | When and Why Congressional Primary Challenges Happen

The data in this and the next two chapters are drawn from all congressional primary elections held from 1970 through 2010 in which an incumbent was running. I categorize all primary challengers who receive more than 25 percent of the vote in these elections (a threshold for which I provide justification in the discussion of my methodology) as being serious enough to warrant study, even though very few of them were actually victorious. Drawing on descriptions of these races and my categorization of the motives behind these challenges (again, explained in further detail under "Methodology"), this chapter poses two sets of questions. First, are there predictable patterns to primary challenges? Are the sorts of ideological primary challenges that are so noteworthy today actually on the rise, or have they always been a feature of congressional elections? The evidence about whether ideological challenges have increased is mixed, but as I document in this chapter, there are other trends of note. Second, do these challenges, irrespective of their results, make sense; that is, are the candidates who get primaried for ideological reasons in fact out of step with their districts? On the Democratic side, they tend to be, but the evidence is more mixed on the Republican side. All of this means that incumbents are no more likely to be primaried today than they were in the 1970s, 1980s, or 1990s. For other types of challenges, there is some evidence to support challengers' rationales and campaign themes, but these challenges do not necessarily break down along partisan lines or exhibit any clear time trend—nor should we expect them to.

In this chapter, I am primarily interested in evaluating the frequency of different types of challenges. In chapter 4, I investigate their results. As noted in the introduction, there are essentially three claims about primary competition today: that there is more of it, that it is of more concern to incumbents, and that it has a pronounced effect on incumbents' behavior. The intent of this chapter is to measure how great the threat of facing a primary opponent is for incumbents of both parties. One might assume from the rhetoric surrounding them that today's primary challenges are ubiquitous, novel, and well deserved, but the evidence in this chapter suggests that they are not necessarily any of these things. There is a logic to the occurrence of primary challenges over the past four decades, but there is some evidence that this logic applies less today than in the past and that it applies less to Republicans than to Democrats.

Primary Competition in Context

As noted in the previous chapter, primary competition has been connected by some researchers to state laws governing ballot access and has therefore been said to be a function of the level of party strength and organization. Most American states have held congressional primaries since the early twentieth century (Galderisi and Ezra 2001), when as many as 25 percent of Democratic House incumbents and 46 percent of Republican House incumbents ran in contested primaries (Schantz 1980). During the early twentieth century, approximately 30 percent of incumbents were renominated with less than 60 percent of the vote (Ansolabehere, Hansen, et al. 2006, 2010). Primaries tended to be most competitive in the South, the border South, and the Midwest and to be least competitive in the Northeast (Turner 1953). Over the course of the twentieth century, primaries became fewer and less competitive; during the period from 1960 to 2000, well under 10 percent of House incumbents' primaries were competitive, according to the 60 percent threshold of Ansolabehere, Hansen, et al. (2006, 2010). Regional differences in competition have declined as well, to the point that there is no difference between the South and the North in the frequency of competitive primaries.

There are few analyses of the causes of this decline. The standard account of the development of primaries identifies two different rationales: that primaries were introduced in the North to limit the power of party machines and in the South to increase competition while retaining Democratic Party hegemony. Galderisi and Ezra (2001) note, however, that the parties adapted quickly to primaries; one adaptation was the creation of ballot access rules that can make it difficult for candidates to run (see also Ansolabehere and Gerber 1996). The dramatic increase in incumbent fundraising has been shown to have discouraged general election competition; the same may hold for primary competition as well. Goodliffe and Magleby (2001) have shown that primary challengers to incumbents raise virtually no money from political action committees and tend to rely primarily on their own funds (see also Steen 2006, 24). Just as incumbents tend to develop large war chests to deter strong general election opponents, so, one can conclude, they also seek to deter primary challengers.

It seems obvious that incumbents would not want primary opposition. The parties, as well, have sought to ward off primary competition. It is conventional wisdom that incumbents' vote shares in a general election are hurt by primary competition. I evaluate such claims in chapter 4. While there is an intuitive logic to noting that parties and candidates may want to avoid primaries, however, it is not possible to measure their success in doing this—there is no way to identify an event that did not happen. We can, however, measure district characteristics. Apart from analysis of vote totals, there are two studies that do this. Herrnson and Gimpel (1995) note that district characteristics can make primary challenges more likely; a diverse district population can increase the likelihood of a primary, and region also can influence primary competitiveness, even though the basic North-South division no longer holds. Some states simply have more competitive primaries than others; Ansolabehere, Hansen, et al. (2006) note, for instance, that Oklahoma has always had contentious primaries, while other analysts have noted the frequency of primary competition in Indiana and several other states. The studies of these analysts at least suggest that it is easier to encourage or discourage primary challenges in some places than in others.

It has been established in the literature, then, that the amount of primary competition had declined as of the early 2000s, that it may well have declined partly because of efforts by incumbents and the parties to ward off competition, and that this effort has been driven by a perception that primary competition is harmful to the party holding the seat. What is not clear, however, is whether this is merely a historical anomaly—that some elections will always be more competitive than others—or whether there has been a decline in certain types of primaries. In other words, we need a baseline not only to measure the occurrence of primary challenges to incumbents in general but also to distinguish between types of primary challenges.

Methodology

To measure changes in the rationale for primary challenges, I compiled the primary election results for all U.S. House and Senate races from 1970 to 2010, using each year's edition of *America Votes*. I then identified all of the primaries in which the incumbent received less than 75 percent of the vote. Using the descriptions of members of Congress provided in each year's edition of the *Almanac of American Politics* (Barone et al. 1971–2011) and *Politics in America* (1971–2011), I coded the reasons for each primary challenge into one of twelve categories: scandal, competence or age of the incumbent, local issues, national issues, ideological challenges from the center, ideological challenges from the extremes (primarying), race, party factionalism, redistricting, ambitious challenger, other reasons, and no reason given.[1] In cases where the *Almanac* did not supply a reason but *Politics in America* did, I used the latter's reason. As a coding rule of thumb, I prioritized the description in the *Almanac* in instances where the *Almanac* and *Politics in America* listed different reasons (there were four such instances). During the 1970 to 2010 period, there were 8,224 races in the House of Representatives where an incumbent was seeking reelection. Approximately one out of ten House incumbents (774, or 9.4 percent) running for reelection during this period faced a primary challenger or multiple primary challengers who garnered more than 25 percent of the vote. Only 329 incumbents, or 4.0 percent, received less than 60 percent of the vote in their primaries.

Table 2.1 lists the frequency of the different types of House primary challenges, according to my coding, with an explanation of each. In several instances, challenges could be placed into more than one category. Most notably, many challenges that likely were inspired in part by race drew on other themes as well; few challengers explicitly argued that the district should be represented by any particular racial or ethnic group. In other cases, arguments about a particular incumbent gradually change; for instance, if one reads the summaries of challenges to Representative Gus Savage, who represented part of the South Side of Chicago from 1980 to 1992, arguments that begin with reference to Chicago political factions gradually shade into arguments based on Savage's competence and then his ethics. In cases where the *Almanac* listed more than one reason, I listed the reason given highest priority as the first reason; where two reasons were given equal attention, I coded the first reason listed as the main reason for the primary. There were fifty-five such cases, and second reasons are spread among the various challenge types with no obvious pattern. In the following discussion, I prioritize the reason given the most attention in the *Almanac* description, with the awareness that multiple rationales may in fact be driving the campaign.

The challenges of the most interest for the analysis in this book—the

TABLE 2.1.   Types of House Primary Challenges, 1970–2010

Category	N	Examples
Scandal	98	Most of these challenges involve allegations of corruption, bribery, or campaign finance violations. Several involve sexual misdeeds. Some years feature a specific scandal, e.g., Abscam (two challenges in 1980) or the House Bank scandal (fourteen challenges in 1992).
Competence, Age	110	Most are straightforward criticisms of the incumbent's abilities, either involving the incumbent's achievements as a legislator or the effects of age. Also included are criticisms of the incumbent's knowledge of the district (some are criticized for living outside the district or spending too much time in Washington). Some challenges also are based on criticism of the amount of time the representative has spent running for higher office.
Local Issue	14	Six of these concern the effects of busing on the district; other issues include power plant siting, timber harvesting policies, crime rates within the district, and policies related to local airports.
National Issue	40	Frequently mentioned issues include the Vietnam War (eight challenges), abortion (thirteen challenges), NAFTA and trade policy (three challenges), and immigration (five challenges).
Ideological Challenge from Center	32	Incumbent criticized for being too extreme or too partisan for district.
Ideological Challenge from Left (Democrats) or Right (Republicans)	101	"Primarying." Incumbent criticized for being too moderate or insufficiently partisan.
Race	57	Challenges in this category are only those that specifically mention race; that is, they are not instances where a white candidate challenges a nonwhite candidate, but only those where the race of the representative is at issue. Many involve claims that only a minority should represent a minority district; others involve challenges among minority groups (e.g., a Latino challenging an African American in a mixed district).
Local Party Factionalism	21	Most of these challenges take place in urban districts (e.g., Chicago, Boston, New York) where competition tends to be between the local machine and antimachine politicians.
Ambitious Challenger	22	Challenges made by prominent local officeholders, focused primarily on the challenger, not any defects of the incumbent. Several of these include challenges made by former representatives of the district who had left the seat to unsuccessfully seek higher office.
Redistricting	36	Challenges waged by opponents who seek to draw support from areas newly incorporated into a House district following redistricting.
Other	8	Includes cases where incumbents retired and then changed their minds and ran again (3), where incumbents switched parties (2), and Lyndon LaRouche supporters (2).

TABLE 2.1.—*Continued*

Category	N	Examples
No Reason Given	240	No explanation given for the motivation of challengers in these races. These races had the highest mean primary vote percentage for incumbents (67 percent) and no successful challenges. Because incumbents were considered to have been challenged if their vote percentage was below 75 percent, there are many cases here where two or more challengers collectively held the incumbent below that amount while failing to receive more than 10 or 15 percent of the vote themselves.
Total	774	

challenges that are generally referred to when one talks about incumbents being "primaried"—are those where a Democratic is challenged on the grounds that he or she is too conservative or where a Republican is challenged for being too liberal. For the most part, these are fairly easy to categorize. However, I have created a separate category for challenges based primarily on one issue. I further separate national issues and local issues. It is possible that some of the issue-based challenges are in fact part of a more general ideological critique. For instance, I categorize Ned Lamont's challenge to Connecticut senator Joe Lieberman in 2006 as an ideological challenge, but Lamont may well have been motivated by one dominant issue, the Iraq War, and it is entirely possible that many Connecticut voters voted for or against Lieberman on the basis of their views on the war. In this case, the issue raised had a left-right dimension in the same manner as would broader claims that Lieberman was too conservative. However, issue-based challenges are not necessarily always made from a similar ideological direction; for instance, both Democrats and Republicans in the data set were subject to challenges based on abortion. To ensure that I am not looking too narrowly at the sorts of challenges of interest here, I refer in my analysis to a restrictive definition of being "primaried," in which only off-center ideological challenges are included, and to a broader definition, which includes centrist challenges and challenges based on national or local issues.

The *Almanac* and *Politics in America* have their own limitations in descriptions of races. Approximately 30 percent of challenges to incumbents are not mentioned at all in those sources or are not described there in enough detail to discern a motive, so the number of challengers' themes presented here is not complete. This is particularly a problem for 2010;

others' estimates of the number of ideological challenges have ranged far higher than mine (see Sobieraj and Berry 2011), and my own quick perusal of candidates' websites confirms that at least ten of the challenges not discussed in the *Almanac* were indeed conservative challenges by candidates running with Tea Party support. To make a special exception for 2010 races, however, would be to skew my findings; for obvious reasons, there is no way to go back and explore campaigns from the 1970s in this manner. I discuss some of the anomalies of 2010 in more detail in this chapter and throughout this book.

Surely many of the challenges classified as "missing" here did fall into one of the categories, but it would be difficult to argue that there is any bias, in terms of the codings, in determining which races are discussed in these sources and which are not. A more serious problem is that some of these descriptions carry over from year to year; a description of one incumbent's primary challenge in one year may appear in subsequent years while descriptions of subsequent primary challenges are not discussed or are cast in the same terms. Absent an exhaustive survey of local media, however, these two compendia are probably the most authoritative sources for discussion of all members' campaigns. At a minimum, as books that attempt to provide authoritative, unbiased descriptions of members of Congress, they provide a consistent and relatively accurate source of information over this period.

The 75 percent threshold was chosen partially with the source for codings in mind. Only two primary challenges where the incumbents were not held to under 75 percent are discussed in the *Almanac* and *Politics in America;* both are attempts by former representatives (Robert Dornan and Mel Reynolds) to return to Congress. This threshold is also useful for campaign finance purposes; virtually no challengers who received less than 25 percent of the vote raised enough money to file with the Federal Election Commission.[2] This threshold is much more generous to challengers than are the criteria for "competitive" campaigns used in other sources (see, e.g., Ansolabehere, Hansen, et al. 2006, 2010), but this ensures that I err on the side of being too inclusive in measuring serious campaigns rather than excluding some legitimate challenges.

In a theoretical sense, my two most substantive decisions here—the decision to use outside elites' descriptions of the challenges as the authoritative verdict on what the challenges were "about" and the decision to set any sort of threshold at all (let alone to justify any particular vote percentage for that threshold)—may strike some readers as being debatable. Beyond the data-driven justifications that I have already offered, a few more words about these decisions are necessary. I begin this explication with the descriptions in the *Almanac* and in *Politics in America,* which tend to be brief summaries of the challengers' campaign themes. Consider the following examples:

- Republican Ken Calvert, first elected in 1996, faced a primary challenger in 1998. During his first term, Calvert was stopped by police while driving, and the police found a prostitute in Calvert's car. Calvert's 1998 challenger accused him of showing a "lack of common decency, sense of right and wrong, concern for the truth, and respect for women." (Barone et al. 1999, 271)
- In 2000, Republican George Nethercutt, who had pledged when elected in 1994 to serve only three terms in Congress, broke his pledge and ran again. The *Almanac* notes that U.S. Term Limits, an advocacy group, pledged to spend one million dollars to defeat him and that Nethercutt faced a talk radio host and term limits advocate in the primary (Barone et al. 2001, 1614).

One could argue that in both cases, the challengers may have simply been ambitious politicians who might well have run even had Calvert not been tarred by scandal or had Nethercutt not taken the term limits pledge. These challengers might simply have found another theme for their campaign. However, one could also argue that the success of these challengers (such as it was—neither won) had something to do with the themes they raised and that the message the incumbent received from this challenge, likewise, was more likely to be linked to the challenger's success in establishing these themes than to beliefs about what the real story behind the challenge might have been. To put matters simply, using the summary provided by neutral outsiders of the primary challenge thus establishes some consistency in coding, provides what is arguably the clearest indication of what voters heard about in the primary, and provides us with the most easily identified piece of information the incumbent might take away from the race.

As I have already stated, critics might quarrel not only with the 75 percent threshold I have used for coding here but with the notion that one should use a threshold at all, as opposed to simply providing a scale—for instance, by developing models that use incumbents' primary vote share as an independent variable. There are three responses to this. First, any threshold is, to some extent, arbitrary. For the most part, the results presented in this chapter use the 75 percent threshold because this strikes me (given, again, the lack of explanation in the *Almanac* and *Politics in America* of challenges that do not hold the incumbent below 75 percent) as a threshold designed to include any challenger to whom an incumbent might pay the slightest attention. Later in this chapter, I compare results using the 75 percent threshold to those using the more conventional, 60 percent threshold; the results are similar. Second, challenger vote share is to some degree endogenous; an incumbent facing a vigorous challenger may exert himself or herself enough in the primary to hold that challenger to a mere 35 percent, but the ultimate failure of the challenger to come close in this instance would not be an indication that this was not a serious challenge. This logic suggests that setting a generous threshold (i.e., including as many challenges as possible) best captures any patterns in competitiveness. Third, some might ask why I do not abandon the notion of thresholds and use some sort of sliding scale. For starters, one would still need some sort of threshold; it seems implausible that there are differences worthy of note between challengers who ultimately receive, for instance, 3 and 10 percent of the vote. In neither case would the incumbent or the media likely pay attention to them. Moreover, if we are seeking to distinguish between the degree that any "message" has been sent to the incumbent, we might make some basic distinctions—again, for instance, between incumbents held below 75 percent and incumbents held below 60 percent—but it is difficult to argue that we can benefit from simply using a scale. Even general election challenges are too idiosyncratic to do this reliably; from one election to the next, many incumbents' vote share fluctuates wildly, according to whether there is party support for their challenger or whether a quality challenger emerges, so many students of Congress use various competitiveness thresholds in distinguishing between general election campaigns. In the case of primaries, there is even more variation, and we have even fewer markers to use (e.g., presidential vote share or the presence of quality challengers). The establishment of any threshold for looking at primary challenges should serve two purposes, then: it should eliminate frivolous or quixotic campaigns, while at the same time guaranteeing that the incumbent and the public have noticed that there has been a challenge.

Before I turn my attention to the data, a few notes on some of the technicalities in coding primary challenges are in order. I exclude races in which two incumbents are forced by redistricting to challenge each other. I count as an incumbent anyone who currently holds a seat in Congress, although there were several cases in which the incumbents had won special elections only weeks before the primary. In instances where runoff elections were held, I consider the primary that preceded the runoff, not the runoff itself. In states that held "blanket" or "jungle" primaries for at least some years in the period covered (Alaska, Louisiana, California, and Washington), I divide the incumbent's vote share by the percentage of the vote received by the incumbent and any other same-party candidate to determine whether the challenge reached the threshold. I leave in the data set states that used their convention to select nominees or to limit ballot access in the primary—indeed, this serves as a variable in some of the analyses to follow.[3] The result of including these states may influence arguments about the total number of primary challenges mounted but does not influence the general trend in the rationales for primary challenges. I exclude instances where incumbents running in Nevada were held to less than 75 percent because of votes for "none of the above." Finally, I take no special notice here of races in which the incumbent faced multiple primary challengers.[4] This is because the unit of analysis in this chapter is the incumbent, not the challenger. There are several cases where an incumbent was held to less than 75 percent by two or more challengers who each received less than 20 percent of the vote; virtually all of these races wound up in the "no reason given" category. It is possible that an incumbent might face two or more challengers who ran for two or more different reasons (i.e., he or she might be challenged by one opponent based on competence in office and by another opponent based on ideology). There are a total of ten races in the data set that feature two primary challengers who received more than 25 percent of the vote;[5] there are no races where the *Almanac* ascribed different reasons to the two challenges (and there are no races where there were three challengers who received over 25 percent).

When do House Incumbents Face Primary Challengers?

Changes in the Reasons for House Primaries

If one turns back to table 2.1, it is worth noting the relationship between ideological challenges and other types of challenges. The table shows that ideology does play a major role in primary challenges, but the most frequent reasons for primary challenges are alleged failures of the incumbent—either scandals or perceived ineptitude. This pattern corresponds with more general research on congressional elections: an incumbent who faces a serious challenge is generally an incumbent who has done something wrong. These types of challenges are also more successful; while 26.9 percent of the incumbents who received less than 75 percent of the primary vote were criticized for scandals or for their competence, more than half (51.3 percent) of the incumbents who received less than 50 percent of the vote fell into these two categories.[6] All of these factors might be expected to be immune to trends over time; scandals break out, incumbents age or demonstrate ineffectiveness, but there is no reason to expect one decade to be different from another in these regards.

As table 2.1 shows, the four types of ideological or issue-based challenges tend to be less frequent and less successful than those based on real or perceived misdeeds or failures on the part of the incumbent. Local issues are often rather idiosyncratic, and changes based on these types of issues exhibit no particular trend. However, challenges based on national issues show a distinct clustering, as I discuss in further detail shortly, and ideological challenges might be more likely to show a trend over time; at least, that is the argument that has been made of late.

Figure 2.1 groups all four of these types of challenges, in order to ensure that all challenges based on issues or ideology can be considered together. If one compares this figure with figure 1.1 in the previous chapter, it is clear that issue-based and ideological challenges have become a slightly larger proportion of primary challenges since 1992, but there has been no dramatic rise, and, again, there are fewer of these races than there were during the 1970s. The years 1996, 2006, 2008, and 2010 feature the largest number of ideological challenges since the 1970s, but the increased number of such races (eight in 1996, six in 2006, seven in 2008, and fourteen in 2010) is not so large as to support a claim that there is an entirely different dynamic. In addition, 1996 would seem outside the range of years in which incumbents were targeted by bundling groups—it comes before the formation of the Club for Growth and MoveOn.org and before the Internet-based calls for primarying mentioned in the introduction to this book. It should be noted as well that the larger number of ideological challenges in 2010 corresponds to an absence of issue-based challenges—as I discuss shortly, the dynamics of this election may have had the effect of casting issues in a larger ideological framework.

In short, figure 2.1 shows that the answer to the question of whether there has been an increase in the number of incumbents facing ideological challenges depends on one's baseline. If one considers data from the past forty years, the answer is no, no matter how elastic one's definition of ideology is. If one's concern is with the past two decades, it does seem that ideology matters more, but this is so in part because the overall amount of pri-

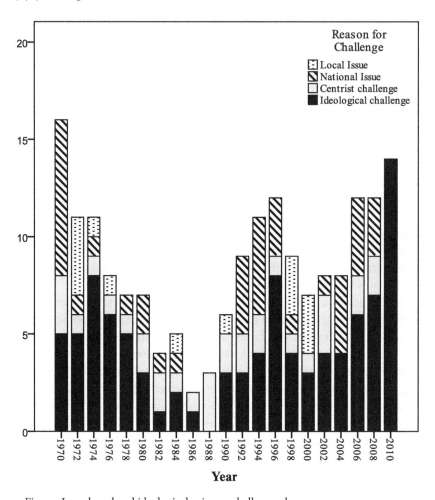

Fig. 2.1. Issue-based and ideological primary challenges, by year

mary competition was so low in the late 1990s and early 2000s and in part because we have just experienced three tumultuous election years. What this portends for the future is unclear, but this is a shaky foundation for any claims that we are truly in an era of increased primary competition.

Comparing Different Years' Primary Challenges

If one is struck by the increase in ideological primary challenges from the 1998 and 2000 cycles to more recent elections, it helps to put the last four elections in the context of other elections in which the number of ideological challenges increased. The overall amount of turnover in Congress in the years since 2006 has two parallels in the past thirty years. In the early 1990s, widespread dissatisfaction with the Democratic Party and with Congress in general produced an unusually competitive set of elections in 1992 and 1994, resulting in a Republican Congress in 1994 and in a serious effort by the Democrats to retake Congress in 1996. Although overall competition in primaries was higher in the 1970s, one might reach back to 1974, where, again, there was substantial turnover in Congress and a forty-nine-seat gain for the Democrats. In figure 2.1, these election years and those immediately before and after them stand out.

Table 2.2 compares the incumbents who faced ideological and issue-oriented challenges over each of these three time periods. The time period from 2004 to 2008 featured seventeen races in which an incumbent faced an ideological challenge (not including challenges from the center) and eleven cases where an incumbent faced a challenge based on an issue of national policy. Of the issue-based challenges, seven were against Republican incumbents, and five of these seven were motivated by the incumbent's perceived leniency on immigration. Of the ideological challenges, nine were waged against Republicans, and eight were waged against Democrats. As one moves through these three years, however, the tables turn: there were no ideological challenges to Democrats in 2004, but there were more ideological challenges to Democrats than to Republicans in 2006 and 2008. This pattern is similar to that of the 1992 to 1996 period, in which there were twelve issue-based challenges and fifteen ideological challenges. Both parties have equal numbers of issue-based and ideological challenges in 1992 and 1994, but eleven of twelve such challenges were waged against Republicans in 1996. In each time period, the party that benefited from the landslide election in the middle year of this sequence saw an increased number of ideological challenges in that year and in the next election cycle.

It is also notable that many of the same incumbents who faced challenges in the 2000s appear on the list of those challenged in the 1990s. Some incumbents, simply put, attract repeated primary challenges, while other incumbents with similar ideological profiles do not. If one considers the data in table 2.2 as a whole, the issues vary from one cycle to the next, even in cases where the primaried incumbents remain the same. Issue-based challenges are more prevalent on the Democratic side, with busing serving as the catalyst for several 1970s challenges and with abortion appearing on both parties' lists. In many of these races, conservative Southern

TABLE 2.2. Comparison of Ideological and Issue-Based Primary Challenges, Three Different Time Periods

Year	Incumbent	Reason	Year	Incumbent	Reason	Year	Incumbent	Reason
1972	Miller (D-CA)	Issue (Vietnam)	1992	Riggs (R-CA)	Issue (pay raise)	2004	Franks (R-AZ)	Ideology
	Rarick (D-LA)	Ideology		Thomas (R-CA)	Ideology		Flake (R-AZ)	Issue (immigration)
	Hicks (D-MA)	Issue (busing)		Porter (R-IL)	Issue (abortion)		Kolbe (R-AZ)	Issue (immigration)
	Nedzi (D-MI)	Issue (busing)		Meyers (R-KS)	Ideology		Lantos (D-CA)	Issue (Iraq)
	W. Ford (D-MI)	Issue (busing)		Sikorski (D-MN)	Issue (abortion)		Gilchrest (R-MD)	Ideology
	Delaney (D-MI)	Ideology		Wheat (D-MO)	Ideology (centrist)		Bartlett (R-MD)	Ideology
	Rooney (D-MI)	Ideology		Swett (D-NH)	Issue (abortion)		Boehlert (R-NY)	Ideology
	Saylor (R-PA)	Ideology		Synar (D-OK)	Ideology (centrist)		Cannon (R-UT)	Issue (immigration)
	Dent (D-PA)	Ideology (centrist)		R. Hall (D-TX)	Ideology			
	J. Young (D-TX)	Issue (busing)						
	R. Casey (D-TX)	Ideology						
1974	McCloskey (R-CA)	Ideology	1994	Thomas (R-CA)	Ideology	2006	Woolsey (D-CA)	Ideology (centrist)
	Hinshaw (R-CA)	Watergate		Calvert (R-CA)	Issue (abortion)		Dreier (R-CA)	Issue (immigration)
	Evans (D-CO)	Ideology		Reynolds (D-IL)	Issue (NAFTA)		Harman (D-CA)	Ideology
	Lehman (D-FL)	Ideology (centrist)		Porter (R-IL)	Issue (abortion)		Bilbray (R-CA)	Ideology
	McClory (R-IL)	Ideology		McCloskey (D-IN)	Ideology (centrist)		Keller (R-FL)	Issue (term limits)
	Kyros (D-ME)	Ideology		Meyers (R-KS)	Ideology		Wynn (D-MD)	Ideology
	Nedzi (D-MI)	Issue (busing)		Barlow (D-KY)	Ideology (centrist)		**Schwarz (R-MI)**	**Ideology**

Year	Incumbent	Reason
	Murphy (D-NY)	Ideology
	R. Casey (D-TX)	Ideology
	Milford (D-TX)	Ideology
	Slack (D-WV)	Ideology
	Cannon (R-UT)	Issue (immigration)
1976	Flowers (D-AL)	Ideology
	McDonald (D-GA)	Ideology
	Mazzoli (D-KY)	Issue (busing)
	Byron (D-MD)	Ideology
	Fountain (D-NC)	Ideology
	Whalen (R-OH)	Ideology
	E. Jones (D-TN)	Ideology (centrist)
	White (D-TX)	Ideology
	McDade (R-PA)	Ideology
	Goodling (R-PA)	Ideology
	Laughlin (R-TX)	**Ideology**
	Bentsen (D-TX)	Issue (abortion)
	N. Smith (R-MI)	Issue (abortion)
	Parker (D-MS)	Ideology
	Clay (D-MO)	Issue (abortion)
	Mann (D-OH)	Ideology
1996	Chenoweth (R-ID)	Ideology (centrist)
	Porter (R-IL)	Ideology
	Morella (R-MD)	Ideology
	Bass (R-NH)	Issue (abortion)
	Kelly (R-NY)	Ideology
	McNulty (D-NY)	Ideology
	Boehlert (R-NY)	Issue (abortion)
	Greenwood (R-PA)	Ideology
	Jones (R-NC)	Issue (Iraq War)
	McHenry (R-NC)	Issue (Iraq War)
	Inglis (R-SC)	Ideology
	Cannon (R-UT)	**Ideology**
	Knollenberg (R-MI)	Ideology (centrist)
	Towns (D-NY)	Issue (tobacco)
	Langevin (D-RI)	Ideology
	Cuellar (D-TX)	Ideology
2008	Lamborn (R-CO)	Ideology (centrist)
	Keller (R-FL)	Issue (term limits)
	Broun (R-GA)	Ideology (centrist)
	Scott (D-GA)	Ideology
	Lipinski (D-IL)	Ideology
	Boswell (D-IA)	Ideology
	Gilchrest (R-MD)	**Ideology**
	Wynn (D-MD)	**Ideology**

Note: Incumbents in bold were defeated in the primary.

Democrats were targeted by liberal insurgents not dissimilar from those who defeated Republicans in 1974. It is striking, however, how few of the primaried incumbents listed in table 2.2 were defeated in the two earlier time periods. Only one of the primaried incumbents in the 1992–96 period was defeated (this primary, in which Ron Paul defeated Greg Laughlin, was, as I noted in chapter 1, an unusual case), and none of those in the 1972–76 period lost, but four lost in the 2004–8 period. Excluding incumbent-versus-incumbent matchups, six incumbents lost their primary bids in the 2004–8 period, 22 lost in the 1992–96 period, and eighteen lost in the 1972–76 period.[7]

If we consider this comparison with reference to the overall shifts in the parties' seat share in Congress, the 1970s and 1990s both show that the partisan trends that brought about turnover in Congress also brought about ideological challenges to moderates in Congress. The same liberal frustration that brought about changes in Congress after the 1974 elections is reflected in the primary challenges of the time, while the conservative frustrations with the Democratic Party in the 1990s also brought about conservative challenges to moderate Republicans. One might read the eight Democratic challenges in 2006 and 2008 as examples of a similar trend.

This is ironic, insofar as the Republican Party is the party most associated with primarying and arguably fears it the most. There is some reason for this, insofar as there have been some noteworthy Republican primary challenges—and, as 2010 has shown, the threat continues to be wielded against several Republican moderates (and not-so-moderates), particularly in the Senate. The 2000s are not atypical in the number of incumbents who are primaried, but they are atypical, at least on the Republican side, in the sense that primarying was not waged amid a strong surge in conservative support within the electorate until 2010. As these data show, actual instances of primarying pose little threat to either party—the number remains small—but one could argue that, if we control for the effects of party surges, primarying remained a bigger problem for Republicans than for Democrats in the 2000s. To put matters numerically, only one Republican was primaried in the 1976 postsurge election, and only one Democrat was primaried in the 1996 postsurge election, but three Republicans were challenged in the 2008 postsurge election (Representatives Gilchrest, Inglis, and Cannon); two of these three (Gilchrest and Cannon) lost their 2008 primaries, and one (Inglis) lost in the primary two years later. The numbers are not large, but the pattern is there.[8]

The story suggested in table 2.2 is easy to tell: when there is substantial unrest within the electorate, potential general election challengers are motivated to run, but so are potential primary challengers. This motivation is more evident within the party out of power—for instance, in a Republican year like 1994, some enthusiastic conservatives run against incumbents of their own party as well as against Democratic incumbents, but in-party challengers also seize on signs of incumbent weakness. Furthermore, this enthusiasm builds and abates over time. To take 1994 as an example again, some conservatives inspired by the 1994 election also ran in the next election, even as political winds begin to blow against them.

This pattern can be shown more clearly than is the case in table 2.2. Table 2.3 shows correlations between the number of primary challenges and the number of defeated incumbents, in the aggregate and within each party. The bivariate correlations here show that there is a relationship between electoral volatility (measured in terms of the number of defeated incumbents)[9] and the number of primary challenges, but, despite the suggestive nature of the 1994 Republican surge, this relationship is driven entirely by Democrats. Democratic primary challenges are more frequent in years when a large number of Democratic incumbents are defeated in the general election, and they are more frequent when the Democrats hold a substantial majority. When the anomalous 1992 election cycle is removed, the correlations for Democrats remain substantively the same, but correlations between Republican primary challenges and some of the variables of seat share (number of Democratic seats, size of majority) reach conventional significance levels.

The correlations here are for all types of primary challenges to incumbents, not merely for the sorts of ideologically inspired primaries that one might expect to correlate with party surges. As table 2.2 shows, a pattern to the occurrence of ideological challenges does track with surge years. The number of ideological challenges in any given year is rarely high—before the fourteen ideological challenges in 2010, the highest number for any year was eight (in 1996)—so correlations here do not tell the whole story. As table 2.4 (presented later in this chapter) shows, the overall mix of primary challenges can be interpreted with reference to political trends in each year, but the overall pattern in the preceding discussion is borne out in much of the subsequent analysis: primaries for Democrats follow a different logic than those for Republicans, but there is some relationship between primaries and political volatility.

To return once more to the most recent election, it is evident from both figure 1.1 in the previous chapter and figure 2.1 that the 2010 election was the high-water mark, thus far, for ideological challenges and that primary

TABLE 2.3. Correlations between Number of Primaries and Characteristics of Election Years

	N of Primaries	N of Democratic Primaries	N of Republican Primaries
N of Defeated Incumbents	.718 **	.555 **	.556**
N of Defeated Democrats	.679 **	.528 *	.521*
N of Defeated Republicans	.082	.055	.076
Size of Majority	.479 *	.700 **	−.126
N of Democratic Seats	.501 *	.733 **	−.134
Number of Observations (years)	21	21	21

**p < .01; *p < .05

competition in that year reached a level seen only once since the 1970s. Though this is noteworthy, I offer three reasons why it is not as noteworthy as one might expect. First, as tables 2.2 and 2.3 show, primary challenges are significantly correlated with turnover in Congress. The 2010 election was unusual in that it followed immediately on the heels of another wave election. This phenomenon is not unheard of; for instance, the Democratic Party won thirty-seven seats in 1964 and lost forty-seven in the next election. But this sort of turbulence does not exist elsewhere in the data considered here—the high turnover elections of 1974 and 1994 were followed by elections with far less turnover. So 2010 represents an extension of a three-election period of volatility. It could signify even more turmoil in future elections, but there is no reason to expect this to be the case, nor should one expect that the number of primary challenges in 2010 signifies anything about future elections. If the pattern shown for the other wave election years holds true, there should be a larger-than-usual number of primary challengers regardless of whether 2012 is a year with high turnover, but if it and the subsequent elections are not high-turnover elections, primary competition should decline.[10]

Second, the reader will notice that there were no primary challenges in 2010 that I coded as being about issues. This may in part be a function of the polarization of U.S. politics, or it may simply be a matter of how challenges are framed by candidates and the media. It is easy to distinguish between a conservative challenger and an anti-abortion challenger, but it is hard to distinguish between a conservative challenger and a challenger running because of an incumbent's vote on the legislation for the Troubled Asset Relief Program. The big issues in the year leading up to the 2010 elections were issues that could only be framed as liberal or conservative.

Third, as the reader will see in subsequent chapters, despite the large number of ideological challengers, very few of these challengers did particularly well in their fundraising. A small number did extraordinarily well, but most did not. It is possible (although it cannot be proven) that what we are seeing in the 2010 data is a number of challengers who enthusiastically sought to curry favor with the Tea Party or with voters unhappy with the state of affairs in Washington and who were able to present somewhat of a threat to the incumbent simply because of the willingness of many voters to register their unhappiness by voting against the incumbent. The fluctuations in the number of competitive races tell part of the story; the changes in the financial support for primary challengers and the consequences of their challenges (discussed in the next two chapters) tell the rest.

Why Do House Incumbents Face Primary Challengers?

Ideological Fit to the District

Given the story line often told about the primarying of incumbents in the past three election cycles, in which conservative groups singled out moderate Republicans while liberal groups responded by singling out moderate Democrats, one might ask whether the targeted candidates deserved to be primaried. Yet matters are not quite that simple. Republican critics of the Club for Growth have sometimes criticized the group for attacking moderate Republicans who represent relatively moderate districts (Cillizza 2005). Indeed, the club has sometimes backed more moderate candidates, arguing that these candidates would fare better in Democratic-leaning districts than would conservatives. Several moderate House and Senate Republicans, most notably those in the New England area, have escaped ideological challenges. On the left, MoveOn.org emphasized in its 2008 campaigns against Maryland Democrat Al Wynn and Illinois Democrat Dan Lipinski that these representatives were out of step not just with their party but with their district. As is the case for Republicans, conservative Democrats in conservative districts have often escaped ideological primary challenges. In instances where the representative is a poor fit for the district, a primary challenger might, if successful, be as likely or more likely to win in the general election than would the incumbent.

Are claims made about the poor "fit" of primaried incumbents accurate? If so, simply comparing the primaried incumbents to their parties

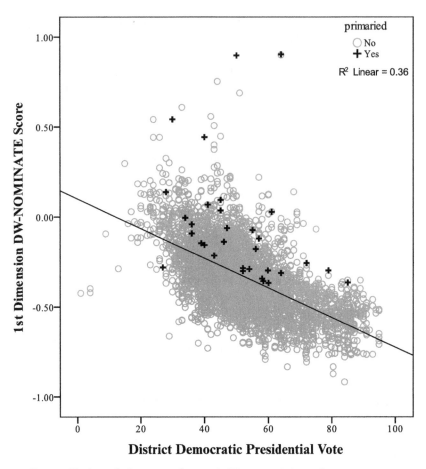

Fig. 2.2. Ideological placement of primaried Democratic incumbents, 1972–2010

would (and does) show that they are more moderate than others in their party, but this by itself is unrevealing. Figures 2.2 and 2.3 show scatter plots of the first-dimension DW-NOMINATE scores (on the y-axis) and district Democratic presidential vote (on the x-axis) for all incumbents seeking renomination from 1972 through 2010, with markers for primaried incumbents. Separate graphs are provided for Democrats and Republicans. If candidates do moderate their positions to reflect their districts, there should be a downward slope for both scatter plots. Furthermore, Democratic incumbents who are more conservative than might be optimal for their districts should appear in upper right-hand quadrant (above

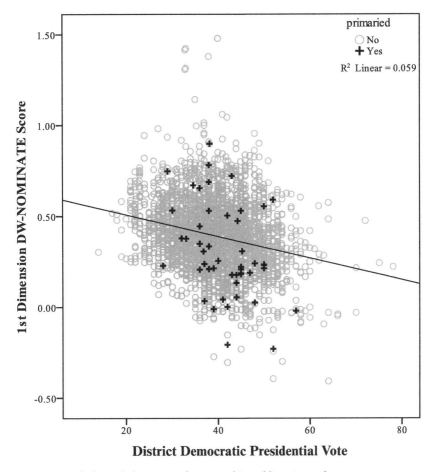

Fig. 2.3. Ideological placement of primaried Republican incumbents, 1972–2010

the fit line), while Republicans who are more liberal than would be optimal should appear in the lower left-hand quadrant (below the fit line).

One should first note that Democrats (see figure 2.2) exhibit more sen-
sitivity to district voting trends than do Republicans; the Republican scatter plot does not fit what would be the regression line nearly as tightly as
would the Democratic scatter plot. In addition, the primaried Democrats
are, as one would predict, almost all to the right of and above what would
be the predicted line; they are arguably too conservative for their districts.
All four of the most extreme outliers on the conservative side were primaried. Most primaried Republicans are below the regression line, again as

one would predict, but a substantial minority of them are not. Primaried Republicans, then, deserve to be primaried less than do primaried Democrats.

Figure 2.4 compares incumbents of both parties primaried in the 2002, 2004, 2006, 2008, and 2010 elections with all incumbents seeking renomination in those years.[11] Here, as in the full data set, all but one of the primaried Democrats are to the right of their party and their district, while less than half of the primaried Republicans (seven of twenty-two) are to the left of their party and district.[12] Of the primaried Republicans, the four who clearly were more liberal than their districts were Gilchrest (primaried three times), Boehlert (primaried twice), Idaho representative Mike Simpson, and Schwarz, all of whom were targeted by the Club for Growth; those five who were not too liberal for their districts included Roscoe Bartlett, Brian Bilbray, Bob Franks, Cannon, and Inglis, of whom only Inglis was a club target. So advocacy groups have indeed chosen candidates who are not just moderates but are perhaps overly moderate for their districts; conservative challengers have, however, run against incumbents who were not out of step with their districts. In 2010, Simpson was the only Republican who appears too liberal for his district; other moderate Republicans who were challenged represented districts that gave Barack Obama a substantial percentage of their votes.

One corollary to this point about fit is that if we simply look at district partisanship, without reference to the incumbent's voting, there is some evidence that district partisanship matters in determining whether Democrats will face challengers, but there is no relationship between district partisanship and Republican primary challenges. For the full 1970–2010 period, the mean Democratic presidential vote share in districts where Democratic incumbents faced primary challengers was 54.7 percent, while it was 52.4 percent in districts where Democratic incumbents were not challenged. This is partially a function of the higher number of challenges in minority districts, but it is still instructive to note that the gap has widened over time; the difference was only 1.6 percent in the 1970s but was 7.0 percent by the 2000s. Republican incumbents who face primary challengers, however, actually represent slightly less Republican districts than do those who are unchallenged. Districts where Republicans went unchallenged averaged a vote share of 39.6 percent for the Democratic presidential nominee, while districts where Republicans were challenged averaged 39.2 percent. The difference among Democratic incumbents is statistically significant; the difference among Republicans is not. When one considers only cases of primarying, the same party difference persists.[13]

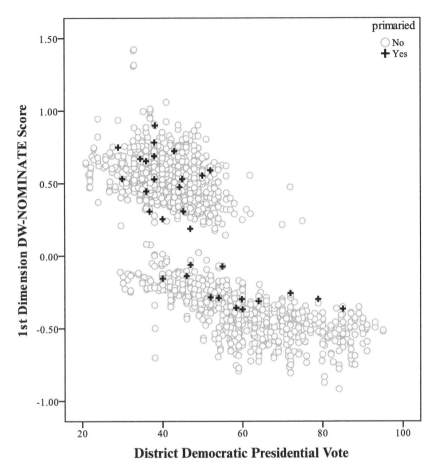

Fig. 2.4. Ideological placement of primaried incumbents, 2002–2010

Other Predictors of Primary Challenges

The preceding discussion suggests that incumbents are no more likely to "get primaried" today than they were in previous years, that the number who get primaried is relatively consistent across time, and that slight increases in the number seem to correspond with surges in one party's power within Congress. The figures discussed thus far, however, do show significant volatility in the number of incumbents facing primary opposition since 1970. If ideological challenges do not account for these changes, what does?

How one interprets table 2.4 depends on whether one takes the short view or the long view. If one is concerned primarily with the past decade or so, the predominance of ideological challenges is unmistakable. There are not a large number of ideological challenges, but they are the plurality winner among my categories. More than half of current House incumbents have been in office for ten years or less, and their tenure has been marked by a steady increase in the number of ideological challenges, so perhaps it is natural for them to worry more about being primaried than it would be for longer-serving representatives.

If one takes the long view, however, table 2.4 shows that many of the sources of primary challenges seem somewhat random. Scandals and allegations of incompetence are the major reasons for primary challenges in

TABLE 2.4. Most Frequent Reasons for Primary Challenges, by Year

Year	Total Number of Challenges	Most Frequent Reason for Challenges (N)	Other Common Reasons (N)
1970	51	National Issue (8)	
1972	59	Competence/Age (13)	Race (10); Redistricting (7)
1974	44	Competence/Age (8)	Ideology (8); Race (7)
1976	45	Competence/Age (10)	Scandal (8); Ideology (6)
1978	45	Scandal (11)	
1980	48	Scandal (12)	Competence/Age (7)
1982	27	Redistricting (7)	
1984	29	Scandal (4)	
1986	15	Competence/Age (4)	
1988	19	Scandal (6)	
1990	31	Scandal (7)	Competence/Age (5)
1992	87	Scandal (19)	Competence/Age (10); Redistricting (10)
1994	46	Race (7)	National Issue (5)
1996	32	Ideology (8)	Race (5)
1998	16	Ideology (4)	
2000	13	*No reason present in more than 3 races*	
2002	31	Redistricting (7)	Ideology (4)
2004	24	National Issue (4); Ideology (4)	
2006	28	Competence/Age (7)	Ideology (6)
2008	33	Ideology (7); Competence/Age (7)	Scandal (4)
2010	51	Ideology (14)	Scandal (6); Competence/Age (5)
Total	774	Competence/Age (110)	Ideology (101); Scandal (98)

the majority of election years; challenges based on race or following a re-districting are also frequent. In reading these data, one must keep in mind that reasons for challenges may be somewhat subjective. For example, an incumbent may be incompetent or too old according to the challenger, or the incumbent may, in fact, be unproductive or old by objective measures. Surely both factors are relevant here. Allegations of incompetence may also be made by candidates who are critical of the incumbent on ideological grounds. If so, this may provide some explanation for the increased number of challenges in the 1970s. Over the course of the decade, there was a rather tumultuous redistricting, one which increased the number of majority-minority districts; the 1970 election is followed by a period of heightened partisanship and ideological fervor, which may explain some of the competence-based challenges in 1972 and 1976. The late 1970s feature a larger-than-average number of incumbents involved in scandals. If the claims to scandal here are at least somewhat valid, these events prolong the unusually high amount of primary competition through the 1980 election. This is just speculation, but absent data on the reasons for primary challenges before 1970, it would cast the 1970s as an aberration, a string of circumstances that brought about heightened competition, rather than as the tail end of a period of greater competition.

Table 2.4 also provides a rather simple explanation of why 1992 is such a clear outlier. This election featured a redistricting that drew many incumbents into somewhat different districts—more so than was the case in 1982 or 2002 (see Jacobson 2004, 172)—and increased the number of majority-minority districts. Like the 1972 election, this election immediately preceded a major change in partisan power within Congress, but it also featured a major scandal (the House banking scandal) which was different from other scandals in that a large number of incumbents were involved. In short, 1992 represented a confluence of several factors that make it unique in the data.

If one accepts this account, there is no gradual trend in primary competitiveness; at most, there is a cyclical trend that corresponds with redistricting, at least in decades such as the 1970s or the 1990s, when districts were substantially redrawn. If an incumbent's ideology is not a particularly good predictor of whether a primary challenger will emerge, what sort of predictors are there? Some states or districts are simply more competitive than others. In some smaller states, if we go simply by the percentage of incumbents challenged, a single incumbent who draws frequent primary opponents over a few elections can lead to a high percentage. Yet there are some cases in which the nature of competition within the state seems to be an issue. Over 16 percent of the races in Arizona, Georgia, Maryland, and Pennsylvania were competitive. These are states that are large enough that a single incumbent could not explain these differences, and there is no obvious geographic story. Meanwhile, not a single Connecticut House candidate faced a primary challenge, and fewer than 5 percent of incumbents in Iowa, Kansas, New Mexico, the Dakotas, Virginia, or Washington faced opposition. There may be some characteristics of state political culture that are relevant here, and in the case of the states with less competition, selection procedures play a role. For much of this period, Connecticut and Virginia selected their nominees at conventions, thus eliminating primary challenges, whereas Washington used a jungle primary to choose candidates and saw frequent primary challenges— there simply were none that were competitive. Idiosyncrasies of the states themselves or even of individual districts may play a role here. We can measure some of this variation, but some of it is likely explained by state-specific or district-specific features.

There are several conventional measurements of state parties and state laws that we can use to get some leverage on the question of whether parties matter for primary competition. Table 2.5 shows that political party strength plays a role, but not necessarily in the manner one might expect. It might be argued that stronger, more organized state parties can discourage primary opposition to incumbents. In fact, the reverse appears to be the case. In table 2.5, I use David Mayhew's (1986) five-point scale of state party organization to compare the percentage of incumbents facing primary opposition according to their state's level of organization.[14] I use two measures of primary competition—the left-hand three columns show the percentage of incumbents who were held to less than 75 percent of the primary vote. The right-hand three columns show the percentage of incumbents primaried (under the restrictive definition)—that is, challenged on ideological grounds from the left (for Democrats) or from the right (for Republicans). Mayhew's party organization categories also include a separate measurement of factionalism (PF, or persistent factionalism) within some of the different levels; I have listed these in parentheses in the table. I also provide percentages for the full 1970 to 2010 data set and for two decades, the 1970s and 2000s. The separate decade estimates are provided here because one might expect the importance of party organization to vary over time and also because one might object to using these scores for the full time period on the grounds that Mayhew's book, published in 1986, might be a better depiction of parties of the decade prior to his book's publication than of subsequent decades.

If one reads down the columns in table 2.5 (ignoring party organization level 3 because there is only one state Mayhew places in that category,
Louisiana), a clear pattern emerges in five of the six columns—incumbents
in more organized states (levels 4 and 5) are actually more likely to face
primary opposition and to be primaried than incumbents in states where
the parties are weaker (levels 1 and 2). The only category in which this is
not true is contested primaries in the 1970s. This pattern is largely driven
by the states with highly organized parties but "persistent factionalism" as
defined by Mayhew (e.g., Indiana and Maryland), but significant differences remain even when the persistent factionalism states are removed.
There may well be explanations for this pattern, yet it seems at odds with
the presumption that parties seek to ward off primary challenges. At a
minimum, the data indicate that parties at the state or local level have little
ability to do this.

Another way to approach this issue is to use direct measures of party
involvement in primaries. Galderisi and Ezra (2001) and Maisel, Gibson,
and Ivry (1998) provide summaries of parties' roles in primary elections.
Maisel and his coauthors group states according to two different measures: first, whether parties play a formal role in primaries (e.g., whether
the party endorsement can replace the primary entirely or limit ballot access), an informal role (e.g., by conferring an endorsement before the primary takes place), or no role at all; and second, whether the primary is
open to all voters, closed to registered party members, or a blanket or
jungle primary. There is no significant correlation between the Mayhew

TABLE 2.5. Primary Competition and Primarying by Party Organization Level

	Contested Primary			Ideological Primary		
TPO	1970–2010 (%)	1970s (%)	2000s (%)	1970–2010 (%)	1970s (%)	2000s (%)
1	8.4	11.9	7.2	0.9	1.1	1.4
2 (PF)	9.1 (8.6)	15.8 (10.5)	6.2 (4.3)	1.2 (0.0)	2.3 (0.0)	1.3 (0.0)
3	13.7	22.9	11.1	0.7	2.9	0.0
4 (PF)	9.8 (12.1)	13.2 (16.7)	7.5 (5.1)	0.5 (0.5)	1.5 (2.1)	0.0 (0.0)
5 (PF)	10.8 (15.2)	11.8 (15.9)	9.0 (21.9)	1.8 (2.9)	1.6 (1.1)	2.7 (6.3)
Total (PF)	9.4 (12.8)	12.6 (16.0)	7.1 (11.6)	1.2 (1.3)	1.5 (1.6)	1.6 (2.2)
N	8,224	1,931	2,388	8,224	1,931	2,388
Chi-square	**	Not sig.	Not sig.	**	Not sig.	**

Note: TPO (Total Party Organization) scores taken from Mayhew 1986. States in each category with
persistent factionalism (PF) as defined by Mayhew are in parentheses. N's are for total number of incumbents seeking reelection.
**$p < .01$; significance tests exclude factionalism measures.

measures of party organization and either of the measurements of Maisel, Gibson, and Ivry or between the two measures of Maisel and his coauthors. In their analysis of the 1994 and 1996 elections, Maisel, Gibson, and Ivry note that in states where parties do play a role in primaries, they can limit the appearance of nuisance candidates (i.e., of uncompetitive primary challengers) but have little effect in warding off serious challengers. These challengers are few enough to begin with, however, that the authors conclude that they simply do not have enough cases to measure the role of parties. Presumably, the larger data set here provides more leverage in measuring the effect of parties and of primary rules. If parties are successful in limiting primary opponents to incumbents, one would expect to see a lower percentage of challenges to incumbents in states where the parties play some role and in states where primaries are closed.

Tables 2.6 and 2.7 show patterns of primary competition according to the measures of Maisel, Gibson, and Ivry, again in the aggregate and for two different decades. They paint a picture that further complicates the analysis based on the Mayhew categories. Considering the party role in primaries first, it appears that parties could once limit challenges to incumbents but have failed to do so during the past decade. Party involvement in the primary has no relationship to the incidence of ideological challenges, however. In terms of the nature of the primary election itself, open primaries actually have fewer primary challengers to incumbents than do closed primaries—again somewhat counter to intuition. One can conclude from these analyses that if parties or primary rules ever did play a role in reducing primary competition, they no longer can do this, except perhaps in deterring frivolous candidacies.[15]

TABLE 2.6. Primary Competition and Primarying by Party Role in Primaries

| Party Role | Contested Primary | | | Ideological Primary | | |
	1970–2010 (%)	1970s (%)	2000s (%)	1970–2010 (%)	1970s (%)	2000s (%)
None	9.5	13.3	8.1	1.2	1.5	1.9
Informal	10.7	13.9	7.4	1.0	1.5	0.9
Formal	6.3	7.7	6.0	1.2	1.7	1.8
Total	9.4	12.6	7.6	1.2	1.5	1.6
N	8,224	1,931	2,388	8,224	1,931	2,388
Chi-square	**	*	Not sig.	Not sig.	Not sig.	Not sig.

Note: Source for party role codings: Maisel, Gibson, and Ivry 1998.
$*p < .05; **p < .01$

TABLE 2.7.   Primary Competition and Primarying by Primary Type

Primary Type	Contested Primary			Ideological Primary		
	1970–2010 (%)	1970s (%)	2000s (%)	1970–2010 (%)	1970s (%)	2000s (%)
Closed	9.8	13.3	7.7	1.2	0.0	1.5
Open	6.4	5.4	6.2	0.8	1.7	2.7
Blanket/Jungle	9.9	17.1	7.6	0.3	1.4	0.0
Total	9.4	12.6	7.6	1.1	1.5	1.6
N	8,224	1,931	2,388	8,224	1,931	2,388
Chi-square	**	*	Not sig.	Not sig.	Not sig.	Not sig.

Note: Source for primary type codings: Maisel, Gibson, and Ivry 1998.
$*p < .05; **p < .01$

Some other determinants of primary competition are more predictable. Majority-minority districts also feature greater primary competition; 16.0 percent of incumbents in these districts faced primary competition, while only 8.7 percent of the representatives of other districts faced a competitive primary opponent. The reasons for such competition are well documented; these districts tend to be lopsidedly Democratic, and as a result, ambitious candidates are far more likely to appear in the primary than in the general election. Another unsurprising characteristic is that redrawn districts are more likely to yield primary competition; 13.2 percent of redrawn districts have primary competition, while only 7.5 percent of districts that stayed the same as in the prior election cycle were competitive.[16]

Age and seniority are also important, but not in the same fashion. One might expect first-term incumbents to be more vulnerable to challenges, not only because they tend to be more vulnerable to general election challenges than more experienced incumbents, but also because they may have recently faced primary opposition in winning the seat or have yet to build up name recognition. Contrary to expectations, however, freshman representatives were not more likely to face primary opponents than were more senior representatives. Overall, seniority exhibits a slight but significant correlation (.037) with having primary competition (perhaps indicating that older representatives are vulnerable to challenges on the basis of their age). Almost all of this relationship is explained by the frequency of challenges based on age or competence. Seniority reduces the likelihood of facing an ideological challenger. So longtime incumbents do not lose touch with their district in an ideological sense, but they may lose touch in the sense that they are no longer regarded as effective advocates for the district. Table 2.8 compares different types of challenges with regard to seniority.

A final potential cause for primary challenges is the pursuit of higher office. While it is difficult to develop a coding for all representatives who have run unsuccessfully in the primary for governor, senator, or president, several of the representatives who faced primary challenges fell into one of these categories. As this evidence indicates, a bid for higher office leaves one vulnerable to the claim that one has been insufficiently attentive to one's district, and the scars of a failed race for higher office can be used against a candidate seeking renomination to a House seat.

Several of these factors can be expected to bring about differences in the number of primary challenges in each party. In particular, because most representatives of majority-minority districts are Democrats, this factor alone might indicate that Democrats are more likely than Republicans to face primary opposition. Overall, 11.0 percent of Democrats faced primary opposition, compared with 7.3 percent of Republicans. If one excludes majority-minority districts, the percentage of Democrats facing opposition declines to 9.9 percent, still a much larger percentage than that of Republicans. However, Republicans are more likely than Democrats to be primaried, according to both the restrictive definition (ideological challenges from off-center) and the less restrictive definition (including issue-based challenges and centrist challenges). While the percentages here are not large (1.6 percent of Republicans versus 0.9 percent of Democrats by the restrictive definition and 2.5 percent versus 1.7 percent according to the less restrictive definition), the differences are significant.

It would be convenient if it were possible to present results of a probit analysis of factors determining primary challenges. However, the most important determinants of primary challenges—the presence of a scandal or ethical transgression, competence or age, being ideologically out of step

TABLE 2.8.   Mean Years in Congress by Type of Challenge

Type of Challenge	Mean Years in Congress	N
Competence/Age	16.0	110
Scandal	12.9	98
National Issue	12.1	40
Ideological Challenge	11.2	101
Race	10.3	57
Local Issue	9.6	14
Centrist Challenge	9.5	32
Other/None	9.9	322
Total	11.6	774

with the district, or being in the wrong on a particular issue—are subjective enough that it is not possible to include measures of these in any analysis.[17] This is an issue that will bedevil us in subsequent chapters as well. I experimented with a number of analyses using some of the indicators previously mentioned, but all of them left out enough of the apparent rationale for challenges that they are not particularly revealing.

Alternate Measurements of Primary Competitiveness

Using a Different Threshold for Defining Competitiveness

Earlier in this chapter, I mentioned that the threshold I have used for defining a primary challenge is debatable. In the preceding analysis, I have categorized a challenge that holds the incumbent below 75 percent as a challenge worthy of analysis; I have deliberately cast my net wide in order to include as many primary challenges as possible, while still seeking to ensure that meaningful data can be gathered about the motive for the challenge. Because other analyses have used a 60 percent threshold, however, it is worth comparing data using the two thresholds. The question in doing so is whether the patterns among highly competitive challenges are similar, across time or according to the rationale for the challenge, to those among less competitive challenges.

It would likely test the reader's patience here to rerun all of the preceding analyses using a 60 percent threshold; let it suffice to say that if one reruns the scatter plots shown in figures 2.2–2.4 using the 60 percent threshold, the plots show similar results.[18] They show that whatever one's measure of competitiveness, ideological challenges tend to be waged against incumbents who are clearly somewhat out of step with the district electorate. If one reconsiders the plot in figure 2.3 using only challenges where the incumbent was held to 60 percent or less of the vote, nine of the thirty primaried Republicans are above the fit line. I suspect this is not a consequential change, but the small numbers here preclude any sort of definitive statement one way of the other. Were it the case that all of the Republicans above the fit line dropped out when using the higher threshold for competitiveness, one might conclude that serious challenges in the Republican Party only take place when the incumbent really is too liberal but that less serious challengers do gain some support by making this argument. Because this is not the case, it seems that, whatever level of competitiveness one uses, Republicans are somewhat different from Democrats in their propensity to have competitive primaries and to have primaries in which the primary challenger runs further from the center than the incumbent.

Quality Challengers

It is conventional in studies of general election competition to use measurements of challenger quality—following Jacobson's (1989) lead and distinguishing between candidates who have held prior elected office and those who have not. Some analyses of primaries have done this as well; Pearson and Lawless (2008), for instance, develop quality measures for primary challengers for the 1992–2006 period.[19] Although Pearson and Lawless find that quality challengers easily outperform those challengers who have not held prior elected office, they note that there are very few such candidates in congressional primaries—fewer than 4 percent of primary challengers have held any sort of prior office. The inclusion of such a variable might add some nuance to this study, but if one is primarily concerned with the frequency of primary challenges or (as we shall explore in chapter 4) the consequences of such challenges, it is unclear what the presence or absence of a quality challenger tells us. To start with, the numbers here are sufficiently small that we would not expect meaningful variation across time. In addition, how does one interpret the signal sent by the performance of a quality challenger? One might assume, on the one hand, that an incumbent would take the appearance of a quality challenger more seriously than the appearance of a challenger without a political track record. On the other hand, the ability of a political neophyte to garner 25 percent or more of the primary vote might actually be more worrisome to the incumbent than the ability of a more seasoned politician to do this. While Pearson and Lawless's findings on the performance of quality primary challengers is beyond dispute, the message their presence might send to incumbents strikes me as being a little bit too difficult to measure for them to be included here. In my analysis, I did explore using a variable to designate quality challengers, but no significant patterns emerged. Prior political experience, it would seem, is simply too rare among primary challengers for it to be of use in understanding why incumbents are challenged.

Repeat Primary Challenges

When this chapter moved beyond looking at the occurrence of primary challengers to explore what we can say about whether incumbent traits or behaviors inspire primary challengers, I noted the difficulties we have in measuring many of the characteristics challengers have seized on. There is, for instance, no objective measurement for corruption or incompetence, and even where we can seek to measure some of these things, there is still a subjective element. Is an incumbent really too old to do the job effectively? Is an incumbent really out of step with the district? We can use measurements of seniority or of ideological placement, but these are only suggestive, not conclusive. The real question here—does the challenger make a good point about the incumbent in his campaign?—is something that is ultimately up to the voters. One way of getting some leverage on this question, however, is to look at repeat primary challenges. If, for instance, an incumbent faces challengers who raise the same issue in successive election cycles, we can at least conclude that the initial challenger who raised this point was not entirely deluded, that he or she was inspired by support in the initial campaign to run again, or that other challengers sought to develop the same themes.

There are some problems with this approach, however, that make it of limited use in terms of analysis. The longer an incumbent stays in office, the more primary challenges he or she is likely to face. An incumbent in office for the duration of this study may have drawn two or three primary challengers over this forty-year span, but this does not definitely mean that this incumbent is more vulnerable or that primary challenges to him or her have more merit than is the case for an incumbent who served for ten years and drew one challenge or no challenges. In addition, a challenger who does have a real point may knock off the incumbent on the first try or inspire the incumbent to retire—thus meaning that there was more merit to this challenge than would be the case for an incumbent who is unsuccessfully challenged in two or three successive election cycles.

A total of seventy-two incumbents faced three or more primary challengers over the 1970–2010 period, and an additional one hundred incumbents faced two primary challenges. In sum, the 774 primary challenges over this period were waged against 480 different incumbents. Nine of the seventy-two who faced three or more challenges had at least one challenger who ran on ideological grounds; these nine include several recent targets of high-profile challenges, such as moderate Republicans Wayne Gilchrest, Sherwood Boehlert, Marge Roukema, John Porter, and Bill Thomas. Gilchrest was challenged six times during his tenure in Congress; three of these challenges were ideological, one appears to have been inspired by the redrawing of Gilchrest's district, and two were uncategorizable. Four of Boehlert's challenges were ideological, and one focused on Boehlert's views on abortion. The most frequent targets of primary challenges, however, were generally representatives who were challenged on account of race (including Missouri Democrat William Clay, who was challenged seven different times; California Democrat Charles Wilson,[20] who was challenged five times; and Pennsylvania Democrat Tom Foglietta, also challenged five times) or scandal (including Illinois Democrat Gus Savage, who was challenged four times because of scandal and twice because of claims about incompetence, and California Republican Ken Calvert, also challenged six times on grounds of scandal and incompetence).

One might use the ideological challenges previously listed to argue that these representatives can truly be said to be out of step with their districts, but such anecdotal claims cannot be taken much further than simply noting that the data here are somewhat messy; a different story could be told for each incumbent. The data do show two things, however. First, the codings here are unavoidably messy. In the case of Gilchrest, for instance, are the uncategorizable challenges really ideological challenges? Is it truly possible to conclusively distinguish between ideological challenges and other types of challenges? Surely there are multiple reasons for any challenge, and it is somewhat reductionist to place challenges solely into one category or another. Second, these repeat challenges indicate that we should be somewhat cautious about reading too much into the trends across time here; the incumbents who faced multiple challenges faced them in years that were good for incumbents and years that were not so good. One might argue that the consequences may vary—in Gilchrest's case, for instance, challengers who seized on Gilchrest's moderate voting record were unsuccessful in several election cycles, but in 2008, a year that featured a larger-than-usual turnover in Congress and a Democratic wave, Gilchrest's challenger was finally able to defeat him (albeit only to lose in the general election). The patterns I have already noted speak for themselves, but there are certainly other reasons in play that are not easy to capture using the coding mechanisms I have explored here.

Senate Primaries

Primary challenges in Senate races are only slightly more frequent than challenges in House races. Between 1970 and 2010, there were 546 Senate races with an incumbent running. Sixty-four incumbents, or 11.7 percent, received less than 75 percent of the vote in their primaries, and 35 incumbents, or 6.4 percent, were held to less than 60 percent. The similarity between the Senate percentage and the corresponding House percentages (9.4 percent and 4.0 percent) is somewhat surprising given that Senate general election races tend to be more competitive than House races and that Senate incumbents are defeated in the general election more often than House incumbents (Jacobson 2004, 99). However, two major causes of House primary contests—majority-minority districts and redrawn districts—are not relevant for Senate races. The numbers are far too small to present a meaningful analysis of reasons in each year, and the time series of contests over the entire time period appears, at first, to be idiosyncratic enough that no real trends are apparent from merely looking at the data. On average, there are two to four cases of primary challenges in each election cycle, with a high of eight (in 1980) and a low of zero (in 1984, 1988, and 2000). In 1992, a year of unusually high primary competition in House races, six Senate incumbents faced primary opposition, and in 2006 and 2010, five incumbents faced primary challengers. Trends in the number of competitive Senate races are somewhat correlated with trends for House races, however: the bivariate correlation is .69, significant at the .01 level. This relationship is apparent when one converts the numbers for House and Senate races into a percentage of races with an incumbent running, as shown in figure 2.5.

Table 2.9 shows a breakdown of Senate races, according to the same categories used in the House. Ideology plays a somewhat larger role in Senate primaries than it does in House primaries. Only five of the sixty-four Senate incumbents in the data set who faced primary competition were challenged on the basis of scandal or ethical problems, and despite the presence of well-known octogenarian senators throughout much of this time, only seven Senate incumbents were challenged on the basis of competence or age. Eighteen of the sixty-four were "primaried," however, and ten of these eighteen were primaried in the past four election cycles— Republican Arlen Specter in 2004 (from the right, as a Republican) and 2010 (from the left, as a Democrat), Republicans Lincoln Chafee and Mike DeWine (OH) and Democrat Joseph Lieberman in 2006, Democrat John Kerry in 2008, and Democrats Blanche Lincoln and Michael Bennet and Republicans Lisa Murkowski and John McCain in 2010. Other noteworthy cases of primarying in earlier years include Illinois Democratic senator Alan Dixon, defeated in the 1992 primary by Carol Moseley Braun; noted liberal Republicans Jacob Javits (NY), Charles Mathias (MD), and Robert Stafford (VT); and Arlen Specter again, in 1998. It does seem plausible that liberal Republican senators face a higher risk of being primaried, even when they represent relatively liberal states.[21]

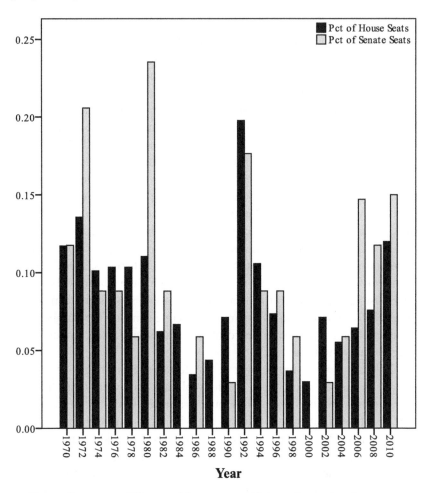

Fig. 2.5. Percentage of House and Senate seats with incumbent primaries, 1970–2010

While ideology may play a larger role in Senate challenges than in House challenges, there are fewer single-issue challenges in Senate races. There are five issue-based challenges, three of which were about abortion, including a vigorous challenge to George McGovern in 1980. Several senators face challengers every election cycle, although the reasons vary— in three of his four reelection bids. Oregon senator Bob Packwood faced primary opposition based on his perceived liberalism and his competence; Specter faced ideological opposition in three of his four bids; and in both of his renomination campaigns, Alaska senator Mike Gravel was held be-

TABLE 2.9. Types of Senate Primary Challenges, 1970–2010

Type of Challenge	N
Scandal	5
Competence/Age	7
Local Issue	3
National Issue	4
Ideological Challenge—Center	1
Ideological Challenge—Left (D) or Right (R)	18
Ambitious Challenger	6
Other	1
No Reason Given	19
Total	64

low 55 percent by challengers who criticized him on the grounds of incompetence. Finally, ambition seems to be a more frequent source of primary competition in the House than in the Senate; the rationale behind challenges such as those to Hawaii's Daniel Akaka in 2006 (by House member Ed Case), South Dakotan James Abdnor in 1986 (by Governor William Janklow), and Arkansas's William Fulbright (successfully challenged by Governor Dale Bumpers) seems to have been simply that the challenger felt he or she was more qualified, not that there was anything in particular wrong with the incumbent.

In sum, the Senate is not dramatically different from the House in terms of the occurrence of primary challenges to incumbents or in the reasons for challenges. Where it is different (in the number of ideological challenges, in the relative paucity of challenges based on competence or age, or in the higher number of challenges that seem to be simply a matter of a qualified challenger emerging), one might attribute these differences to the higher prestige of being in the Senate or to different standards that voters or political elites may use in evaluating the performance of senators. As is the case in so many treatments of congressional elections, however, the smaller number of Senate races to consider ensures that it is difficult to make generalizations and that one is limited to using anecdotal support drawn from a small number of high-profile Senate races.

Conclusions

The reader of this chapter might be forgiven for feeling a little bit overwhelmed at this point by the sheer amount of data presented here. The point of all of this, however, is that few arguments about primary competition draw on such data and that an understanding of trends in primary competition is necessary in order to understand what is taking place today. In chapter 1, I focused on the stories of races that have garnered media attention. It is easy to be misled by these stories or to seize on unmeasurable details of particular races. In this chapter, I relied solely on characteristics of primary challenges that one can measure.

Despite all of the effort that has gone into quantifying the nature of congressional elections and congressional election results, much about these elections eludes political scientists' efforts to understand elections. This is the case even though many aspects of electoral campaigns are the fodder for punditry. There have been advances in measuring campaign discourse (see Simon 2002) and in understanding why some candidates run for office while others do not (Stone and Maisel 2003). In my own work, I have aimed at a better understanding of what those who challenge incumbents in the general election talk about in their campaigns (Boatright 2004). Yet all of these studies are attempts to systematize what many savvy political insiders believe they already know. The data presented here are another attempt to measure political decisions that largely take place under the radar but that are said to have profound effects on Congress.

Through the analysis in this chapter, I have sought to demonstrate that the instances of "primarying" noted by so many observers over the past few election cycles are neither unprecedented nor demonstrably as frequent as some have argued. Primary challenges follow predictable patterns. They are more frequent when there is greater turnover in the partisan composition of Congress, but this has been the case in past election cycles, not just in the 2000s. Somewhat counterintuitively, primary challenges are more likely in areas of the country where the parties have wielded more power. If parties ever did limit serious primary competition for incumbents, there is little evidence that they do so today. It is hard to measure whether some incumbents deserve primary opponents, but there is some evidence that some types of incumbents do. Challengers who gain some traction in their campaigns do not invent campaign themes out of whole cloth; either they are inspired to run because of real flaws on the part of the incumbent, or they are savvy enough to choose a theme that will resonate with the public whether or not that is their actual reason for running.

Perhaps most noteworthy in this chapter's analysis are the party differences. Primary challenges across the 1970–2010 time period are more likely in the Democratic Party than in the Republican Party, and in terms of ideology, the Democrats who are primaried appear to be more out of step with their districts than are primaried Republicans. Whether this is a function of the greater heterogeneity of the Democratic Party or the consequence of a higher standard of purity among conservative activists is not clear, but this should be somewhat troubling for Republicans. A Democratic incumbent may at least know how to vote if he or she is to ward off a challenger from the left, while some Republicans may wonder just what they have to do in order to represent their districts while avoiding being branded as traitors to the cause. Traditional theories of the differences between party coalitions (see, e.g., Freeman 1986) have posited that the Republican Party is the more hierarchical of the two parties while the Democrats are a messier, group-driven coalition. The more haphazard occurrence of Republican primary challenges provides evidence to support the notions that the Republican establishment has become less able to protect its members from its conservative flank (a phenomenon noted in treatments of the Tea Party, as in Bullock 2012) and that so-called cross-pressured legislators (Carson et al. 2010) must increasingly worry about protecting both their right and left flanks.

Few incumbents have very much to fear from primaries, however, whatever their rationale. As this chapter shows, primary challenges are still relatively infrequent, and as I shall argue in future chapters, far fewer primary challenges are successful. These conclusions may be cold comfort for the handful of incumbents who are successfully primaried. For anyone else, the rhetoric behind primarying may be either frightening or invigorating, depending on one's point of view. The reality, however, is that when we put the level of primary competition today and the reasons for it in the context of congressional elections over the last forty years, it is by no means clear that the number of competitive primaries is any different from what it has been in years past.

3 | The Financing of Congressional Primary Challenges

As the previous chapter demonstrated, there is little evidence that the number of primary challenges to incumbents is greater today than it was in previous decades. A conclusion one might draw from the discussion so far is that all of the most prominent cases of incumbents "getting primaried" are cases in which interest groups have targeted incumbents for defeat. On the Republican side, the Club for Growth has regularly singled out RINOs (Republicans in Name Only) and encouraged challenges to these candidates; on the Democratic side, MoveOn.org and smaller organizations, such as the Working for Us PAC, have singled out Democrats who have "actively stepped away from the Democratic caucus, to the detriment of constituents in their districts."[1] The involvement of these types of groups, each of which has members throughout the country and has a track record of raising small contributions via the Internet for its favored candidates, has the potential to substantially alter the financing of primary challenges. An incumbent who might have previously faced a feisty but underfunded challenger now may face a challenger capable of raising money quickly through national networks of political activists.

In this chapter, I look at changes in the financing of different types of primary challenges, paying particular attention to changes in the total funding for primary challengers, PAC support for primary challengers, the average size of contributions over time, and the geography of contributions. The data presented in this chapter show that a select number of primary challengers have been able to substantially exceed the amounts of money traditionally raised by candidates in the primaries and that ideological primary challengers have done far better than other types of challengers at raising money. Furthermore, most of this money has come from individuals. While some of these changes are undoubtedly a consequence of the increase, following the 2002 elections, in hard money contribution limits for individuals, primary challengers have benefited in ways that general election challengers have not. This provides at least strong circumstantial evidence that primary challenges have been nationalized to a degree, that there are donors out there interested in sending a message to Congress by unseating incumbents, and that primary challengers have found new ways to reach these donors, ways that they did not have in previous elections. While the average incumbent has no more reason to worry about "getting primaried" today than he or she did in the 1980s or 1990s, the incumbents who do face primary challengers may have greater reason to worry than they once did.

I can say only that these incumbents may have greater reason to worry, because difficulty exists in identifying a trend in the past decade's election cycles. From 2002 through 2008, it is evident that spending by primary challengers was increasing and that this spending was concentrated among a small number of challengers. Even as the number of serious challengers fluctuated (as shown in chapter 2) according to trends in party competition, it seemed that there was a general upward trend in the amount of money being channeled into primaries. In 2010, however, the number of candidates increased, but few of these challengers had very much money, and those who did were not necessarily the sorts of ideological candidates who emerged in past elections. Was 2010 an aberration, or was it a sign that what we will see in future elections is not spending that is concentrated in a few high-profile challenges but, rather, a profusion of underfunded but competitive challengers of the sort loosely connected to the Tea Party? This is a question that I cannot answer, but as should become evident in the ensuing pages, I am inclined to believe that 2010 was an aberration and that we should pay more attention to the spending increases in 2006 and 2008.

It must be emphasized, however, that the 2006–10 period is unprecedented in the data here and effectively wipes out any effort to make comprehensive statements about the effects of changes in campaign finance law during the earlier years of the decade. In chapter 2, I noted that primary competition increased in the years surrounding "wave" elections. In the other wave elections considered here, such as 1974 and 1994, the wave subsided in the following year. For the 2006–10 period, however, we had three consecutive high-turnover elections, featuring very different types of challengers. In 2006 and 2008, the Democrats were the beneficiaries of the wave, and Democratic primary challengers raised substantial sums of money. In 2010, in contrast, the Republican primary challengers seeking to ride the wave did so despite the fact that most of them raised relatively little money. In short, we can speculate about party differences in financial support for primary challengers—something I shall do later in this chapter—but we can infer little about what these elections portend for future primary challenges. Perhaps we will know more once the tumult of the past three election cycles has subsided.

The Scant Body of Research on Campaign Finance in Congressional Primaries

Few studies have focused on the role of campaign finance in primary elections, and fewer still have focused on changes in primary fundraising over time. Political scientists have, of course, noted the dramatic increase in incumbent fundraising over the past three decades, and they have generally concluded that incumbents have increased their fundraising in order to amass large war chests that can deter general election competitors. It stands to reason that many potential primary opponents are deterred from running for the same reason. This causes some problems for our analysis; after all, primary competition is not the norm, so we cannot measure the decisions of potential primary opponents not to run. Because general elections are usually contested, we can take the paltry fundraising of many general election challengers as evidence that stronger candidates were deterred (see, e.g., Jacobson 2004, 38–51). A corollary of this argument is that incumbents tend to cement their advantage by raising money from access-oriented PACs and, when necessary, from the party committees.

In one of the few studies of campaign finance in primaries, published in 2001, Goodliffe and Magleby have shown that primary challengers to incumbents raise virtually no PAC or party money and tend to rely primarily on their own funds. In her 2006 study of self-financed candidates, Jennifer Steen (2006, 24) reaches similar conclusions. We can take the Goodliffe and Magleby study as prima facie evidence that potential primary challengers are at such a disadvantage that the ones we actually do observe—those who run at all and those who raise enough money to even file with the Federal Election Commission—are an unusual bunch.

It is difficult, for a variety of reasons, to assess the extent to which incumbent fundraising changes based on the potential or actual threat of a primary challenge. While some incumbents may raise extra money to ward off a primary challenge, it is impossible to distinguish between fundraising aimed at warding off a primary challenge and fundraising geared toward warding off a general election challenge, let alone fundraising that is undertaken based on other considerations—for instance, fundraising based on an expected run for higher office, with an eye toward redistributing the money to other candidates, or simply contributions received from donors who wish to support prominent or like-minded members of Congress. Incumbents can raise and spend money during the primary season for the purpose of helping themselves in the general election; this is the case whether or not these incumbents actually have a serious primary challenger. We cannot, in other words, benchmark the spending of primary challengers directly against incumbent spending or even against the spending of incumbents who face primary opposition.

Challengers' fundraising, however, might be expected to vary across time, particularly if there is indeed a trend toward increasing ideological competition in congressional primaries. There are several questions of interest here that can be addressed through analysis of primary challengers' fundraising:

- Have the aggregate sums of money raised by primary challengers increased? Or, to be more precise, have they increased at a greater rate than has the cost of campaigning for other types of candidates?
- Following Goodliffe and Magleby's contention, has there been a change in challengers' propensity to spend their own money?
- Again following Goodliffe and Magleby's claims, do primary challengers raise a different amount of money or percentage of their money from PACs (or even from the parties) today than they did in previous years?
- Has the propensity of challengers to raise small or large contributions changed over time?
- How has the ability of primary challengers to raise money from outside of their home district or state changed over time?

All of these questions can be answered with reference to measuring changes in the financing of all primary challenges as well as with reference to distinguishing between different motivations for challenges, using the categories of the previous chapter. In this chapter, I address the ways in which one can answer these questions.

Measuring Campaign Finance for Primary Challengers

I have supplemented the previously discussed data on the vote share of primary challengers to incumbents and the reasons for these challenges with campaign finance data drawn from the Federal Election Commission's candidate summary files and itemized contribution files. In the case of unsuccessful primary challengers, I have used the candidate summary files for each cycle; in the case of successful challengers (of which there are thirty-two), I have used the successful candidates' reports of primary fundraising.[2] This is necessary because unsuccessful candidates will have only primary money to report, while successful primary challengers will receive money during both their primary and their general election campaigns; we need to be certain to exclude money received during the general election from our calculations here. Candidate summary files are available electronically for all elections from 1980 to the present. These files include data on total receipts, PAC receipts, contributions from party committees, contributions from the candidates themselves, and loans from the candidates. I have created a self-funding variable that includes both contributions and loans that were not repaid before the primary. The itemized individual contribution files for these years allow one to add data on the size of contributions (the amount of money raised in contributions of less than $250, from $250 to $499, from $500 to $749, and $750 or more). These figures are useful in analyzing changes in the donor base of primary challengers, but they are complicated somewhat by the passage of the Bipartisan Campaign Reform Act and the increase in the contribution limits for individuals. The percentage of funds raised in each of these categories can give one a sense of any changes in the types of donors, although the FEC files do not aggregate by donor; that is, a donor who gives multiple contributions of less than $250 may properly belong in a higher contribution category, but the FEC data do not allow one to do this without manually combing through each candidate's donor list (as is done in the data from the Center for Responsive Politics).[3] I have also used the address of contributors in the itemized files to measure contributions from inside and outside of the candidate's home state.[4] Throughout this chapter, I use the dollar numbers provided by the FEC (i.e., I do not inflation adjust), because the reporting threshold of $200 does not change, nor do contribution limits for PACs or, until the 2002 passage of BCRA, individuals.

There are numerous complications to using FEC data to describe primary challengers, partly because of the variation in the fundraising of primary challengers and partly because of changes in campaign finance law during the period covered here. A number of decisions must be made about which candidates to include and which to exclude. In chapter 2, the lone threshold decision that was required was when to consider a candidate a "serious" challenger; here, there are a number of cut points, dictated by the availability or lack of campaign finance data for different primary challengers. Another analyst might easily make different decisions about how to present the campaign finance data on these candidates. Even so, the data here present clear evidence of what has changed in the funding of primary challengers over the past three decades. In this chapter, I note changes in the finances of primary challengers with reference to broader changes in the fundraising of incumbents and general election challengers where appropriate, and I note the decisions I have made in order to show these changes.

The unit of analysis here is the challenger, not the incumbent, so the number of candidates here is different than it is in chapter 2. While I do include multiple challengers in a very small number of races (five), the number of cases is much smaller than in the previous chapter, for several reasons: I am only able to consider races from 1980 on; I omit candidates who did not file with the FEC; and whereas I was concerned in chapter 2 with incumbents who received less than 75 percent of the primary vote, I am concerned here with challengers who receive more than 25 percent. In other words, incumbents who, for instance, received 70 percent of the vote in running against two challengers who each received 15 percent of the vote were included in chapter 2, but neither of the two challengers in that hypothetical example is included here. The following analysis of House primary challengers is based on a total of 373 cases.

Changes in the Finances of House Primary Challengers

Total Receipts

Figure 3.1 shows changes in total receipts for incumbents, general election challengers, and primary challengers during the election cycles from 1980 through 2010. As the figure shows, receipts for competitive primary challengers increased substantially during this period, particularly in 2004 and 2006; the rate of increase cannot simply be explained by inflation or by a general increase in campaign costs, because while incumbent receipts increased steadily during this period, receipts for general election challengers did not. There are two anomalously expensive primary campaigns during the 1980s and 1990s, both on the Republican side and both in California; these were the races featuring successful primary challengers Tom Campbell in 1988 and Michael Huffington in 1992. The first graph for mean spending by primary challengers includes these two races; the second graph excludes them.[5] The second graph may better illustrate the

Primary Challengers to House Incumbents

All Challengers

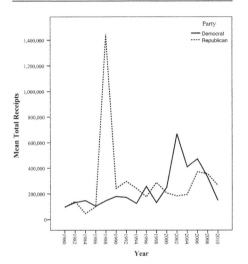

Anomalous 1988 and 1992 Challenges Excluded

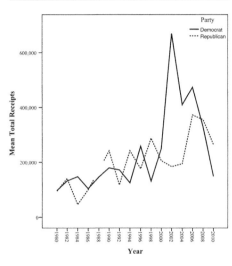

House General Election Races

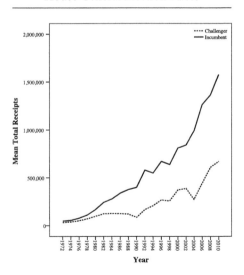

Fig. 3.1. Mean receipts by year, 1980–2010

trend in fundraising by primary challengers. The average competitive primary challenger in 1980 raised $96,472; the average had doubled by 1990 to $196,494. Average receipts for primary challengers increased another 18 percent by 2000 (lagging behind inflation) and went up another 75 percent (with some ups and downs) by 2008, before declining back to slightly over $200,000 in 2010. The average primary challenger in 2008 raised $345,000—almost four times as much as the average primary challenger in 1980.[6]

As figure 3.1 shows, spending increased for challengers of both parties. Some of this increase can be accounted for by a general increase in campaign costs, and much of it is driven by the types of candidates who appear in any given year. However, the rate of increase for spending by primary challengers is quite different from the rate of increase for other types of candidates—the line is flat for much of the 1980s and 1990s, takes off sharply in the 2000s, and plummets in 2010. Mean spending by incumbents increases steadily throughout this time, while fundraising for general election challengers increases far more slowly, with the exception of a burst in 2008. As I previously noted, it is problematic to try to match the fundraising of primary challengers directly against incumbents' pre-primary spending, so one cannot posit a direct relationship. These graphs indicate, however, that primary challenges—in the races where they do in fact occur—have become more consequential over the past three decades, while general election challenges have not.

Not all of the increase in spending by primary challengers resulted from the rise of ideological challenges. During the 1980s, there were relatively few ideological challengers who raised enough money to file with the FEC; in the years in which there were any ideological challengers at all, these challengers lagged behind nonideological challengers in fundraising. In fact, only two ideological challengers during the 1980s raised over $100,000, and these two (both unsuccessful) barely exceeded that amount. It was not until 1996 that ideological challengers as a group raised more than nonideological challengers, and this was largely a function of the spending in one idiosyncratic challenge, the bid of former representative Ron Paul to reclaim the seat he had abandoned to run for president.[7] In 2004, 2006, and 2008, however, ideological challengers raised far more than nonideological ones; in 2004, the four ideological challengers raised an average of $281,000 while nonideological challengers raised only $255,000. The ratio was $678,000 to $348,000 in 2006 and $454,000 to $301,000 in 2008. This increase was not the result of any individual idiosyncratic race; ten of the sixteen ideological challengers over these three elections raised well over $300,000, and an additional three

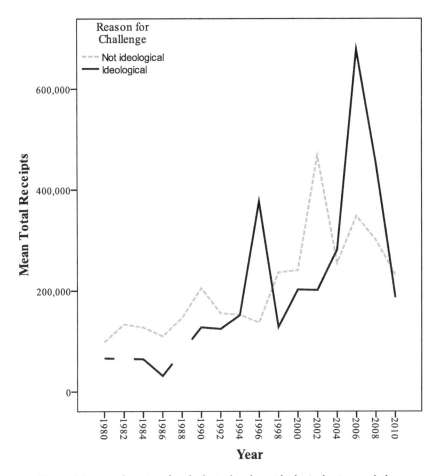

Fig. 3.2. Mean total receipts for ideological and nonideological primary challenges, 1980–2010 (anomalous 1988 and 1992 cases excluded)

(including one victorious challenger) raised over $100,000. The increase, in other words, is widely spread among candidates. By 2010, however, ideological and nonideological candidates were again spending similar amounts.

If anything, patterns in fundraising for nonideological challengers are more idiosyncratic over this period than is fundraising for ideological candidates. The average for nonideological candidates is boosted substantially by the presence of six candidates who raised over $400,000. Figure 3.2 shows the patterns for ideological and nonideological challengers from 1980 through 2010, with the Campbell and Huffington races excluded.

Contribution Sources

Figure 3.3 shows changes in the sources of contributions for primary challengers for 1984 through 2010. FEC summary files for 1980 and 1982 do not include data on unitemized or aggregate individual contributions, so I exclude those years here.[8] Unsurprisingly, the increase in total receipts for primary challengers was driven almost entirely by an increase in individual contributions, but candidates also increased their contributions to their campaigns. Party contributions were negligible, and PAC contributions varied across elections but showed no real increase. Some of the increase can no doubt be attributed to the increase in individual contribution limits, but given the lack of a corresponding increase for general election challengers, it seems that something more must be going on. The sharp increase in 2006 cannot solely be attributed to BCRA's increase in individual contribution limits, insofar as the raised limits did not produce a surge in 2004. It is conceivable that BCRA's effects were felt one election later, but if this is the case, it would seem that there are other contributing factors.

Figure 3.4 shows the sources of contributions for ideological primary challengers. For these challengers, individual contributions also became far more important across the decade considered here; PAC contributions did not increase substantially, and candidate contributions increased in 2004 but declined in 2006. As figure 3.5 shows, ideological challengers largely fueled the increase in overall receipts for primary challengers; compared to other types of primary challengers, ideological challengers raised less, on average, in 2000 and 2002 but far more in 2004, 2006, and 2008. This disparity went away in 2010 as well.

Another anomalous change in contribution patterns occurs in 2006, when PAC contributions to ideological challengers spike upward. This is shown in figure 3.6. In 2006, four primary candidates raised over $100,000 in PAC money, including African American Democrats Hank Johnson (running against Cynthia McKinney) and Karen Carter (running against William Jefferson); Timothy Walberg, running from the right against first-term Michigan Republican Joe Schwarz; and Juan Vargas, a California Democrat and veteran San Diego city councilman, running against Representative Bob Filner. I categorized Walberg and Vargas as ideological candidates, so the spike is entirely due to their fundraising. As we shall see when we discuss in-state and out-of-state contributions, ideological challengers in recent years have tended to draw their money from out-of-state donors. Walberg did this (raising only 15 percent of his money from

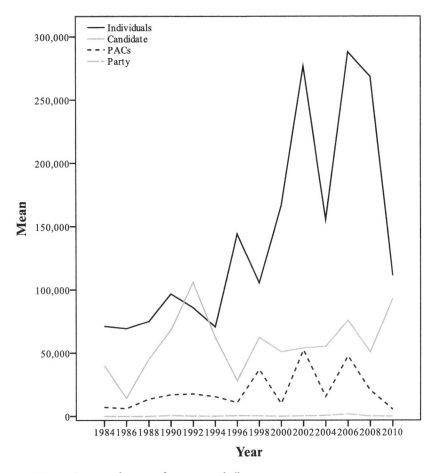

Fig. 3.3. Sources of receipts for primary challengers, 1984–2010

Michigan donors), while Vargas did not (raising only 91 percent of his money from California donors). The other ideological challengers in 2006, Rhode Island's Jennifer Lawless, California's Marcy Winograd, and Maryland's Donna Edwards, did less well with PACs but did raise a substantial percentage of their funds from out-of-state donors. Walberg skews the data, then, partly because he did well with PACs and out-of-state donors, while other challengers generally have not succeeded in raising money from these sources.

Although literature on primary challengers has generally noted that these candidates often self-finance their campaigns, there are no clear

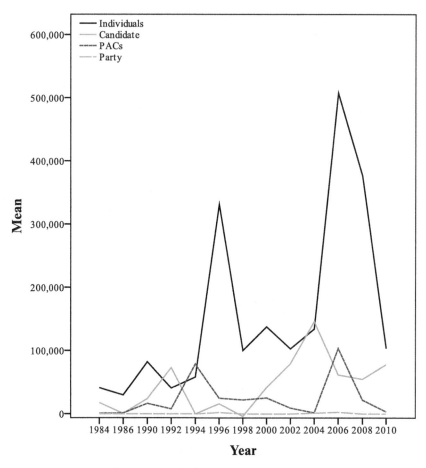

Fig. 3.4. Sources of receipts for ideological primary challengers, 1984–2010

changes over time in their propensity to do so. Throughout the thirty-year time period considered here, the personal funds of ideological and non-ideological challengers have tended to constitute approximately one-third of the candidates' total receipts. Ideological candidates of the 2000s have contributed more money to their campaigns, but they have also raised more money from individual donors, so the role of personal funds has not necessarily increased over time. There are several instances of almost entirely self-financed candidates in the data; Michael Huffington is the obvious case, but there are several other instances where primary challengers have bankrolled virtually their entire campaign but also wound up spend-

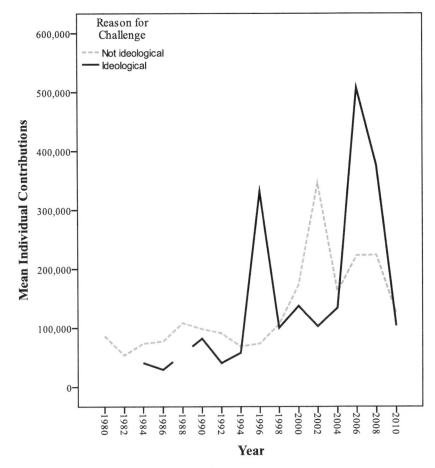

Fig. 3.5. Mean individual contributions for ideological and nonideological primary challengers, 1980–2010

ing very little in sum. Unsurprisingly, given the literature on self-financing, there is no correlation between the amount of personal money spent by candidates and their primary vote percentage, but there is a negative relationship ($R = -.193$; $p < .01$) between the percentage of the total campaign receipts supplied by the candidates and their vote percentage.

In sum, we know that there was an increase during the 2000s in the amount of money raised by primary challengers and particularly in the amount raised by ideological challengers. It is clear that most of the increase came in individual contributions. I now turn to a consideration of the nature of these individual contributions.

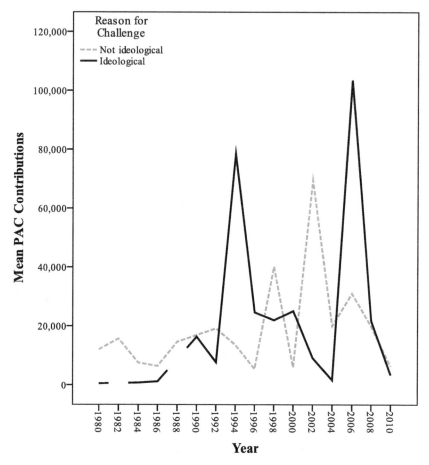

Fig. 3.6. Mean PAC contributions for ideological and nonideological primary challengers, 1984–2010

Small and Large Contributions

Many studies of campaign finance have sought to track the role of small donors in campaigns (see, e.g., Francia et al. 2003). The assumption in many of these studies has been that strong candidates with a grassroots following have tended to raise larger sums of money in small donations than have candidates with stable donor bases. To put matters in other words, "insider" or "establishment" candidates can generally finance their campaigns with contributions of $1,000 or more from wealthy repeat donors, while "outsider" or "insurgent" candidates are better positioned to raise money in small amounts from a more diverse donor base. The types of ideological challengers discussed in the previous chapters would be obvious candidates for such "outsider" status; presumably, then, a larger number of strong ideological candidates would correspond to a larger percentage of small contributions.

Changes in campaign finance law render measuring large contributions problematic. For the period from 1980 through 2002, the maximum permissible individual contribution was $1,000 per election. BCRA raised individual contribution limits and indexed them to inflation; the maximum individual contribution in 2004 was $2,000, rising to $2,150 in 2006, $2,300 in 2008, and $2,400 in 2010. Throughout this time, candidates who raised at least $5,000 for their campaigns were required to report the names of contributors of $200 or more.

For figures 3.7–3.10, I created a variable for individual contributions of $250 or less; this includes itemized contributions of $200 to $250 and all unitemized contributions. As figure 3.7 shows, large contributions (those over $750) have become more important to primary challengers over the past decade, while the percentage of funds raised in small contributions has declined. This may be partly a function of BCRA's increased individual contribution limits, but BCRA itself cannot explain this, as the percentage of funds raised in larger amounts began to surpass the percentage raised in small amounts in 1998, three elections before BCRA took effect. There is an increase in the percentage of money raised in larger amounts in 2004 (the election in which the increased contribution limits took effect), but in figure 3.7, this increase looks more like the continuation of a trend than a radical shift. This is one aspect in which the crop of 2010 primary challengers does resemble the crops of 2006 and 2008.

The lines in figure 3.7 represent the average percentages of money raised in small and large amounts for all primary challengers; candidates who received several hundred thousand dollars in individual contributions and candidates who barely received enough money to bother filing are counted equally. This may lead to some distortion in the averages across years. To limit our attention to candidates who made some effort to solicit donations, figure 3.8 shows the average amounts by year for candidates who received at least fifty itemized contributions—this cut point includes roughly half of the 373 primary challengers who filed with the FEC over this period of time. The basic pattern remains the same in figures 3.7 and 3.8, except that the point at which large contributions begin to surpass small contributions in their importance occurs two elections earlier in fig-

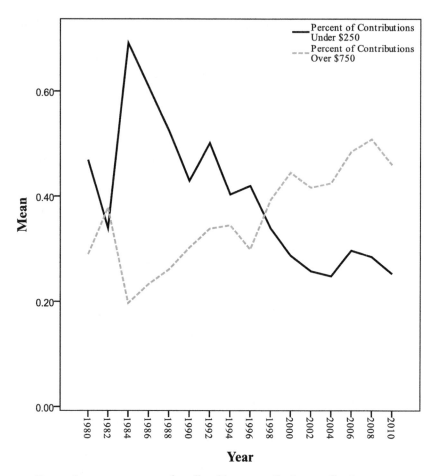

Fig. 3.7. Average percentage of small and large contributions to all primary challengers (as a percentage of all individual contributions), 1980–2010

ure 3.8. It must be reiterated here that FEC data list individual contributions but do not aggregate by individual contributor. This means that the measure of small contributions here slightly overestimates the role of small donors; some of the small contributions may have been given by donors who made subsequent contributions and ultimately gave more than $250.

These aggregations of primary challengers do not tell us anything, however, about the difference between ideological and nonideological primary challengers in their propensity to raise contributions in smaller

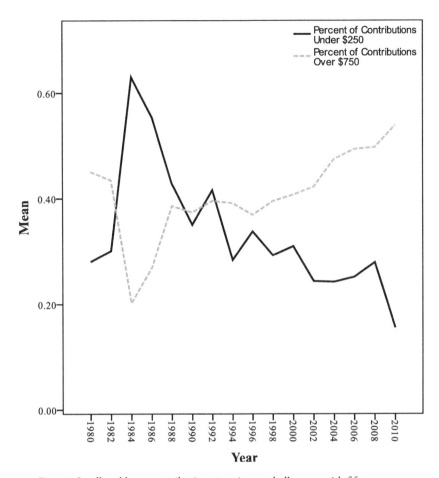

Fig. 3.8. Small and large contributions to primary challengers with fifty or more itemized contributions (as a percentage of all individual contributions), 1980–2010

amounts. Figure 3.9 shows the average percentage of funds raised in amounts of under $250 for ideological and nonideological challengers; the graph on the left shows yearly averages for all primary challengers, while the graph on the right shows averages for challengers who received at least fifty itemized contributions. The graph on the left shows few differences between the two types.[9] In the graph on the right, however, the percentage for ideological challengers exceeds that of nonideological challengers in most years, and in two elections, 1996 and 2008, the difference is quite large. The difference in 1996 is entirely a function of the Ron Paul cam-

All Primary Challengers

Challengers with Fifty or More
Itemized Contributions

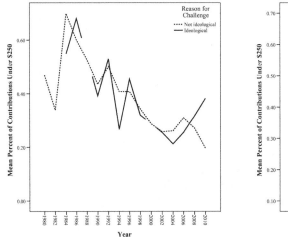 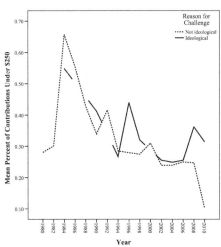

Fig. 3.9. Small contributions to ideological and nonideological challengers (as a percentage of all individual contributions), 1980–2010

paign's success in raising small contributions. The difference in 2008, however, is not driven by any one candidate; five of the seven ideological challengers raised over one-third of their money in contributions of under $250, and of the two who did not, one raised less than $6,000 in total from individual contributors. The other, Maryland Republican Andrew Harris, actually raised the second-largest amount of money from small donors of any 2008 candidate, $234,000; his percentage is low because he raised over $1 million in total individual contributions. Figure 3.10 shows the mean annual total of small contributions for ideological and nonideological candidates. Here, the surge from Ron Paul's 1996 candidacy remains, but the increase in 2006 and 2008 is also evident. If there is any difference between today's primary challengers and those of years past, then, it is that ideological challengers today are better funded, they rely more on individual donors, and those funds are raised in smaller amounts. This was not the case in past elections. Despite the efforts of the Tea Party and other groups, these differences also vanished in 2010.

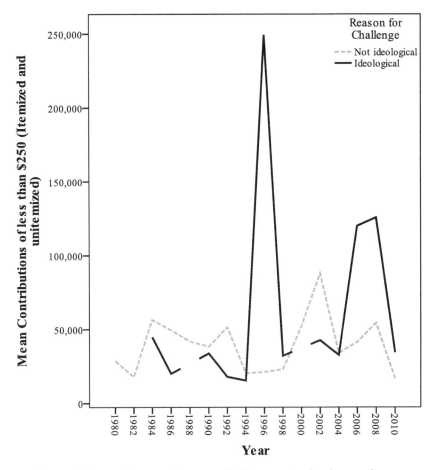

Fig. 3.10. Mean total amount of money raised in amounts of under $250 for ideological and nonideological challengers, 1980–2010

In-State and Out-of-State Contributions

The logical final step in looking at the fundraising of primary challengers is to see whether these funds come predominantly from constituents or from contributors outside of the district. As noted earlier, it is difficult to identify the district in which contributors reside, in part because one would need sophisticated mapping software in order to determine who resides in the district and who does not, but also because many contributors may reside in one district but work in another, and there is no consis-

All Primary Challengers

Challengers with Fifty or More
Itemized Contributions

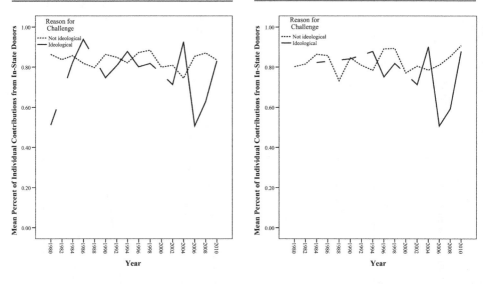

Fig. 3.11. In-state itemized contributions to ideological and nonideological challengers, 1980–2010

tency in which addresses are used for contributions. One can obtain a rough measure of these patterns, however, by distinguishing between in-state and out-of-state addresses. If a candidate excels in raising contributions from individuals who reside in other states, this would be a sign that there is some sort of national fundraising effort afoot, either on the part of the candidate or on the part of bundling groups. Ideological or cause-oriented challengers might be expected to raise more money from out-of-state sources than will candidates motivated by the incumbent's competence, ethical problems, and so forth.

Figure 3.11 shows differences across time in the mean percentage of itemized contributions raised from in-state donors.[10] Here again I provide two graphs, one showing all primary challengers, the other showing only challengers who received more than fifty contributions. In both graphs, the percentage of money raised in state remains relatively constant from 1980 through 2004, regardless of whether a candidate is motivated by ideology or not. In 2006, the percentage of individual contributions raised from in-state donors plummets for ideological challengers, but not for nonideological candidates (another way to put this, of course, is that the percentage of money raised out of state by ideological challengers increased in 2006). This figure demonstrates that throughout the 1980s and 1990s, ideological challengers tended to raise relatively paltry sums of money from outside of the state in which they were running. Apart from the anomalous Ron Paul campaign of 1996, the percentages were consistently low, and the total amount of money raised out of state rose only very slowly. In 2002, both types of candidates did particularly well (an increase investigated later in this chapter). In 2006, however, the percentage of funds raised out of state and the total amount of money raised out of state exploded for ideological challengers and maintained that level in 2008, while remaining relatively low and consistent for nonideological challengers. As in the figures for small contributions, this increase is not driven by any individual candidate but is a function of the fundraising prowess of these two years' classes of ideological challengers. The average amount of money raised from out-of-state donors declined in 2010, however, to the level it had been at in the 1980s and 1990s.

The sources of contributions are part of the narrative of the campaigns themselves; that is, we would expect some instances in which candidates either make a point of declining to accept out-of-state contributions or take issue with their opponent's receipt of such contributions. Consider, for instance, the 2008 primary challenge to Dennis Kucinich in Ohio. Kucinich's opponent, Joseph Cimperman, made Kucinich's inattention to the district a central theme of his campaign. Because Kucinich had run a quixotic bid for the presidency in 2008, Cimperman argued, he had not spent sufficient time tending to his district's needs (see, e.g., Naymik 2008). Unsurprisingly, Cimperman raised 96 percent of his campaign budget of $600,000 from Ohio donors. For a very different case, consider the 2010 Delaware Senate primary. While this was not an incumbent-versus-challenger race, Delaware House member Mike Castle, the presumptive nominee in this one-district state, was, in many ways, cast as the incumbent in the race. When Castle was upended by political neophyte Christine O'Donnell, his campaign aides argued bitterly that her campaign was largely funded by out-of-state donors (Catanese 2010a). In both instances, the contributions of those who are not constituents is a sign not merely of national attention to the race but of the interests the candidates are presumed to represent.

The figures on in-state and out-of-state contributions complete the story we can tell using campaign finance data about changes in the nature of House primary challenges. It is easy to see why congressional primaries have garnered so little attention in the past; during the 1980s and 1990s, there was little change in the financing of congressional primaries, and apart from a few anomalous cases, there was little of interest to be said. There is something different about the challengers that have emerged in the past decade—they have raised more money in sum and in individual contributions, small contributions, and out-of-state contributions than have past candidates. It is hard to say at what point a candidate's fundraising prowess shifts from being merely idiosyncratic to being part of a trend (do three, five, or ten candidates constitute a trend?), but when one puts together the various features of the fundraising of primary challengers, it seems evident that a different dynamic is in play over the past three election cycles. We cannot prove why this is the case, but it seems reasonable to assume that Internet fundraising, the nationalization of congressional elections, and the rise of new ideological interest groups on the left and right are likely causes.

The time trends in this chapter tell a different story than do the data in chapter 2, but when put together, these two patterns make perfect sense. That these stories point in different directions means that we cannot develop any statistical models that point to the consequences of primary challenges, of well-funded primary challengers, and so forth—the numbers are, as of yet, too small, and it is not even clear what our dependent variables in any such model would be. There are no more primary challengers today than there were in previous years, but candidates and outside groups now have the ability to raise more money and to have more of an impact on congressional primaries than in the past.

The Candidates

There are two major weaknesses involved in looking at time trends by using aggregations of campaign finance data for primary challengers. First, one must remember that we are dealing with small numbers of candidates in each of these years; as the Campbell and Huffington cases show, one anomalous case can distort the data for a time trend. Second, one must also keep in mind that the classifications of candidates are not perfect; the difference between an ideological challenger and a challenger who runs for other reasons is not always clear. The data presented so far in this chapter are intended to be suggestive, not definitive; there does appear to have been a change in the funding of primary challenges, and this change is reflected in many different aspects of candidate fundraising. Any reader who has followed congressional elections closely for the past decade, however, will undoubtedly think of individual candidates when looking at the aggregate data.

Table 3.1 lists the thirty-five best-funded primary challenges from 2000 through 2010, with ideological challengers in bold font. The list shows the surge in all types of challenges in 2006 and 2008. Equally revealing, however, is the nature of the types of challenges listed here. Only two of the challenges listed for the period from 2000 through 2004 are clear cases of ideological challenges, and these two are not the most prominent challenges in either year. The two most costly challenges in this period were both instances where liberal African American Democrats were challenged by more moderate African American opponents. The two incumbents challenged in these races, Alabama's Earl Hilliard and Georgia's Cynthia McKinney, were generally cast by the media as outspoken or abrasive, and their challengers received heavy support from the business community. Hilliard's challenger, Artur Davis, was among the few Democrats to receive the endorsement of the Business Industry Political Action Committee and other business groups in 2002; he received the endorsement partly because these groups concluded that the Alabama district could not be won by a Republican and that the best chance to influence the district's representation would be to support a more centrist Democrat. The supporters of McKinney's challenger, Denise Majette, likely felt the same way. Not all of the highest-profile challengers from these years even make this list, however; New Jersey Republican Scott Garrett, for instance, received support from the Club for Growth in his 2000 campaign against moderate incumbent Marge Roukema, but Garrett reported raising only a total of $306,000 in his race.

All three of the challengers listed for 2002 raised more than one-third of their individual contribution money from out-of-state donors, perhaps indicating a concerted strategy. Maryland's David Fischer ran as a conservative challenger to centrist Republican Wayne Gilchrest; Gilchrest would go on to be defeated by a conservative challenger six years later. Fischer received the endorsement of the Club for Growth; although the club did not report bundling money for him, the club's endorsement likely aided him in raising out-of-state money.

The best-funded candidate of 2004 was Henry Cuellar, a veteran member of the Texas legislature. Cuellar's race is an unusual case because he does not appear to have been motivated to run by disagreement with the incumbent, Ciro Rodriguez. Cuellar had narrowly lost a general election bid in 2002 and was redrawn into Rodriguez's district in Texas's 2003 redistricting. Cuellar had a large contributor base from which to draw but

TABLE 3.1. Top Thirty-Five Fundraisers among House Primary Challengers, 2000–2010

Year	Candidate	Party	District	Primary Vote (%)	Individual Contributions	Small Contributions	Out-of-State Contributions[a]	Total Receipts
2000	Collen, Martin J.	Rep	CA 43	29	14,045	1,795	0	348,115
	Obama, Barack H.	Dem	IL 1	39	475,235	119,205	39,650	508,640
2002	Davis, Artur	Dem	AL 7	56	1,231,231	412,451	615,627	1,578,640
	Majette, Denise L.	Dem	GA 4	58	1,560,532	314,489	759,140	1,980,218
	Fischer, David W.	**Rep**	**MD 1**	**36**	**251,884**	**74,009**	**136,150**	**567,798**
2004	**Murphy, Rick L.**	**Rep**	**AZ 2**	**36**	**248,265**	**46,811**	**39,366**	**798,265**
	Delgrosso, Michael	Rep	PA 9	49	357,047	136,551	16,650	365,853
	Cuellar, Henry	Dem	TX 28	50	608,781	5,802	2,250	1,407,409
	Rosenberg, Andrew	Dem	VA 8	41	355,771	90,788	173,167	420,526
2006	Nation, Joe	Dem	CA 6	34	657,148	91,299	6,250	718,570
	McCloskey, Paul	Rep	CA 11	32	522,044	98,493	82,050	573,301
	Winograd, Marcy	**Dem**	**CA 36**	**38**	**157,326**	**71,589**	**8,348**	**373,395**
	Vargas, Juan	**Dem**	**CA 51**	**43**	**816,810**	**47,298**	**55,050**	**1,051,848**
	Johnson, "Hank" Jr.	Dem	GA 4	44	527,987	122,195	66,150	797,997
	Carter, Karen R.	Dem	LA 2	27	821,723	1,464	102,350	979,488
	Walberg, Timothy	**Rep**	**MI 7**	**53**	**947,775**	**363,891**	**461,185**	**1,260,111**
	Godchaux, Patricia	Rep	MI 9	30	152,921	72,770	10,800	468,271
	Mcewen, Bob	Rep	OH 2	43	381,124	53,649	210,675	834,520
	Lawless, Jennifer	**Dem**	**RI 2**	**38**	**307,031**	**42,343**	**164,975**	**358,5972**
	Jacob, John	Rep	UT 3	44	42,049	7,649	5,850	591,830

2008	Parnell, Sean	Rep	AK al	45	587,138	158,496	328,751	604,253
	Crank, Jeff	Rep	CO 5	30	379,364	66,996	37,214	418,431
	Fleming, Barry	Rep	GA 10	29	751,202	160,881	44,301	952,476
	Pera, Mark	**Dem**	**IL 3**	**25**	**393,205**	**163,627**	**55,901**	**770,703**
	McGoff, John P.	Rep	IN 5	45	360,511	78,052	21,250	473,664
	Moreno, Helena	Dem	LA 2	43	293,028	133,778	21,550	349,375
	Harris, Andrew P.	**Rep**	**MD 1**	**43**	**1,009,017**	**234,386**	**381,865**	**1,092,771**
	Edwards, Donna	**Dem**	**MD 4**	**59**	**764,977**	**286,263**	**393,464**	**793,577**
	Cimperman, Joseph	Dem	OH 10	35	595,012	83,173	21,850	621,512
2010	Liberatore, Philip	Rep	CA 42	37	60,930	14,342	2,250	795,930
	Messer, Allen	Rep	IN 5	28	559,680	72,374	41,150	580,892
	Hawkins, B. Lee	Rep	GA 9	45	600,192	238,452	10,050	1,042,707
	O'Brien, Corey D.	Dem	PA 11	34	383,917	29,071	29,440	412,682
	Gowdy, Trey	**Rep**	**SC 4**	**39**	**464,120**	**23,893**	**13,499**	**468,620**
	Clark, Steve	**Rep**	**TX 4**	**30**	**21,341**	**5,091**	**1,000**	**618,236**

Note: Ideological challengers are in bold.

[a]The out-of-state contribution totals only include itemized contributions.

raised virtually no money outside of Texas. The only candidate who did raise a substantial amount of money outside of his home state in 2004 was Virginian Andrew Rosenberg. His district was in the suburbs of Washington, DC, however, and many of his out-of-state contributions came from the District. Arizona's Rick Murphy is the strongest ideological challenger of 2004, but most of his campaign money came from his own pocket.

The difference between ideological challengers in 2006 and those of previous years is striking. Three of the five ideological challengers in 2006 raised substantial sums of money from outside of their home states. Michigan's Tim Walberg raised almost $500,000 from donors outside of Michigan, and Rhode Island's Jennifer Lawless, while receiving less national media attention than other ideological challengers, still raised almost half of her money from out-of-state sources. Maryland's Donna Edwards, a favorite of MoveOn and liberal bloggers, narrowly missed making the list; in her unsuccessful 2006 race, Edwards raised $190,250, more than half of her $345,000 total, from out-of-state sources, and she would go on to do the same in her successful 2008 race. The three strongest candidates who were *not* ideological challengers were former Ohio representative Bob McEwen and two challengers in African American districts: Hank Johnson, running against McKinney in Georgia,[11] and Karen Carter, who was challenging scandal-tainted Louisiana representative William Jefferson. Perhaps proving the limits of the base of liberal donors for primary challengers, however, Marcy Winograd, an anti-war candidate challenging Representative Jane Harman, raised only $8,000 outside of California, despite being touted on many of the same blogs that discussed the Edwards and Lawless challenges in the House and Ned Lamont's challenge to Joseph Lieberman in the Senate.

In 2008, three of the four best-financed challengers were ideological challengers. Again, these were candidates who benefited from national bundling efforts, and these efforts are reflected in the out-of-state contribution totals. MoveOn supported Donna Edwards and Mark Pera, and the Club for Growth supported Maryland's Andrew Harris and Alaska's Sean Parnell.[12] Pera's contribution totals from small and out-of-state donors are not particularly high, but Edwards, Parnell, and Harris did do quite well. Concerning the other well-funded primary challengers, it is interesting to note that Georgia's Paul Fleming was running a centrist challenge against an incumbent supported by the Club for Growth, Paul Broun.

Table 3.1 includes most, but not all, of the House primary challengers who have garnered attention over the past decade. The individual fundraising numbers make it clear that no single uniform story fits all of them—some did well among individual contributors, small donors, and out-of-state donors, but some did not. Fundraising success, as this table shows, is not correlated with vote share or with particular types of campaigns. Nonetheless, it does appear that the strongest ideological challengers of 2006 and 2008 raised a substantial amount of money from individual, small, and out-of-state donors. This is clear evidence of a nationalization of their races. Such a form of nationalization has happened before, as in the Davis and Majette races in 2002, but for both the 2002 races and the 2006 and 2008 ideological challenges, this nationalization suggests a level of coordination. It would seem to be beyond the means of individual primary challengers to inspire large out-of-state donations, but such coordination has become a hallmark of ideological interest groups.

Finally, this table gives the most vivid evidence thus far of the shift in spending in 2010. Though 2010 featured the largest number of primary challengers in almost two decades, there were fewer well-funded challengers than there had been in 2006 and 2008. The three candidates with the most money were self-funded. None of these challengers raised very much money outside of their home states. Two of the year's fourteen ideological challengers made the list, but their totals are lower than those of the strongest ideological challengers in the past two election cycles (the Democratic ideological challenger who received the most out-of-state money and arguably the most national media attention, Massachusetts's Mac D'Alessandro, narrowly missed the cutoff for the list). Perhaps money did not matter as much in the 2010 primaries—after all, three of the four victorious primary challengers in 2010 did not make the list at all. Or perhaps the Senate primaries were more important to ideological donors—as we shall see in the next section of this chapter, there were Senate challengers who excelled at raising contributions nationally. Whatever the reason, however, the 2010 primary challengers were a pretty unremarkable bunch when it came to fundraising.

Senate Primaries

For a variety of reasons—including the varying cost of Senate campaigns across states, the smaller number of primary challenges, the absence of any challenges during some years, and the fact that any time series can easily be skewed by one or two unusual races in any given year—the fundraising patterns in Senate primaries do not show as clear a pattern as do House primaries, but a look at the campaign finance data for primary challenges to incumbents does show some similarities. Table 3.2 shows the sources of campaign contributions for all competitive challenges since 1980 where the candidates filed with the FEC.[13] The table shows substantial variation in the aggregate fundraising and the sources of funds for these races.

Self-financing is not uncommon in Senate challenges, but PAC and party contributions are rare, just as they are in House challenges. With one exception, the only candidates who financed more than 10 percent of their campaign through PACs were candidates who did not raise very much money in the aggregate. The one exception is New Hampshire Republican representative John Sununu, who received substantial support from the Republican Party and traditional Republican donors in his challenge to renegade Republican Bob Smith in 2002. As in the House, the challengers who have emerged in the past decade have raised substantially more money than did challengers in the past—eleven of the sixteen competitive challengers since 2002 raised over $1 million, while only three of twenty-four challengers between 1980 and 2000 did so. In addition, two of the three well-funded candidates of the 1980s and 1990s raised over $1 million only because of their own contributions to their campaigns. Since 2002, only one of the eleven well-funded candidates contributed more than a token amount of his own money to his campaign, and that candidate, Connecticut's Ned Lamont, nevertheless raised $1.7 million from individual contributors. Several Senate challengers (including six of the eleven well-funded challengers since 2002) were current or former House members, and several of these candidates (most notably New Jersey's Rob Andrews and Pennsylvania's Joe Sestak) were able to transfer substantial amounts of money from their House campaign accounts to their Senate campaigns.[14]

Table 3.3 shows the amounts of money raised in contributions of under $250 and from out-of-state donors for all competitive Senate primary challengers since 1980. Here again, as in the House data, there is not an evident pattern in the proportion of funds received from small donors, but recent challengers have raised a much larger amount of money from these donors. As in the House data, however, the most striking difference between recent Senate challengers and those of the 1980s and 1990s is the amount and proportion of individual contributions from out-of-state donors. Only three candidates from the 1980s and 1990s raised more than $50,000 from out-of-state donors, and none of these three raised more than $200,000 from such donors. Two of these three—Alaska's Clark Gruening and South Dakota's William Janklow—were running in low-population states and may have been forced to raise money from out of state because of this. The only anomaly here is James Miller, a former Reagan administration official who ran against John Warner in Virginia's 1996 Republican Senate primary. Miller raised $1.3 million in individual contributions, far more than any other pre-2002 candidate, and he received just under $200,000 from out-of-state donors.

In contrast, eleven of the fifteen most well-funded challengers since 2002 raised more than $200,000 from out-of-state donors. Of particular note here are the highest-profile ideological challengers: Patrick Toomey, Ned Lamont, Steve Laffey, and the group of 2010 challengers. Toomey, Lamont, Laffey, Joe Sestak, and Bill Halter all raised more than one-quarter of their individual contribution money from out-of-state donors, and Laffey raised nearly half of his money from such donors. It is hard to generalize from such a small number of cases, but it does seem evident that these three candidates, each of whom had substantial support from bundling groups (Lamont, Halter, and Sestak from MoveOn.org, Laffey and Toomey from the Club for Growth) did succeed in nationalizing their election bids.

The data in tables 3.2 and 3.3 also help to put some of the events of 2010 in context. Among the 2010 challenges were those of Pennsylvania's Arlen Specter (who was opposed by well-financed primary challengers in 1992 and 2004) and Alaska's Lisa Murkowski (note that Alaska is the most frequently represented state in these tables, with five challenges from 1980 through 2008). In chapter 2, I noted that House primaries have become more frequent over the past three election cycles but that this appears to be part of a regular cycle. While there clearly were more competitive Senate primaries in 2010 than at any time in the past thirty years, it may well be that this was as much a confluence of unusual events as it was a trend.

If there is a trend, however, it may well be one that develops because of changes in the financing of Senate races and of the perception of prospective candidates that they can capitalize on this trend. In a piece entitled "Why Senators Are Falling," published after the end of the 2010 primary season, Ronald Brownstein (2010b) notes that while, in historical terms, the number of primaries remains small, the financial impact of primary challenges is far different than it was in the years of previous incumbents' defeats. Brownstein quotes AFL-CIO deputy political director Michael Podhorzer as saying that "it has for a while been easier to do this, but no one's done it. It was sitting there waiting to happen. This year, it became apparent to everybody." In the same article, the Club for Growth's David Keating predicts that the new fundraising abilities of challengers will lead

TABLE 3.2. Fundraising by Senate Primary Challengers, 1980–2010

Year	Challenger	Party	State	Incumbent	Primary Vote (%)	Receipts ($)	Funds from Individuals (%)	Funds from Candidate (%)	Funds from PACs (%)
1980	Folsom, James	Dem	AL	Stewart, Donald	51	131,600	79	19	2
	Gruening, Clark	Dem	AK	Gravel, Michael	55	348,606	98	1	0
	Jenkins, Louis[a]	Dem	LA	Long, Russell	39	142,369			1
	D'Amato, Alfonse	**Rep**	**NY**	**Javits, Jacob**	**51**	**424,170**	**92**	**12**	**2**
	Schumaker, Larry[a]	Dem	SD	McGovern, George	37	61,737			19
1982	**Bond, Michael**[a]	**Dem**	**MT**	**Melcher, John**	**27**	**67,182**			**0**
	Ledbetter, Stewart[a]	**Rep**	**VT**	**Stafford, Robert**	**35**	**264,760**			**2**
1986	Lutz, Joe	Rep	OR	Packwood, Robert	42	465,862	94	0	6
	Janklow, William	Rep	SD	Abdnor, James	45	438,111	84	0	14
1988	Kelleher, Robert	Dem	MT	Melcher, John	25	69,239	11	82	0
1990	Bird, Robert	Rep	AK	Stevens, Ted	30	69,211	72	6	4
1992	McNair, Christopher	Dem	AL	Shelby, Richard	28	105,512	71	0	24
	Jones, Julia	Dem	AR	Bumpers, Dale	35	73,164	74	1	21
	Moseley Braun, Carol	**Dem**	**IL**	**Dixon, Alan**	**38**	**230,006**	**93**	**0**	**7**
	Hofeld, Albert	**Dem**	**IL**	**Dixon, Alan**	**27**	**4,897,538**	**5**	**94**	**0**
	Woods, Charles	Dem	NV	Reid, Harry	39	402,494	0	98	0
1994	Friend, Stephen	Rep	PA	Specter, Arlen	35	517,356	93	0	6
	Post, Thomas	Rep	RI	Chafee, John	31	64,462	87	9	2
	Goode, Virgil	Dem	VA	Robb, Charles	34	222,453	84	9	7

Year	Challenger	Party	State	Incumbent					
1996	Cuddy, David	Rep	AK	Stevens, Ted	32	1,522,815	12	87	0
	Lowe, Daniel	Rep	OK	Inhofe, James	25	123,300	7	90	0
	Worley, Harold	Rep	SC	Thurmond, Strom	30	444,097	1	96	0
	Miller, James	Rep	VA	Warner, John	34	1,476,944	89	7	3
1998	Eggert, William	Rep	CO	Campbell, Ben	29	106,159	85	11	3
2002	Sununu, John	Rep	NH	Smith, Robert	53	1,536,463	46	0	15
2004	Miller, Michael	Rep	AK	Murkowski, Lisa	38	262,107	21	76	3
	Toomey, Patrick	**Rep**	**PA**	**Specter, Arlen**	**49**	**3,925,894**	**90**	**4**	**3**
2006	**Lamont, Edward**	**Dem**	**CT**	**Lieberman, Joseph**	**52**	**4,173,847**	**40**	**60**	**0**
	Case, Edward	Dem	HI	Akaka, Daniel	45	1,364,411	77	0	9
	Laffey, Steve	**Rep**	**RI**	**Chafee, Lincoln**	**46**	**1,840,058**	**95**	**2**	**3**
2008	Cuddy, David	Rep	AK	Stevens, Ted	27	759,003	4	96	0
	O'Reilly, Edward	**Dem**	**MA**	**Kerry, John**	**31**	**366,660**	**40**	**59**	**0**
	Andrews, Robert	Dem	NJ	Lautenberg, Frank	35	4,039,692	47	0	3
	Witherspoon, Buddy	Rep	SC	Graham, Lindsay	33	441,452	49	0	0
2010	**Miller, Joseph**	**Rep**	**AK**	**Murkowski, Lisa**	**51**	**283,473**	**62**	**37**	**2**
	Hayworth, J. D.	**Rep**	**AZ**	**McCain, John**	**32**	**3,063,180**	**98**	**0**	**1**
	Halter, William	**Dem**	**AR**	**Lincoln, Blanche**	**42**	**2,639,472**	**92**	**3**	**6**
	Romanoff, Andrew	**Dem**	**CO**	**Bennet, Michael**	**46**	**2,597,969**	**85**	**14**	**0**
	Sestak, Joseph	**Dem**	**PA**	**Specter, Arlen**	**54**	**6,108,380**	**31**	**0**	**1**

Note: Ideological challengers are in bold.
[a]The FEC did not list total individual contributions in its 1980 and 1982 candidate summary files. Totals for victorious candidates (D'Amato, Folsom, Gruening) in these years are estimated from their preprimary filings.

TABLE 3.3. Fundraising by Senate Primary Challengers, 1980–2010

Year	Challenger	Party	State	Incumbent	Primary Vote (%)	Individual Contributions ($)	Small Contributions ($)	Out-of-State Contributions ($)[a]	Total Receipts ($)
1980	Folsom, James	Dem	AL	Stewart, Donald	51	104,400	82,637	0	131,600
	Gruening, Clark	Dem	AK	Gravel, Michael	55	341,214	249,357	54,905	348,606
	Jenkins, Louis[b]	Dem	LA	Long, Russell	39	69,564		13,000	142,369
	D'Amato, Alfonse	**Rep**	**NY**	**Javits, Jacob**	**51**	**388,560**	**157,860**	**10,250**	**424,170**
	Schumaker, Larry[b]	Dem	SD	McGovern, George	37	26,000		20,000	61,737
1982	**Bond, Michael**[b]	**Dem**	**MT**	**Melcher, John**	**27**	**4,300**		**0**	**67,182**
	Ledbetter, Stewart[b]	**Rep**	**VT**	**Stafford, Robert**	**35**	**23,553**		**8,000**	**264,760**
1986	Lutz, Joe	Rep	OR	Packwood, Robert	42	435,949	384,591	6,000	465,862
	Janklow, William	Rep	SD	Abdnor, James	45	367,283	122,928	104,250	438,111
1988	Kelleher, Robert	Dem	MT	Melcher, John	25	7,700	0	0	69,239
1990	Bird, Robert	Rep	AK	Stevens, Ted	30	49,511	40,911	4,250	69,211
1992	McNair, Christopher	Dem	AL	Shelby, Richard	28	74,782	19,032	7,450	105,512
	Jones, Julia	Dem	AR	Bumpers, Dale	35	54,144	24,143	9,660	73,164
	Moseley Braun, Carol	**Dem**	**IL**	**Dixon, Alan**	**38**	**214,305**	**173,955**	**1,250**	**230,006**
	Hofeld, Albert	**Dem**	**IL**	**Dixon, Alan**	**27**	**237,795**	**17,395**	**19,300**	**4,897,538**
	Woods, Charles	Dem	NV	Reid, Harry	39	530	0	0	402,494
1994	Friend, Stephen	Rep	PA	Specter, Arlen	35	479,476	317,988	30,038	517,356
	Post, Thomas	Rep	RI	Chafee, John	31	56,322	52,997	1,900	64,462
	Goode, Virgil	Dem	VA	Robb, Charles	34	187,379	87,088	3,950	222,453

Year	Incumbent	Party	State	Challenger					
1996	Stevens, Ted	Rep	AK	Cuddy, David	32	180,109	84,937	5,500	1,522,815
	Inhofe, James	Rep	OK	Lowe, Daniel	25	8,240	2,940	1,000	123,300
	Thurmond, Strom	Rep	SC	Worley, Harold	30	444,097	1,110	0	444,097
	Warner, John	Rep	VA	Miller, James	34	1,321,310	857,158	191,550	1,476,944
1998	Campbell, Ben	Rep	CO	Eggert, William	29	89,756	47,071	7,735	106,159
2002	Smith, Robert	Rep	NH	Sununu, John	53	699,829	—c	514,048	1,536,463
2004	Murkowski, Lisa	Rep	AK	Miller, Michael	38	54,592	7,337	10,550	262,107
	Specter, Arlen	Rep	PA	**Toomey, Patrick**	49	3,515,820	1,177,337	1,318,643	3,925,894
2006	**Lieberman, Joseph**	Dem	CT	**Lamont, Edward**	52	1,663,909	665,910	485,551	4,173,847
	Akaka, Daniel	Dem	HI	Case, Edward	45	1,046,255	390,037	228,040	1,364,411
	Chafee, Lincoln	Rep	RI	**Laffey, Steve**	46	1,745,243	747,244	816,271	1,840,058
2008	Stevens, Ted	Rep	AK	Cuddy, David	27	31,062	2,783	8,198	759,003
	Kerry, John	Dem	MA	**O'Reilly, Edward**	31	148,462	74,790	3,900	366,660
	Lautenberg, Frank	Dem	NJ	Andrews, Robert	35	1,883,696	849,320	323,949	4,039,692
	Graham, Lindsay	Rep	SC	Witherspoon, Buddy	33	216,729	165,704	25,970	441,452
2010	**Murkowski, Lisa**	Rep	AK	**Miller, Joseph**	51	174,553	166,040	53,182	283,473
	McCain, John	Rep	AZ	**Hayworth, J. D.**	32	3,013,405	2,303,849	609,089	3,063,180
	Lincoln, Blanche	Dem	AR	**Halter, William**	42	2,426,220	2,187,984	708,268	2,639,472
	Bennet, Michael	Dem	CO	Romanoff, Andrew	46	2,214,901	1,278,333	122,294	2,597,969
	Specter, Arlen	Dem	PA	**Sestak, Joseph**	54	2,837,917	756,918	1,498,727	6,108,380

Note: Ideological challengers are in bold.

aThe out-of-state contribution totals only include itemized contributions.

bThe FEC did not list total individual contributions in its 1980 and 1982 candidate summary files. Totals for victorious candidates (D'Amato, Folsom, and Gruening) in these years are estimated from their preprimary filings.

cData not provided by candidate.

to more primary challenges in the future: "I think more people are going to run. And if you have better-quality candidates, you have a better chance of winning." As in the House, the story in the Senate includes not just the fact that a few strong challengers emerged in the primaries but the fact that money did not go hand-in-hand with success. Two primary challengers won their primaries in 2010 (although both lost the general election); one spent over $6 million, while the other spent $283,000.

Measuring Group Influence

The preceding analysis has drawn on extant hypotheses in the literature about primary candidates and limited itself to data whose meaning is not subject to debate—that is, a difference in total contributions or PAC contributions across candidates is a finding in itself; it does not necessarily have to "mean" anything. It should be clear that one of the major reasons why primarying has received substantial attention in recent elections is that the groups who support primary challengers have been very vocal about their support and have sought to use these candidates as a vehicle to increase their own visibility. The data here provide substantial circumstantial evidence that outside groups have sought to nationalize House and Senate races and that they have been successful in doing so. In chapter 5, I explore group activities in more detail. Here, however, it is worth noting the data we can acquire on bundling and independent expenditures for primary challengers.

The FEC requires groups that bundle contributions to report their bundling to the FEC, and it also requires candidates to report bundled contributions. Using these disclosures, the Center for Responsive Politics provides a list of major bundlers, by recipient, for elections since 2002.[15] Several recent primary candidates are on this list, including Steve Laffey (recipient of $443,918 in bundled contributions from the Club for Growth), Ned Lamont (recipient of $251,126 of contributions bundled by MoveOn.org), and Tim Walberg (recipient of $241,995 in contributions bundled by the Club for Growth). The Club for Growth also bundled over $300,000 for Andrew Harris and Sean Parnell in 2008. One could piece together estimates of aggregate group support (e.g., one could add to Laffey's bundled contributions the $485,061 in independent expenditures by the Club for Growth against Laffey's opponent, Lincoln Chafee; the $45,554 in independent expenditures for Laffey; and the $2,598 contributed to Laffey by the Club for Growth's PAC). Similar estimates could be made for Lamont,

Walberg, and others. These estimates, though, lack an easy point of comparison; similar data are not available for candidates in earlier elections, and these groups' endorsements may also inspire other individual contributions that are not easily detected or measured.

These data do suggest, however, that the candidate fundraising reports for recent primary challengers are the tip of the iceberg in many instances. The 2010 bundling data provide some instructive evidence: Bill Halter received $179,156 from MoveOn.org, Joe Miller received over $150,000 from the Club for Growth (given Miller's primary fundraising numbers, most of this was undoubtedly received after his primary victory), and Joe Sestak received a total of over $150,000 from three different bundling sources. These bundling figures show how out-of-state money finds its way into campaigns. If, for instance, one makes the assumption that few of the MoveOn contributions originated in Arkansas, MoveOn alone accounted for over one-fourth of Halter's out-of-state money. In 2008, the Club for Growth numbers account for almost all of the out-of-state money for Parnell and Harris. When such groups decide to become involved in a race, they can tap into a donor base far larger than even the strongest primary challengers might hope to reach on their own. Such groups provide a service to candidates, however, that is not easily quantified or reduced to fundraising numbers.

Conclusions

Congressional primaries have received scant attention from students of congressional elections, and the campaign finance data from the 1980s and 1990s indicate that this lack of attention has, for the most part, been deserved. In chapter 2, I argued that there are no unambiguous signs that the level of primary competition today is any different from what it has been in the past. The data in this chapter show, however, that the past decade has been different. Primary challengers, particularly ideological primary challengers, are raising more money, and they are raising much of that money from donors who do not reside in their states or districts. This change is driven by enough candidates that I believe it to be a consequential change, but it is not driven by enough candidates that we can make confident predictions about the future, especially given the coincident increase in the number of primary challengers and decline in fundraising by primary challengers in 2010. Average fundraising for primary challenges dipped sharply in 2010, and due to the fact that most of the primary challengers in 2010 were Republicans, its decline meant that a large number of Republican challengers appear to have overperformed in terms of their vote share per dollar. Does this say anything about the two parties? We shall know more about this in future elections.

The financial success of several primary challengers in recent years will not, however, necessarily render congressional primaries easier to study. We can look at data on the receipts of these candidates and the sources of contributions, but it may continue to be difficult to adequately gauge the relationship between primary challengers and their supporters. While primary challengers have been happy to classify themselves as part of a movement, they have not always been willing to provide details on the financial arrangements of their dealings with their supporters. For instance, in his autobiographical book on his campaign, Steve Laffey (2007, 45, 160), who, as we saw, received over $400,000 in contributions bundled by the Club for Growth, briefly refers to the club as having "lots and lots of money," but he has virtually nothing to say about his relationship with the club. He is silent about whether the club encouraged him to run, whether he was aware of how much money the club was spending, and whether he saw himself as a kindred spirit to other primary challengers. It may be asking too much of candidates to request that they place themselves in the broader historical context of any shift in how activists and politicians view congressional primaries, but one suspects, after reading Laffey's book, that candidates may be reluctant to divulge too many of the details of their fundraising. Recent changes in campaign finance law will likely also obscure some of the spending on behalf of primary challengers; we will still be able to observe individual contributions, but, as I shall explain in chapter 5, group expenditures will become harder to measure.

Future elections will indicate whether there will be a sustained increase in the competitiveness of incumbents' primary renomination bids or whether the call for primarying candidates is a function of the narrowly divided Congress and some of the partisan anger generated by the fight for control of Congress. As has been demonstrated by far more visible campaigns, at the presidential level or, in a few cases, in general elections for Congress, changes in fundraising options and strategy have allowed a few candidates to go far beyond the norm in raising money quickly and in large amounts. Candidates and groups with a good story to tell about themselves or about their opponents have shown the ability to do this in congressional primaries as well.

4 | The Consequences of Congressional Primary Challenges

As I have shown in the two previous chapters, there is little evidence to suggest that the amount of primary competition we see today is novel. Primary competition, whatever the motivation of the challenger, comes and goes in waves that correspond, to some degree, with voter unrest. There are, however, two unusual features of the primary competition for incumbents that we have seen in the 2000s. First, as chapter 2 showed, it corresponds less to the role of political parties than it once did; all wayward incumbents are equally vulnerable. Second, as I argued in chapter 3, there is a class of primary challengers today that is better funded and draws on more of a national fundraising base than was the case in the 1970s, 1980s, and 1990s.

At the beginning of this book, I posed three questions. First, is there more primary competition today than there once was? The answer to this question depends on one's baseline—are we concerned here about history or about how today's members of Congress (few of whom were in office in the 1980s) perceive primaries. Second, are primary challengers more of a threat to incumbents today than they once were? If one construes "threat" to entail some measure of campaign financing, the answer seems to be a qualified yes. Third, do primaries have consequences for incumbents' behavior in Congress; that is, are incumbents running scared, and do they make adjustments to ward off potential challengers or to respond to actual challengers? In this chapter, I seek to answer the third question.

Since it appears, from chapter 2, that it is difficult to find ways in which parties can effectively discourage primary competition, we should look at what incumbents do in response to it. As I shall note at the end of this chapter, however, it is not possible to conclusively measure whether incumbents modify their behavior to ward off challenges; in that case, we would be measuring the effect of potential challenges that may not actually occur. We cannot collect data regarding nonevents. We can, however, measure the consequences of the primary challenges that do happen. If incumbents who have problems treat primary opposition as a wake-up call, we might look at their responses to see if the incumbents have indeed heard the call.

As I have documented in the previous two chapters, not all primaries contain the same message. The coding of primary challenge types I have provided in the previous two chapters, however imprecise it may be, should correspond to the messages incumbents have gotten from their opponents. The incumbent Democrat who survives a strong challenge from the left or the incumbent Republican who survives a challenge from the right gets a message about his or her behavior and can respond by changing that behavior. An incumbent whose primary challenger has argued that he or she is too old, however, obviously cannot become younger; the incumbent might seek to demonstrate his or her vigor, but this is difficult to measure. A white incumbent who represents a predominantly African American district and who faces an African American challenger might seek to pay greater attention to the needs of his or her African American constituents, but again, this is difficult to measure and may not be enough to ward off future challengers, who may simply argue that the district should be represented by an African American. In other words, incumbents sometimes can and sometimes cannot respond to the message. In addition, incumbents may choose to ignore the message. Perhaps some districts are sufficiently heterogeneous that an incumbent is doomed always to face primary competition, in which case a strategy that antagonizes some portion of the primary electorate is the only strategy that will yield a general election triumph.

Previous Research on the Consequences of Primaries

Let us begin by reviewing past studies of primary competition, in order to disaggregate the effects of different types of primary challenges. To be certain, some incumbents lose their bids for renomination. Beyond these rare cases, however, what can we say about the consequences of primary challenges? One claim in literature dating all the way back to the 1950s has been that primary competition hurts incumbents in the general election. The evidence on this is mixed—some early articles (e.g., Hacker 1965) contended that primaries had little effect on incumbents' general election totals, while others (Kenney and Rice 1984, 1987; Kenney 1988; Born 1981; Piereson and Smith 1975; Bernstein 1977; Johnson and Gibson 1974) have found some effects. Most of the latter studies conclude that candidates are hurt slightly in competitive districts or states but are relatively unscathed in districts or states where one party is dominant (Piereson and Smith 1975). As Kenney (1988) notes, a primary challenge is often more a symptom of a weak incumbent than a cause of weakness; Kenney finds that challenges tend to occur when incumbents are implicated in a scandal, switch parties, are drawn into new districts, or show other signs of weakness.[1]

More recently, some studies of primary competition have tried, as I do here, to explain how different types of primary challenges can yield different results. These studies have differentiated primary challenges according to their competitiveness or according to attributes of the challenger. Pearson and Lawless (2008), for instance, measure changes in party unity scores among incumbents who faced primary challengers in the previous election, controlling for the race and gender of the incumbent, the initial party unity score of the incumbent, and their measure of whether or not the challenger is a quality challenger (i.e., has held prior elective office). Hirano et al. (2008) consider Senate primary challengers, seeking to identify changes in DW-NOMINATE scores for threatened incumbents, with various controls for the nature of the state's primary electorate. Both of these studies conclude that primaries have little effect on incumbents' voting habits or their success in general elections. Brady, Han, and Pope (2007) present a theoretical rationale for why primaries may pull candidates away from the median position of their district, but they caution that this is generally done through defeat, not through incumbent movement, and that defeats are rare enough that the effect in Congress is not dramatic. Sulkin (2011, 171) asks whether primary opposition increases legislators' responsiveness to voters and willingness to keep campaign promises, and she concludes that it has no effect.

The conclusions we can draw from these studies are ambiguous, because there is no a priori reason why competitive primary challenges should always be consequential for incumbents. There is certainly anecdotal evidence that challenges can hurt; it is a staple of literature on presidential elections, for instance, that primary challenges to incumbent presidents Jimmy Carter and George H. W. Bush were harmful and pulled these candidates away from the general electorate's median.[2] The notion that a candidate's base may be demoralized by the mudslinging of a primary race certainly seems plausible. It is not at all clear, however, that all competitive primaries are necessarily divisive, nor can we measure divisiveness lest we engage in Monday-morning armchair quarterbacking, scouring election results for ad hoc evidence of divisiveness. There is no reason to assume, for instance, that an incumbent deemed too moderate by the primary electorate will lose votes to a general election opponent, unless voters of the incumbent's party are so disillusioned by his or her performance that they refrain from voting at all in the general election. In an overwhelmingly partisan district, a primary challenge may simply be a sign of healthy electoral competition. In some instances, the issues raised in the primary will resonate with general election voters; in others, they will not.

In short, looking at primary competition in the aggregate or even through measures of the type of challenger does not allow us to identify the reason for the challenge. In addition (and this is admittedly a more controversial assumption), there is little reason to suspect that differences in a primary challenger's vote share should matter once the challenger has passed a threshold level of competitiveness, unless the incumbent is defeated in the primary. Looking at differences in the reasons for challenges complicates our effort to identify consequences with great precision, but it does allow us to narrow our attention to the types of challenges (as opposed to challengers) that matter and to talk about how they matter for incumbents across future election cycles. Using a binary measure of competitiveness also seems more intuitive—incumbents either are or are not scared by their primary opponents. The drawback identified by Kenney (1988) remains, however: in using such measures, we cannot prove that changes in incumbent behavior are consequences of the primary challenge itself. They may, instead, be responses to the incumbent's problems that brought on the primary in the first place. I am skeptical, however, that more subtle treatments of challenger vote share, challenger financing, and so forth solve this problem or give us any greater leverage in assessing the degree of threat faced or perceived by the incumbent.

This chapter seeks to provide a comprehensive statement on the consequences of primary challenges. In the following pages, I consider primary defeats, general election defeats following a contested incumbent primary, and reductions in general election vote share following a contested primary. Incumbents do face a small reduction in vote share following a competitive primary, but the decline in vote share is rarely lethal to incumbents. I also consider shifts in voting behavior following a contested primary that are, again, slight but do occur, particularly when the primary competitor has run on the basis of the incumbent's perceived lack of ideological fit to the district. I also consider the longer-term consequences of primary challenges: while events of two, three, or even four elections past the primary challenge do not necessarily indicate that the primary challenge caused injury to the incumbent, challenged incumbents often do tend to retire sooner than those who are not challenged, and they tend to be replaced by incumbents who provide a better fit for the district. The chapter is organized such that I first consider data on the causes of primary challenges, with an eye toward what, if anything, an incumbent might do to respond. I then catalog potential consequences of different types of challenges, and I measure the extent to which these consequences—reduced vote share, retirement, and change in an incumbent's voting habits—correspond to primary challenges. Following this analysis, I briefly turn to the problem of looking at the challenges that do not actually happen, to the possibility that the behavior of unchallenged incumbents and perhaps even of Congress as a whole is influenced by the threat of primary opposition.

Measuring the Causes and Effects of Primary Challenges to Incumbents

In this chapter, I assess the consequences of the most prevalent types of primary challenges, according to the coding system presented in the previous two chapters. I group these consequences of different types of challenges into two broad types. First, incumbents may face *electoral consequences*. Their primary challenges may precede a decline in general election vote share or a more serious primary or general election challenge in the next election. The primary challenge may signal to the incumbent that he or she is likely to face increasingly difficult campaigns, and the incumbent may thus be inspired to retire or to seek other office. Such consequences may have little to do with measurable characteristics of the incumbent's behavior while in office.

Second, there may be *behavioral consequences* to primary challenges. Some of these are measurable; some are not. An incumbent accused of being inattentive to his or her district may increase travel back to the district or may otherwise seek to dispel the notion that he or she is not responsive. These sorts of changes, however, are difficult to measure. In cases where incumbents are accused of being out of step with their district or with their party on matters of policy or ideology, however, incumbents may shift their positions, moving away from the center in response to being "primaried" or moving toward the center if they are challenged for being too partisan.

These behavioral consequences dovetail with the central motif of this book, the exploration of the rise of "primarying." It is important to note several complications in simply positing ideological shifts for incumbents, however. First, such shifts may well be rare. If incumbents who judge their primary challenger to be unrepresentative of the district's median voter survive the primary, they may continue to behave as they had before the primary. Second, behavioral and electoral consequences can interact with each other. Incumbents may shift away from the median in response to a primary challenger, thus affecting their general election vote percentage in their current election or in subsequent elections. Incumbents may also retire rather than change their positions. As the recent case of Arlen Specter shows, an ideological challenge may even inspire them to change parties. Third, the consequences of an ideological challenge may be felt even after the challenged incumbent has left office—they may result in a different type of representative for the district. Fourth, as noted in the previous chapters, the threat of primary challenges may have as strong an effect on incumbents' position taking as does an actual challenge.

In the previous chapters, I grouped primary challenges into ten categories. Here, I focus on the consequences of the six most common reasons for primary challenges, grouped according to whether their consequences can be expected to be electoral or behavioral. These six types comprise 58 percent of all competitive primary challenges and 85 percent of those that could be coded. Table 4.1 lists these types of challenges and some expectations about their consequences.

Primary challenges can arise for multiple reasons, and the dominant reason that the challenger presents for the challenge may not truly be the most important reason. Even where the reason for the challenge is clear, it is not always easy to measure the consequences of the challenge. I offer to examples of complicated challenges for consideration here.

First, consider the four-way Democratic primary in Illinois's third congressional district in 2008, which we visited in chapter 1. Representative Daniel Lipinski was elected to the seat in 2004 to succeed his father, William Lipinski. One could code the challenge to Lipinski as an ideological challenge, an issue-based challenge, or a challenge based on competence. Although I coded this as an ideological challenge, it is somewhat reductionist to distill this challenge into only one category or to place too much stock in the stated reasons of the challenger. Lipinski won the race rather easily—surprisingly so, given the mobilization of groups such as MoveOn .org behind Lipinski's strongest primary challenger, Mark Pera. Perhaps Pera overstated Lipinski's poor fit for the district, perhaps Lipinski simply ran a better campaign, or perhaps Lipinski managed to recast himself as a

TABLE 4.1. Expected Consequences of Primary Challenges to Incumbents

Type of Challenge	Electoral Consequences	Behavioral Consequences	Other
Scandal	Decreased general election vote share Greater likelihood of retirement	None	
Competence/Age	Decreased general election vote share Greater likelihood of retirement	None measurable	
Issue-Based		Position change on primary issue; depending on issue, this may mean movement toward or away from center	
Ideological—Noncentrist	Greater likelihood of retirement	Movement away from center	More partisan/ noncentrist successor
Ideological—Centrist	Decreased general election vote share	Movement toward center	More centrist successor (same party) Greater likelihood of other-party successor
Race	Greater likelihood of retirement	Movement away from center	Successor of different race (minority challenger)

more liberal candidate. At any rate, it is not clear that Lipinski suffered any adverse consequences from this challenge in the short run, and if he did get a message from the campaign, it may have been that liberal groups took a good shot at him and did not succeed.

Second, consider Scott Garrett's two primary challenges to moderate New Jersey Republican Marge Roukema in 1998 and 2000. Roukema clearly was more liberal than most Republicans, but she was popular in her district by many accounts; she received over 65 percent of the general election vote during each of her elections in the 1990s. Garrett clearly ran from the right, garnering 48 percent of the primary vote each time. When Roukema retired in 2002, Garrett easily won the seat, and he has been comfortably reelected ever since (although, interestingly, his general election vote share has been consistently lower than Roukema's). Did Garrett's challenges cause Roukema to retire? Although Roukema did not say so and may have had many other reasons to retire after twenty-two years in Congress, it seems evident that she would have continued to face primary opposition, from Garrett or from another conservative Republican. Roukema won her general election campaigns easily in both years, however. The consequences of these challenges, then, are not crystal clear. The challenges did not affect the positions Roukema took or her general election performance, and one cannot prove that her retirement was a consequence of being challenged.

What lessons did Lipinski and Roukema learn from their challenges? Ultimately, we cannot be certain. Perhaps Lipinski did something different following the 2008 election that enabled him to run for the Democratic nomination in 2010 with less opposition, or perhaps he was just lucky the next time. Perhaps Roukema retired because she was tired of being challenged, or perhaps she had other reasons. The simplest approach to such races is to at least use the challengers' interpretations of the incumbents as a starting point for analysis and to look for patterns in the incumbents' fortunes over the subsequent years. Part of the rhetoric of "primarying" involves claims about changing the voting habits of members of Congress—either by replacing some members or by encouraging incumbents to change their positions in order to ward off challenges. The rhetoric of those who challenge scandal-prone members or supposedly inept members implies no such change. To measure the consequences of challenges, then, it is necessary to separate out the intentions of challengers and connect them with changes in Congress. In the analysis that follows, I loosely group challenges into those that seek to replace individual members and those that seek to alter the policies pursued or enacted by Congress.

Expectations about the Consequences of Primaries

If one is to use the challengers' arguments as a starting point for analysis, one must at least subject these claims to objective examination. This is quite easy in some cases and more difficult in others. In the analysis that follows, I match my coding of challengers' rationales with characteristics of the challenged incumbents. If we expect consequences from primary challenges, we must at least be able to say that the challengers were not off base in their arguments.

Causes of Electoral Change

Scandal

Ninety-eight incumbent House members were challenged on the basis of scandal or perceived scandal during the 1970 to 2010 period. Of the six types of challenges listed in table 4.1, those based on scandal would seem most likely to correlate with a decreased general election percentage for incumbents. This does not, however, mean that the primary challenge *causes* the decreased general election percentage. Both are merely signs that the incumbent is in trouble.

Welch and Hibbing (1997; see also Peters and Welch 1980) explore the effects of corruption charges on incumbents' general election and primary election fortunes. They conclude that corruption charges lead to a reduction in the incumbent's general election vote share of slightly over nine percentage points. They show, as well, that incumbents accused of corruption are more likely to be defeated in their primaries than are other incumbents, but they limit their consideration of primaries to primary defeats, not to reduced primary election vote share or to any interaction for these incumbents between primary challenges and weakened general election performance.

The analysis by Welch and Hibbing shows several difficulties in exploring the effects of scandal-related primaries on incumbents. First, as the authors note, many incumbents expecting to be accused of corruption may retire preemptively; as a consequence, those who are charged and yet run for reelection may have already calculated that they can withstand such charges. Second, Welch and Hibbing's data set includes all incumbents who become embroiled in scandals; their data set thus includes many incumbents who did not face primary challenges at all, and it excludes some who did face primary challengers who alleged that the incumbent was, in some way, corrupt.[3] In short, they seek to develop objective measures, while the reasons I consider here are somewhat more subjective.

These two issues make it difficult to measure the consequences of scandal-related primary challenges. Nonetheless, the very nature of such a challenge implies not that the incumbent is wrong on the issues or represents the district poorly but that the incumbent has made poor ethical choices. Scandal-related challenges should thus correlate with a reduced general election vote percentage but should have little effect either on the incumbent's voting behavior in Congress (should the incumbent survive the challenge) or on the ideological positioning of subsequent representatives of the district (should the incumbent retire or be defeated). Scandal-related challenges may also encourage incumbents to retire, but only if the scandal is not one that can be expected to diminish in importance over time.

Competence/Age

In the data set I use here, there are 110 primary challenges that involve criticism of the incumbent's effectiveness: either the incumbent is deemed to be incompetent or insufficiently attentive to the district, or he or she is deemed by the challenger to be too old. As is the case for scandal-based challenges, these reasons are not always easy to quantify. A claim that the incumbent is incompetent is subjective, and while one might hypothesize that age is a somewhat more objective factor, there is no evidence that primary challenges become more prevalent with age or seniority—although, as chapter 2 shows, challenges based on competence or age do tend to be waged against more senior incumbents. An alternate interpretation would be that an incumbent who has served eight terms or so (the average for incumbents challenged based on their competence or age) must be relatively in step with the district on ideological issues, and competence may thus be the most plausible issue to raise for a challenger; that is, the issue is not that the incumbent does not represent the district but that he or she just does not do it actively enough.

Literature on congressional retirements suggests, however, that among the most senior incumbents, there is often more of a threat of defeat from primary challengers than from general election challengers (Bullock 1972;

Hibbing 1991, 35–37).[4] Incumbents expecting to be challenged because of their age or competence may, as is the case for those involved in scandals, retire preemptively, making it again difficult to argue for any causal relationship stemming from primary challenges. As is the case for scandals, though, age and competence are issues that have little to do with ideology. Shifts in voting behavior do not seem related to such challenges, but changes in general election vote percentage do.

Causes of Behavioral Change

Ideological Challenges
In the data set I use here, there are 101 cases where the challenge is based on the allegation that the incumbent is insufficiently partisan. These cases of so-called primarying are in many ways the easiest to look at in order to explore changes in incumbents' behavior, but the ultimate consequences of these races have much to do with the overall state of partisan competition in the district. Consider the following three different potential responses by incumbents to a challenge from a more partisan opponent.

- A Democrat in a strongly Democratic district is challenged in the primary by an opponent who claims that the incumbent has not voted in a liberal enough manner. The incumbent may have reason to fear that this challenger or future challengers will be successful in this tactic, but the incumbent has little to fear from Republican opponents in the general election. The incumbent may, then, shift his or her positions to the left in order to ward off primary challenges, with little cost in the general election. The same logic holds for Republican incumbents in heavily Republican districts.
- A Democratic incumbent in a competitive but relatively homogeneous district[5] faces a challenger from the left. If the incumbent shifts to the left in the primary, he or she may suffer in the general election or in future general elections, if confronted by a moderate Republican candidate,; that is, there are more votes at the center than at the ideological extremes. The incumbent therefore continues to take moderate positions.[6]
- A Democratic incumbent in a competitive but heterogeneous or polarized district faces a challenger from the left. The incumbent, who will suffer if he or she shifts to the left in the primary, gains little in the general election from taking a moderate posi-

tion. The cost of shifting to the left, then, is lower than the cost of taking a moderate position, and warding off primary opposition may become more important. Whether or not the incumbent survives the general election, the district's representative will take relatively partisan positions.

In each of the preceding scenarios, the incumbent measures the relationship between two different electorates—the primary electorate and the general electorate—and seeks to take a position that maximizes the chances of winning both. In such cases, one must assume that the out-party candidate is unlikely to capture any of the other party's primary voters in the general election or to reverse positions with the incumbent (i.e., that it is unlikely for the Republican candidate to take a position to the left of the Democrat). Something like this may happen in the rare instances where incumbents who fear challenges switch parties; there were two such cases in 2010. But this is generally such a rare occurrence that I give it no further attention here.

Thus ideological challenges, whether from the margins or the center, are the cases where a shift in incumbent behavior may be most likely, but the degree of the shift depends on the nature of the district. It is difficult to use voting statistics to sort districts according to the types listed in table 4.1, because there are few agreed-on measures of district-level polarization[7] and because the degree of threat posed by the challenger is difficult to quantify. There is a range even among the races considered here, in which the challenger has at least reached a threshold of 25 percent of the vote. One can, however, assess the degree of general election threat to the incumbent based on prior general election vote performance or the performance of the incumbent's party at the district level in presidential races. One can look at any change in the incumbent's voting with these factors in mind.

In the political science literature, there is much discussion of the extent to which there are many remaining districts in which moderate candidates tend to emerge from party primaries. Burden (2004) contends that competitive primaries (without regard to the challenger's intent) tend to pull candidates away from their district median—although Ansolabehere, Snyder, and Stewart (2001) argue exactly the opposite. General election competition does, for Burden, have a moderating effect on candidates, but insofar as primary electorates are more likely to value ideology than are general electorates, the ability of primary candidates to take centrist (relative to the district) positions is limited by the different nature of primary elections. King (2001) brings together primary and general election competition in an entirely different way, arguing that the most ideologically extreme members of Congress actually tend to come from moderate districts. His rationale for this claim is that primary election competition poses more of a threat to incumbents because these incumbents are initially less secure. This creates a sort of seesaw effect, in which the most competitive districts in the country shift, over time, from representatives of one ideological extreme to another.

Changes in behavior are thus of the most importance in looking at ideological challenges, but the effect of the challenge on the incumbent's general election performance is an important secondary consideration. Anecdotal evidence—particularly that of the races between Roukema and Garrett—also suggests that incumbents may be pushed to retire by strong primary challenges. The literature is ambiguous about whether conventional wisdom regarding incumbents' responses to more partisan challengers is actually correct, but it does provide a clear rationale for considering the effects of ideological challenges on incumbent behavior and for separating out different types of districts in analyzing any behavioral changes.

Causes of Electoral and Behavioral Change

Centrist Challenges

Challenges to incumbents from the center—accusations of being too partisan—are less prevalent among the races considered here than are ideological challenges; there are only thirty-two such cases in the data set. The spatial logic of these challenges is somewhat simpler than that of ideological challenges. If voters weigh ideology at all in their considerations, dissatisfaction among the more moderate members of the primary electorate should correspond with diminished general election performance; that is, we should expect to see both behavioral consequences—movement toward the center—and electoral consequences.

Issue-Based Challenges

Table 4.2 lists the issues that inspired primary challenges during the 1970 to 2010 period. Issue-based challenges are among the most difficult to analyze here, partly because it is difficult to measure whether members have shifted on these issues and partly because many issue-based challenges closely resemble ideological challenges. In the previous two chapters, I sought to make some distinctions among these challenges by separating challenges based on national issues—such as abortion, war, or immigration—from challenges based on local issues. Reasons for challenges I categorize as being based on local issues include such matters as an incumbent's stance on logging (in a rural California district), an incumbent's friendliness with Rudolph Giuliani during Giuliani's tenure as mayor of New York (in a New York City Democratic primary), an incumbent's violation of a pledge concerning a term limit (in several cases), and an incumbent's actions regarding expansion of the Dallas Love Field Airport. In such cases, the reason behind a challenge to an incumbent does not necessarily correspond to the incumbent's overall ideological orientation.

In the case of national issues, some issues might be expected to be used against the incumbent in the general election, while others would not be. Where, for instance, a pro-choice primary opponent challenges an anti-abortion Democrat, it seems unlikely that such a challenge would have an effect in the general election. Some issues (e.g., an incumbent's stance on social security or free trade) could be expected to endure for several election cycles, thus either affecting the incumbent's vote share in subsequent years or inspiring the incumbent to change positions over time. Some issues are consequential enough that a position change on them might show up in broader ideology scores, while other position changes might not. For instance, in 2006 and 2008, two Republicans and one Democrat were challenged on the basis of their support for the Iraq War; in the framework of a Democratic primary, opposition to the war may correlate with liberalism on other issues, while this seems unlikely to be the case within the framework of a Republican primary. One could argue that a serious issue-based challenge could inspire the incumbent to change his or her position on that issue, but it is difficult to measure how often this is the case among the candidates considered here. The most one might hope for

TABLE 4.2. Issue-Based Challenges

Issue	Party	N	Years	Direction
Vietnam	Dem	8	1970–72	Left
Abortion (anti-)	Rep	7	1992–98	Right
Abortion (pro-choice)	Dem	3	1978, 1980, 1992	Left
Abortion (anti-)	Dem	3	1992, 1994, 1996	Right (centrist)
Immigration	Rep	5	2004, 2006	Right
Iraq	Dem	1	2004	Left
NAFTA/Trade	Dem	1	1994	Left
NAFTA/Trade	Rep	1	2002	Left (centrist)
No Clear Direction	4 Dem, 7 Rep	11	1974–2008	
Local Issues	11 Dem, 3 Rep	14	1972–2008	

in investigating the consequences of issue-based primaries is to look at whether incumbents shift away from the center on those issues where the criticism is raised by more liberal challengers (for Democrats) or more conservative ones (for Republicans). One might treat some issue-based challenges as more focused ideological challenges, with the acknowledgment that the consequences of these challenges, in terms of overall movement, are likely to be weaker than those of broader ideological challenges. I have selected the most likely cases of this here, but their small number will, at best, only add to a more complete listing of ideological challenges.

Race/Ethnicity
Finally, in fifty-seven of the challenges in the data set I use here, race is explicitly mentioned. In most of these cases, these are districts where a white representative represents a majority-minority district or at least a district where nonwhites comprise a sizable percentage of the electorate. In a small number of cases, however, the incumbent and the challenger are of different nonwhite ethnic groups—for example, Latinos are challenging African Americans, or vice versa. In one example (that of Chicago Democrat Luis Gutierrez), the conflict is between a Puerto Rican incumbent and three different Mexican American challengers. In elections such as these, the arguments made by challengers tend to be about descriptive representation—arguments that the district's representative should be of the same background as his or her constituents—but there is sometimes an ideological dimension. Given that nonwhites tend to take policy positions that are more liberal than the positions taken by whites, the challenger may supplement claims about descriptive representation with claims about substantively representing the district's purportedly more liberal views. As is the case for issue-based challenges, however, measuring ideological change for the district's representative (be that representative a successful challenger or an incumbent who survives the primary) requires, first, that the ideological direction of the challenge be ascertained and, second, that one acknowledge that any positioning effects should be weaker than the effects of a strictly ideological challenge. Table 4.3 shows a rather conservative estimate of how race-based challenges might relate to ideological change.

All of the fifty-seven race-based challenges in the data set occurred within the Democratic Party, and only one of the seats so challenged (in South Carolina in 1972) changed party control in the general election. This renders somewhat implausible the notion that there might be general election consequences for challenged incumbents. One other consequence that bears investigating, however, is the possibility that such challenges lead to a greater likelihood that the incumbent will retire in the subsequent election cycle. I have established a separate category for challenges based on redistricting,[8] so the most dramatic cases of shifts in racial composition of the district are not present among these challenges.[9] Nonetheless, incumbents who survive redistricting but face districts where a majority of constituents are of a different race may see primary competition as a sign that they will face increasing difficulty in years to come and may opt to retire.

Instances of the remaining categories of reasons for primary challenges—party factionalism, ambitious challenger, and redistricting—are smaller in number and difficult to fit into table 4.1. Absent an ideological dimension to party factionalism, it is difficult to forecast behavioral consequences, and as suggested in chapter 2, factionalism is endemic to some districts regardless of the incumbent. Challenges based on redistricting are also largely out of the incumbent's hands, and insofar as they generally occur (except in unusual circumstances) in one election cycle per decade, they seem unlikely to have long-term consequences if the incumbent survives them. In the following analyses, however, I have sought to minimize the interaction between redistricting and other changes in the incumbent's electoral performance or voting behavior; I discuss these decisions where they are relevant. Finally, challenges based simply on the ambition of the challenger appear likewise to have little effect on the incumbent, should he or she survive.

Evidence of Change Following Primary Challenges

There is much overlap among the potential consequences of primary challenges previously described. In short, incumbents can be affected in four

TABLE 4.3. Race-Based Challenges

Type of Challenge	N	Direction
Black Challenger, White Incumbent	36	Left
White Challenger, Black Incumbent	10	Center
White Challenger, Latino Incumbent	4	Center?
Latino Challenger, White Incumbent	3	Left?
Latino Challenger, Black Incumbent	2	??
Latino Challenger, Latino (different nationality) Incumbent	2	??
Total N	57	

different measurable ways: they may lose the next election, they may see a decrease in general election vote share, they may choose to retire, or they may choose to change their voting behavior. They may also, of course, be completely unaffected. We cannot always be certain of the reason for such changes—for instance, an incumbent's declining fortunes in the general election may be completely unrelated to a primary challenge—but we can at least see whether different types of primary challenges are correlated with different observable actions by incumbents. Table 4.4 recasts the expectations summarized in table 4.1, in order to show the relationship be-

TABLE 4.4. Possible Results of Primary Challenges

Possible Consequences of Primary Challenge	Cause
Defeat in Primary	Any type of primary challenge
Defeat in Current General Election	Any type of primary challenge—except for ideological challenges
Defeat in Next General Election	Any type of primary challenge—except for ideological challenges
Change in Current General Election Vote Share	Any type of primary challenge—except for ideological challenges
Change in Next General Election Vote Share	Any type of primary challenge—except for ideological challenges
Retirement in Next Election	Any type of primary challenge
Retirement in Next Election, with Different Type of Successor	Depends on type of challenge: • More centrist same-party successor if centrist challenge in previous election • More ideological same-party successor if ideological challenge in previous election • Greater likelihood of other-party successor if centrist challenge in previous election • Successor of different race if race-based challenge in previous election • More ideological same-party successor if race-based challenge by nonwhite candidate in previous election • More centrist same-party successor if race-based challenge by white candidate in previous election • Greater likelihood of other-party successor if race-based challenge by white candidate in previous election
Shift toward Center in Voting Behavior	Centrist challenge
Shift away from Center in Voting Behavior	Ideological challenge

tween types of observable reactions to primary challenges and the previously summarized reasons for such challenges.

Primary Losses

Primary defeats are rare for incumbents, but they are the only unambiguous cases of consequences that challenges have for incumbents. Table 4.5 compares the proportion of categorizable challenges of each type to the proportion of primary defeats of incumbents of each type. The vast majority of primary challengers are unsuccessful (86 of the 774 challengers considered here actually won their primaries), but some types of challengers are more successful than others.[10] Challengers who run because of the incumbent's age or incompetence, who run centrist challenges, or who run in substantially redrawn districts are overrepresented among primary winners, compared to their proportion among all primary challengers. Challengers running further from the ideological center than the incumbent or running because of local issues are underrepresented among primary winners. The appearance of primary challengers is too idiosyncratic for one to contend that particular types of incumbents tend to lose their primaries or even to be challenged (a point made in Hirano et al. 2008 as well), but some types of challenges are more successful, when merited (another unmeasurable factor), than others.

TABLE 4.5.   Primary Defeats by Type of Challenge

Reasons for Challenge	Categorizable Challenges (%)	Primary Defeats (%)	N of Primary Defeats
Scandal	18.4	17.4	15
Competence/Age	20.7	24.4	21
Local Issue	2.6	0	0
National Issue	7.5	9.3	8
Centrist	6.0	10.4	9
Ideological	18.0	12.8	11
Race	10.7	9.3	8
Party Factionalism	3.9	2.3	2
Ambitious Challenger	4.1	2.3	2
Redistricting	6.4	10.4	9
Other	1.5	1.2	1
Total N			86

General Election Losses

There is some evidence that incumbents who face primary challenges are more likely to lose their seats than are those who do not face such challenges. Throughout the period considered here, the reelection rate for incumbents was 94.3 percent; incumbents with primary challengers were elected at a rate of 90.8 percent.[11] In other words, the number of incumbents who lost reelection after facing primary challengers was twenty-seven more than would have been expected had there been no challenges. This is a statistically significant difference ($p < .001$), but in no case can we be certain that the primary challenge caused the defeat. Of the incumbents who lost, a disproportionately large percentage were challenged based on scandal (the reelection rate for such incumbents was 81.6 percent). Five candidates who faced ideological challenges were defeated in the general election, and three who faced centrist primary challengers were defeated. The difficulty in finding a clear causal relationship is discussed in the 2008 studies by Hirano et al. and Pearson and Lawless, but it is a point worth reiterating in regard to the different types of reasons identified here.

Declining General Election Vote Share

As table 4.6 shows, primary challenges, in the aggregate, are substantially more harmful to Democrats than to Republicans (or, if one is to avoid references to causality, they coincide with more difficult general election campaigns for the former). Republicans can expect a decrease of approximately 1.5 percent in their general election vote share if they have a primary opponent, while Democrats can expect a decrease of 3.3 percent in vote share. The difference in means also reaches a higher level of statistical significance for Democrats than is the case for Republicans. These estimates are made by considering primary opposition as a binary variable—an incumbent either has a primary challenger who won over 25 percent of the vote or does not, and I do not use dummy variables for year or other control variables. Other studies (e.g., Pearson and Lawless 2008) have used more subtle measurements of primary vote share for challengers; the intuition here, however, is that if an incumbent has an opponent who is sufficiently visible to bring up issues about the incumbent, this may influence general election voting. I exclude here, of course, successful primary opponents—in these cases, there is no general election for the incumbent. These measures, then, underestimate the actual consequences of primary elections for incumbents by considering only those who survived. The party differences may be related to the nature of the challenges within each party or may be indicative of the types of primary challenges waged in each party. As subsequent rows in the table show, not all types of challenges are equal in their consequences for incumbents.

In table 4.6, I have excluded challenge types with fewer than ten cases. This leads to some difficulty in interpreting effects on the parties—because there are more Democratic incumbents throughout this period, there are simply more of each type of challenge, so we can be more confident in interpreting Democratic results than in interpreting Republican results. The results, however, are, with two noteworthy exceptions, as one might expect. Primary challenges unrelated to ideology—those based on scandal or the competence of the incumbent—hurt the incumbent in the immediately following general election. Democrats and Republicans alike lose approximately two percentage points in the immediately following general

TABLE 4.6. Changes in General Election Vote Share, Current and Subsequent Election, by Type of Primary Challenge

Reason for Challenge	Change in Vote Share, This Election (%)	N	Change in Vote Share, Next Election (%)	N
Democrats				
All Challenges	−3.30**	286	.69	266
All Strong Challenges[a]	−1.41**	91	.80	90
Scandal	−7.37	49	−.08	33
Competence/Age	−2.16	63	−2.54	40
National Issue	−3.41	17	1.02	12
Centrist Challenge	−3.15	12	.02	10
Ideological Challenge	−.78	28	−1.55	18
Race	−.17	38	−.67	28
Republicans				
All Challenges	−1.53**	227	.69*	143
All Strong Challenges[a]	−2.89*	155	1.85**	59
Scandal	−1.11	25	.88	19
Competence/Age	−1.77	25	−2.97	17
National Issue	−.80	17	.67	12
Centrist Challenge	−3.34	10	2.10	6
Ideological Challenge	−.12	47	.11	24

*$p < .01$ in F-test compared with change in vote share for unchallenged incumbents of same party.

**$p < .05$ in F-test compared with change in vote share for unchallenged incumbents of same party.

[a]Strong challenges: Incumbent held to less than 60 percent of primary vote.

election (compared to the election before the primary challenge) if their primary opponent discusses issues of competence. Democratic incumbents suffer substantially if accused of scandal or ethical misdeeds, losing over seven percentage points in the general election. Republicans, interestingly, lose barely more than a percentage point when they have a primary challenger who discusses any sort of scandal. As expected, centrist challenges are associated with a decrease in general election vote share for both parties; Democrats and Republicans each lose slightly over three percentage points. Ideological and issue-based challenges have minimal effects in both parties, and race-based challenges do not correspond to substantial reductions in vote share for Democrats.

The two right-hand columns show the relationship between general election vote share in the year that the primary challenge occurs and vote share in the subsequent general election.[12] The intuitions here are either that the candidate will bounce back or that a strong other-party challenger will observe the incumbent's troubles and choose to run in the next election. For the most part, it is evident here that incumbents suffer no further damage in the next election; they rebound in a few instances, but their vote share changes little overall. The one exception is incumbents who are challenged on the grounds of competence or age; these incumbents lose further vote share in the next election in both parties. There is some evidence as well that Republicans bounce back a bit more quickly than Democrats.

Because these are aggregate estimates, they do not take into account year-specific effects. I have removed election dyads in multidistrict states that coincide with redistricting years (e.g., I have not sought to isolate the effects of primary challenges in 1992 on vote share, because a decline in vote share from 1990 to 1992 may be related to redistricting; one cannot isolate the effects of redistricting, since different incumbents will be running in districts that are redrawn to different degrees). Also, if particular types of challenges tend to occur in different years (e.g., ideological challenges happen more in midterm elections, and issue-based challenges are clustered around elections where particularly salient or divisive issues affect voters' choices), they will have an influence on vote share. While the proportion of different types of challenges fluctuates across years, there is little evidence in the data of predictable, systematic differences that can be pegged to, for instance, the redistricting cycle, the presidential election calendar, or other such factors. That the effects of different types of primaries generally accord with intuition is a sign that different types of challenges indeed yield different types of general election results.

Retirement

Incumbents also do not seem to be inspired to retire because of primary challenges. Throughout the 1970–2010 period, 93.9 percent of incumbents sought reelection. This number included 93.9 percent of those who did not face competitive primary opponents in the previous election and 93.5 percent of those who did. Patterns are relatively consistent across types of challenges—95.8 percent of those challenged because of scandal sought reelection the next year, as did 92.9 percent of those challenged on the ground of incompetence, 88.2 percent of those who faced a centrist primary challenger, and 89.5 percent of those challenged because of local or national issues. Of those who faced ideological challengers, 89.9 sought reelection—a slight and statistically insignificant difference, but one that (were it significant) would translate into only four more retirements than would be expected for all who faced primary challenges and four more than would be expected for those who did not face challenges.

What happens, however, when incumbents who face primary challenges that have any relationship to the incumbent's ideology do eventually retire? In many ways, the Scott Garrett challenge to Marge Roukema (already briefly discussed earlier in this chapter) is the paradigmatic case of what ideological challengers hope for if they cannot actually win in their challenges. Garrett challenged the moderate Republican Roukema twice from the right, in 1998 and 2000, and when Roukema retired (allegedly out of frustration with being challenged in the primary), Garrett easily won the seat in 2002. Garrett established a substantially more conservative voting record than Roukema, with a first-dimension DW-NOMINATE score of .77 in his first year, compared to Roukema's final-year score of .19 and her set of scores between .13 and .19 during her tenure in office. Does this pattern hold true for other ideological challenges? Do they eventually yield a more ideological successor? Do we see a similar pattern with centrist challenges? There are several permutations to this logic, as described in table 4.4.

Table 4.7 shows some of the longer-term consequences of various types of challenges with an ideological component. Reading across the table, it becomes evident that a large minority of the incumbents who are challenged wind up being replaced by representatives whose views are more in line with those of the primary challengers. For this table, I have expanded my focus to what happens to the incumbent within the subsequent three elections. This means that the cases here include incumbents challenged between 1970 and 2004. This expanded look means that the incumbents

TABLE 4.7. Successors to Challenged Incumbents

Type of Challenge	N	Remained in Congress	Retired within Six Years	Replaced by More Moderate Same-Party Representative	Replaced by Less Moderate Same-Party Representative	Replaced by Similar Same-Party Representative	Replaced by Other-Party Representative	Retired, District Redrawn	Lost General Election	Lost Primary
Centrist	24	5	8	2	1	4	1	1	4	7
Ideological	66	23	23		8	9	4	2	10	10
Issue/										
Ideological	27	5[a]	8			5	2		5	8
Issue/Centrist	5	1	4			4				
Race/Left	33	10[a]	19		9	9		1	1	2
Race/Right	7	5	1				1		1	
N	162	51	63	2	18	31	8	4	21	27

Note: "Moderation" is measured by a movement of the district's representative's DW-NOMINATE score of more than .10 from the challenged incumbent's final term to the new representative's first term. Succession is measured across the subsequent three election cycles. If summing across rows, the first "retiree" category is the sum for the subsequent five columns.

[a] Two incumbents died within six years—one in the "Issue/Ideological" category and one in the "Race/Left" category.

may not necessarily leave office because of the primary challenge—the primary challenge may simply be a symptom of the incumbent's larger problems. There is some variation, however, in the fates of incumbents according to the nature of the initial challenge. To measure whether the candidate replacing the challenged opponent represents a shift for the district, I have categorized a shift in first-dimension DW-NOMINATE scores of over .10 as a movement, either to the center or away from it. This is an admittedly arbitrary categorization, but it does represent a change more substantial than the fluctuation for incumbents' scores from one Congress to the next tends to be.

In the case of centrist challenges, nine of twenty-four incumbents who faced such challenges were eventually replaced by a more moderate candidate of the same party—either through a subsequent primary defeat or through retirement and replacement by a more moderate candidate of the same party.[13] In nine other cases, the incumbent either remained or was replaced by a similar candidate upon retirement; in five cases, the opposing party eventually won the seat; and in one case, the incumbent was replaced by a less centrist candidate upon retirement. Centrist challenges, then, work a little bit less than half the time. Ideological challenges yield results that accord slightly less with intuition: seventeen of sixty-six incumbents were replaced by a more partisan candidate; for thirty, there was no change; and in fourteen instances, the opposition party gained the seat. We would expect more replacements by more partisan same-party candidates than by the opposition party, which is indeed the case, but the difference is not substantial. Issue-based challenges with a possible ideological dimension—as presented in table 4.2—have somewhat less positive results for the challenger, as do race-based challenges.

As a final note on retirement, there are five instances among the race-based challenges in which a white representative was subsequently replaced by an African American representative. There are no instances where the race of the district's representative changed from a minority representative to a white representative.

Shifts in Voting Behavior

One of the most frequently cited claims about ideological primary challenges is that they pull the incumbent away from the political center. As I argued in chapter 2, not all incumbents challenged from the extremes (from the right for a Republican incumbent or from the left for a Democrat) are demonstrably far from the rest of their party initially. One might still expect, however, that the average incumbent challenged in this manner would be tempted to become more partisan.

I measure shifts in voting behavior by using a simple comparison of DW-NOMINATE scores from one Congress to the next.[14] For an incumbent challenged in one election year, I measure the change in the DW-NOMINATE score from that year to the subsequent election year. For every incumbent, whether challenged or not, I thus construct a series of dyads, of measurements of change across each two-year cycle. To ensure that redistricting effects are not a factor, I exclude dyads that include a redistricting year, unless the district in question is an at-large district; for instance, the dyads considered for the 1990s are 1994–96, 1996–98, and 1998–2000. I also exclude the dyad ending in the first year of this study (1968–70), and I exclude, for obvious reasons, dyads in which the representative was not the same (i.e., where there is a defeat in the first year) and dyads at the end of which the incumbent retired. This limits the number of primary challenges considered: we are down to a total of 4,940 cases, or 54 percent of all House elections over the 1970–2008 period, and 407 primary challenges.

Table 4.8 shows the changes in DW-NOMINATE scores for Democratic and Republican incumbents, for all challenged and unchallenged incumbents and then according to the motivation for the challenge. A positive mean change indicates a shift to the right, while a negative change indicates a shift to the left. While none of the coefficients here are statistically significant, the table does show a general movement away from the political center for incumbents of both parties, irrespective of whether they face a primary opponent or not. The movement is more pronounced, however, for incumbents who faced a strong primary opponent in the first year of the dyad. The differences here, however, are trivial, evidence that primary challenges do not change the incumbents who are challenged. To assume for a moment that the coefficients were significant and to put this change in contemporary context, the shift in voting behavior among Democrats facing strong challenges would—if one subtracts the general ideological shift of unchallenged Democrats from the shift of challenged Democrats—leapfrog most conservative Democrats over one or two of their slightly less conservative colleagues. The median member of the 2008 House, Colin Peterson of Minnesota, would, if showing the mean response to a challenge, have moved from having the 218th highest DW-NOMINATE score to having the 216th. To put the differences for Republicans in context, the two most liberal Republicans, Chris Shays of Connecticut and Wayne Gilchrest of Maryland, ranked 237th and 238th, would both have moved to the 243rd spot. This is hardly the sort of change that one might expect would ward off future challenges.

We have here a variety of different independent and dependent variables, a variety sufficient to deter an effort to boil down the previously presented material into any sort of multivariate presentation of the consequences of primary opposition. If we are seeking to measure retirement, defeat, or ideological movement on the part of incumbents, we must conclude from the preceding discussion that the contribution of primary challenges is small. I conducted a variety of different tests of the effects of different types of primary challenges; all showed no significant results. This may partly be because, as noted in chapter 2, primaries are often a symptom of a problem that a legislator faces (e.g., age or diminished competence, scandal, an unpopular stance on an issue or an unpopular ideological position in general), for which developing objective measures is

TABLE 4.8. Changes in Incumbent Voting Behavior

	Mean Change in DW-NOMINATE Score	Standard Deviation	N
Democrats			
Unchallenged	−.0103	.091	2,167
Challenged	−.0120	.107	278
Strong Challenge[a]	−.0183	.121	91
Scandal	−.0023	.023	26
Competence/Age	−.0044	.019	37
Issue-Based	−.0440	.119	9
Centrist	−.0137	.018	9
Ideological	−.0087	.024	23
Race	−.0273	.173	38
Republicans			
Unchallenged	.0209	.106	2,038
Challenged	.0199	.166	129
Strong Challenge[a]	.0289	.209	50
Scandal	.0770	.240	16
Competence/Age	.0039	.040	13
Issue-Based	−.0167	.281	15
Centrist	−.0063	.023	4
Ideological	.0140	.084	24

Note: Mean change in DW-NOMINATE score = DWN in first election year of dyad— DWN in second election year. Uncategorizable challenges or challenges for reasons not considered in this chapter are omitted from the table, so the totals for challenger motivation do not sum to the total number of challenges.

[a]Strong Challenge: Incumbent held to less than 60 percent of primary vote.

problematic. Ultimately, again, the decision to run on the part of a primary challenger is based on a subjective assessment of the incumbent's weakness, and the message the incumbent takes from this challenge is also somewhat subjective.

Alternative Thresholds for Competitiveness

As in the previous chapters, it is also worth considering the consequences of strong primary challenges, using the more conventional threshold of holding the incumbent to 60 percent or less of the vote. In tables 4.6 and 4.8, I showed the differences between all primary challenges used in this study and those that reduce the incumbent to less than 60 percent of the vote; the lines for strong challenges in each table show the effects of these latter types of challenges. In the case of both consequences—general election vote share and voting behavior in the subsequent Congress—we have relatively few cases to work with, partly because such strong primary challenges are rare and partly because some challenges that pass this threshold actually result in a primary defeat for the incumbent.

Tables 4.6 and 4.8 show that, unsurprisingly, the incumbents who do survive such strong primary challenges tend to be hurt somewhat more in the general election than are all challenged incumbents, and they tend to shift their voting further away from the political center than do all challenged incumbents. The numbers for the different challenger rationales are sufficiently small that they are not particularly illuminating—for only two rationales (scandal and competence, both among Democrats) are there more than eight cases. The mean decline in vote share is slightly larger in each category for the incumbents who face strong challengers than for all challenged incumbents. The same odd partisan pattern remains, however—Democrats are hurt far more than are Republicans.

The numbers are likewise small when we seek to measure changes in incumbent voting behavior. What is most striking, however, is the shift among the handful of incumbents who garner 60 percent of the vote or less against an ideological challenger. Among Democrats who managed to remain in Congress for another term after their challenge, the mean shift in DW-NOMINATE score was about the same as for those with less competitive challengers. Republicans who survived such challenges, however, had a mean shift of .063; to use the same reference points as those used earlier, such a shift would mean that most liberal Republican House members in 2008 would have leapfrogged twelve of their colleagues. The very small number of Republicans who have faced strong ideological challenges appear, then, to have noticeably pulled to the right in response. These incumbents were initially at least perceived to be somewhat out of step with their party, so they may actually be less savvy about responding to threats within their own party than are other incumbents—the ones who have already made adjustments in order to ward off competition. In this sense, it is remarkable that the small class of primaried Republicans responds at all, rather than retiring or simply persisting in their moderate voting until defeated.

Because of the small numbers here, these data are merely impressionistic. Were they not, we might be able to go beyond the comparison of means here and use scaled primary vote share as an independent variable. The same goes for the possible use of any sort of measure of challenger quality; if incumbents were to face a primary challenger with prior electoral experience, perhaps they would shift their positions more or be hurt more in the general election—although a strong performance on the part of an inexperienced challenger might be more worrisome for incumbents. Because quality challengers are so rare in primaries, however, we can only speculate or, at best, use isolated examples to explore such occurrences.

Time Trends

The claim generally made about the consequences of primary competition for incumbents is not only that primaries can hurt incumbents but that today's primaries hurt incumbents more than they did in the past. As chapter 2 showed, there is little evidence of an increase in the number of primary challenges, and most of the rationales for primary challenges do not lend themselves to the assumption that there would be increases in such challenges across time. As this chapter has shown, there is little strong evidence that primary challenges, in the aggregate, have substantial effects on incumbents. The challenges that do appear to hurt are challenges predicated on scandal or other misdeeds of the incumbent, and there is little reason to suppose that these challenges should be any more or less consequential in one decade than in another. Only ideological challenges might be expected to increase across time. Despite the fact that this book has shown no such increase, it is still possible that primary challenges in the 2000s have greater consequences than past primary challenges or that ideological challenges today have greater consequences.

Unfortunately, there are simply not enough challenges in any of the rationale categories for one to conclusively address this possibility. It is possible to compare the effects of challenges in different decades; in neither the Democratic Party nor the Republican Party have primaries had greater consequences in terms of general election vote share in the 2000s than in prior decades. Republican challenges have had consistently small effects on general election vote share (again if one assumes that a decline in general election vote share in the election following the primary can be attributed to the challenge). Democratic challenges decline slightly in their effects from the 1970s to the 2000s; the thirty-seven Democratic challenges between 2000 and 2010 correspond to an average decline in general election vote share of only two percentage points, while the challenges of the 1970s, 1980s, and 1990s all corresponded to declines of between three and six percentage points.

The same pattern holds true for ideological shifts following primary challenges. There was little initial evidence that such changes occur. In both parties, although the numbers for the different categories are small, there is actually a trend toward lower responsiveness to these challenges; that is, incumbents of both parties actually shifted further from the center in the term following the primary challenge during the 1970s than they did during the 1990s. If contemporary primary challenges have a greater effect on Congress than challenges did in previous years, we must look at something other than the electoral fortunes or legislative activities of the incumbents who face these challenges.

Senate Primaries

As was the case in the two previous chapters, there are simply not enough challenges to Senate incumbents for one to say anything with certainty about patterns in Senate primaries. For the most part, however, it appears that, given the limited data we have on Senate primaries, challenges to Senate incumbents yield results similar to those of challenges to House incumbents. Senate incumbents who face primary challengers fare less well in the general election than do incumbents who win renomination without opposition; incumbents who win over 75 percent of the primary vote go on to win an average of 60.6 percent of the general election vote, while those who garner less than 75 percent in the primary go on to win, on average, 53.2 percent of the general election vote. These averages exclude, of course, the seven incumbents who were defeated in their primaries. Incumbents who win their primaries with 60 percent or less of the vote go on to win only 51.2 percent in the general election. Given our inability to measure causality in these elections, this may simply mean that incumbents who are fated to perform less well in the general election with or without primary opposition are more likely to have serious primary challengers. In the case of House elections, one can measure change from one election to the next in order to come up with some sense of causality. In the case of Senate incumbents, however, the last election for these candidates was, except in some unusual cases, six years ago, which makes prior vote share a less reliable predictor. In addition, longer Senate terms mean that there are fewer incumbents who have at least one reelection bid prior to the primary challenge, again making problematic any measure of the relationship between primary opposition and current and prior general election vote share.

Table 4.9 shows patterns in general election vote share according to the reason for the challenge. I do not break this table down by party, because there are no significant differences between Democrats and Republicans in any of these categories. It must be emphasized that the numbers for many of these cases are quite small and may speak more to idiosyncrasies on the part of the incumbent or the election cycle than to broader patterns of competition. Nonetheless, the data here do yield some interesting patterns. First, they show that incumbents who are opposed in the primary perform less well in the general election than those who are not, regardless of the reason for the challenge. Second, the category here with the largest number of cases is incumbents challenged on the basis of ideology. The incumbents in this category are slightly worse off than those challenged for other reasons, but not dramatically so; the mean general election vote share for these incumbents is 51.1 percent, compared to an average of 53.2 percent for all challenged incumbents. While this does not indicate that such incumbents are necessarily hurt by their primary challengers, it certainly does not provide evidence that these challenges are benign, as one might hypothesize if using a spatial logic in analyzing these elections' consequences. To return to the logic presented earlier in this chapter, one could assume that a moderate incumbent Democrat challenged unsuccessfully from the left would not lose vote share in the general election, because supporters of the liberal primary challenger would still vote for the incumbent in the general election. The general election performance of these candidates provides no support for this assumption.

Beyond the information in table 4.9, however, the most one can do in exploring the effects of primary challenges is to name names. Most of the incumbents who were unsuccessfully challenged for being insufficiently partisan—Arlen Specter (three times), Lisa Murkowski, Charles Matthias, Joseph Lieberman, Robert Stafford, John Melcher, and so on—were demonstrably moderate in their Senate voting records, but there is little evidence that these candidates changed their voting habits following their reelection. I do not present ideology measures here, partly because there are so few senators who faced primary challengers and partly because it is unclear, given the six-year Senate terms, which terms one might use if one were to measure any shift in ideology. Most of these senators represented states where moderates of their parties tend to win office more often than partisans, so perhaps they simply regarded primary opposition as an occupational hazard and felt that a moderate stance was the only way to win the general election.

A senator in office throughout the 1970–2010 period faced the general electorate seven times at most. This means that looking at repeat primary challenges is also problematic. Only two senators faced primary opponents three times, and five others faced primary opponents twice. One might argue that these primary challenges were a symptom of weakness—of these seven senators, one is still in office, three were defeated in the general election of the year of their final primary challenge, one (Robert Packwood) retired under a cloud of scandal, and another (Pennsylvania's Arlen Specter), left the Republican Party in 2010 in order to avoid a rematch of his bitter 2004 primary, only to lose in the Democratic primary instead. Only one of these seven (Oregon senator Mark Hatfield) retired without appearing to have been forced to do so.

In sum, one cannot make claims about primary competition in the Senate with anywhere near the level of precision one can attain in discuss-

TABLE 4.9. Senate General Election Vote Share by Type of Challenge

Challenge Type	Mean General Election Vote Share (%)	Standard Deviation	N
Unchallenged	60.6	10.1	467
Challenged*	53.2	8.5	58
Strong Challenge*	51.2	7.8	29
Scandal	52.0	14.2	5
Competence/Age	52.8	5.4	6
Local Issue	54.0	7.2	3
National Issue	56.5	12.1	4
Ideological	51.1	9.6	17
Ambitious Challenger	52.8	9.9	4

Note: Challenges where the issue could not be categorized and challenger rationale categories for which there were fewer than three cases are not included.

*$p < .01$ in F-test compared with change in vote share for unchallenged incumbents.

ing the House, but there is little in the Senate data to suggest that the general patterns in the House are different than those in the Senate.

The Challenges That Don't Happen

As the data in this chapter and the preceding chapters show, despite all of the patterns in primary competition, many incumbents, including many who might appear vulnerable to a challenge, never face primary competition. Not all scandals result in primary challenges, not all moderate incumbents draw primary opposition, and not even all incompetent incumbents draw primary opponents. One of the great unmeasurables in this study is the effect of the *threat* of a primary challenge. One can think about this on three different levels.

First, many (perhaps most) incumbents worry enough about potential primary opposition that they raise campaign funds or vote on legislation with this possibility in mind. One cannot prove this, but virtually all treatments of Congress assume that incumbents are continually "running scared," thinking about the electoral consequences of their behavior in Congress. Surely they are not thinking only of the general election.

Second, claims are often made that incumbents today worry more about primary opposition than they once did, that they are pressured into ideological orthodoxy because of this concern. Claims of this nature can be straightforward assertions—witness political scientist Merle Black's claim that "increasingly, [incumbents] have to worry about the politics of the primaries as well as the politics of the general election" (quoted in Brownstein 2010a). They can also be made in a more theoretical fashion, as in David Karol's (2009) argument that some issue advocacy groups can capture political parties and enforce homogeneity on particular issues.

Third, during election season, one can often identify particular incumbents who are faced with particular threats. These threats include potential challengers who explore running but ultimately choose not to, calls from party activists for a primary challenge, or simply media reports that a challenger might file. I explore one such prospective challenge, the race against Massachusetts Democrat Stephen Lynch, in the next chapter.

For the most part, these claims are not measurable, although logic would dictate that there is something to the first and third claims and possibly to the second. This has consequences for the claims here about ideological movement. In the preceding analysis, I hypothesized that one goal of ideological challenges, apart from actually defeating the incumbent, is to pull the incumbent away from the political center, to put pressure on members of both parties not to break with their party. If one believes that members of Congress are sufficiently worried about primary opponents that they are already doing this, what we are measuring here is essentially the tip of the iceberg, the members who are simply moving less quickly away from the center than are their colleagues. Congress has clearly become more polarized over the past decade. Theriault (2006) estimates that one-third of the growth in polarization has come from movement to the extremes by members (the other two-thirds comes from member replacement). Possibly some of this movement results from fears about primaries. This poses the possibility, however, that the incumbents whose challenges we actually observe are *less* responsive to any sort of potential threat than are their unchallenged colleagues—some incumbents were able to head off any sort of threat, while these incumbents either were unable or unwilling to do so. If this is the case, we might argue that these are candidates who have reasons for being unresponsive to the themes raised by challengers.

In addition, the threat of primary opposition poses the possibility that what matters is not movement after the election but movement before the election. This is particularly plausible in the case of Senate elections; if one takes the 2010 election season as an example, the small number of high-profile challenges (e.g., those to John McCain, Arkansas Democrat Blanche Lincoln, and Colorado Democrat Michael Bennet) all unfolded early enough in the year that the incumbents had plenty of opportunities to respond. In the Bennet case, for instance, Bennet's primary opponent began his campaign in September of 2009, although the Colorado primary was not until August of 2010. With almost a yearlong campaign, Bennet had plenty of time to respond to claims made by his opponent. If there were any doubts about Bennet's loyalty to the Democratic Party, he could have spent much of 2010 establishing a voting record that might be used to counter such claims.

If measuring primary effects is messy, measuring the effects of the threat of having a primary is even messier. In a way, this serves the purpose of those who support primary challengers. Claims about these threats, claims that are, in many ways, the strongest claims made about the role primary challengers play in contemporary politics, are unfalsifiable.

Conclusions

There are consequences to primary challenges, but they are far more nuanced than one might expect. In this chapter, I have presented two different approaches to looking at primary challenges. First, I have explored the fit between what challengers say in their campaigns and the circumstances of the incumbents they challenge. Any challenger may allege that an incumbent is ethically tainted, incompetent, or inappropriate for the district. It may well be that a strong challenger can make such charges stick, but it is easier to make them stick if they are, in fact, true. The nature of the charges raised by the challenger, however, determine the response of the incumbent. In discussing the veracity of challengers' claims, I thus outlined the sorts of responses we should see from the voters or from the incumbent. I then proceeded to look at a variety of consequences—in terms of both the incumbent's subsequent electoral fortunes and the incumbent's own behavior in subsequent terms if the incumbent survived the challenge.

To summarize, apart from the rare instances where incumbents are defeated in the primary (in which cases the consequences of the challenge are clear), incumbents are affected by primary challenges in a number of different ways but are not affected very much overall. Incumbents tend to lose a few votes in their general election campaigns, but they generally do so in cases where the challenge is nonideological or is from the political center. Incumbents challenged in primaries are no more likely to retire shortly after their challenge than are unthreatened incumbents. But more often than not, in cases when incumbents retire after their challenger raises issues of ideology, their successor is closer to the position of the challenger than was the incumbent. We cannot be certain that the primary challenge brought about retirement, but it was likely a contributing factor. To return to the Roukema example, Marge Roukema discussed her frustration with being a moderate Republican during the Bush administration and her failure to acquire a committee chairmanship (also a consequence of her moderate record) as reasons for her retirement (Hernandez 2002). Surely, facing conservative primary opponents went along with her record and contributed to her frustration, but perhaps she would have retired anyway—many members of Congress who do not face primary opposition have noted similar reasons upon retiring. Primaries, then, correspond to retirement and general election difficulty, but it is not clear that they cause it.

In terms of behavior, evidence that incumbents who survive their primaries do somewhat modify their voting is rather flimsy. The changes shown here are probably not sufficient to ward off future allegations that these incumbents are "RINOs" (Republicans in Name Only) or among the "worst" Democrats?[15] These changes probably do not account for increasing polarization in Congress (as some have argued), although we cannot be certain that concern about the possibility of a challenge does not drive Republicans rightward and Democrats leftward. It is not clear whether or not these shifts are politically wise. In several instances, primarying corresponded with gains for the opposition party. To provide a few examples, Rhode Island senator Lincoln Chafee, truly a moderate Republican, survived a strong conservative challenge in the 2006 primary, only to lose the seat to a Democrat in the general election; New York representative Sherwood Boehlert survived a string of conservative challenges during his final decade in Congress, but a Democrat took the seat when Boehlert retired; and after Maryland representative Wayne Gilchrest was defeated in the 2008 primary, his conservative challenger went on to lose to a Democrat in the general election (although he won a rematch with that Democrat in 2010). In all three of these cases, it is difficult to argue that a shift to the right by the incumbent would have been politically wise. It is clear, however, that the conventional claims about ideological challenges are likely overblown. Media coverage of John McCain's 2010 primary race contended that McCain "increasingly tilted to the right" in response to the challenge (see, e.g., Viser 2010).[16] Incumbents probably do not really do this enough for voters to notice.

Finally, this chapter supplements the discussion of differences between Democratic and Republican primary challenges that has been a recurring feature of the past two chapters. Democratic primary challenges tend to be more consequential than Republican challenges, if one is to assume that a decline in general election vote share has anything to do with the primary challenges. This finding, when combined with the data on the frequency of primary challenges in chapter 2, indicates that there is a different logic to primary elections in the Republican Party than there is in the Democratic Party. The next chapter will explore some reasons why this might be the case.

Literature on primary elections often takes its cue from particularly notorious primary challenges, at the congressional level as well as at the presidential level. This literature has generally concluded that primaries have minimal effects on the incumbents who survive them. This chapter, as well, concludes that they do not have substantial effects, but they do have some effects. These effects are best understood if one differentiates between primaries according to the reason for the primary. This chapter shows that, although it is often difficult to attribute a strong primary showing to measurable attributes of the challenger, one can at least identify different types of effects and map them out over the ensuing election cycles. For the most part, however, primary challengers appear to be epiphenomenal. When an incumbent has a problem, it is manifested in the primary as well as in the general election. I noted in chapter 2 that it is debatable whether there has been any epidemic of "primarying" in recent years. The data in this chapter show that when they do occur, primary challenges rarely have the sorts of dramatic consequences that are often attributed to them.

5 | Interest Groups and
Congressional Primaries

Chapters 2 and 3 of this book showed that congressional primary challenges are still somewhat rare but that there has been a change in the fundraising base of many ideological challengers over the past few decades. There is more money coming in to ideological primary challengers in small amounts, and there is more money coming into their campaigns from out of state than was once the case. It is virtually impossible to imagine this happening without the existence of some sort of entity coordinating the efforts of donors nationwide. To return to the example of the Arkansas Senate primary discussed in chapter 1, it is inconceivable that citizens from around the country could be motivated to care about the Arkansas race unless someone convinced them to care, and the challenger in that race showed no sign of having the ability to single-handedly make the non-Arkansan public care. In short, the financial data suggest that nonparty groups are increasingly focusing their efforts on congressional primaries.

Traditional theories on interest groups provide little insight into why groups would do this, and as I argued in chapter 3, direct group contributions are a negligible part of challengers' funds. As we shall see in this chapter, the task of nationalizing primary challenges has been taken up in many instances by interest groups such as MoveOn.org or the Club for Growth. Less formal political movements, such as the Tea Party movement, can also fulfill this function, as can such blogs as DailyKos or RedState. Even an individual political actor—such as South Carolina senator Jim DeMint or former Alaska governor Sarah Palin—can call the attention of a nationwide audience to a primary challenge. It is difficult to take fingerprints from an individual primary challenger's donor file to see who has drawn the attention of donors to that campaign. Yet the undeniable fact that some combination of groups, online communities, and individual political activists has touted the campaigns of several primary candidates over the past few election cycles indicates that we should narrow our focus somewhat. While it is evident that most PACs are skittish about becoming involved in congressional primaries, the decisions of one or two interest groups or other political actors can elevate the profile of a small number of primary challengers.

The broad generalizations frequently drawn about politicians' motives do not apply to all politicians or all groups. To say that, as a rule, incumbent members of Congress will not support primary challengers to their colleagues is not to say that there will not be one or two renegade members who throw caution to the wind and get involved in primaries. To say that most interest groups do not get involved in primaries is not to say that one or two groups will not seek to distinguish themselves by focusing on primaries. Because of the rarity of such steps, a group or politician doing this draws attention. Some groups or politicians may benefit from this attention; most will not. For the Club for Growth or MoveOn to do this is to serve notice of their independence from the parties; likewise, for Sarah Palin to do this is to serve notice of being a different kind of politician, of seeking reform above and beyond party labels.

If we are to identify instances of this throughout the time period I consider here, we must limit ourselves to what is measurable, but we can focus on the signals sent by endorsements or contributions. Instead of looking at contributions in the aggregate, as I have done in chapter 3, we can look at the behavior of individual groups. There were many attempts to do this in 2010—the national media periodically issued scorecards on how candidates endorsed by Sarah Palin or by groups related to the Tea Party did— but these are rather idiosyncratic events and cannot be compared across time.[1] A more systematic way to do this is to identify PACs that have contributed to multiple primary challengers across time and to follow their behavior from one election to the next. This sort of analysis uses PAC contributions as a signal, of the sort that so-called lead PACs seek to send, not as determinants in themselves of a candidate's level of overall group support.

This chapter proceeds, first, by illustrating the role of individual groups or politicians in several recent congressional primaries, noting the activities of these groups or politicians in bringing about a challenge, in supporting the challenger, and in using the primary challenge to broadcast a larger, national message about the threat primary competition may pose to other incumbents. I then turn to an analysis of the types of groups that have given money to primary challengers since 1980 and the types of primary challengers who have received some PAC support. This analysis shows that the universe of groups that give to primary challengers is not dramatically different from the larger interest groups population but that a very small number of groups have distinguished themselves for their willingness to wade into ideological challenges. I follow this section with a look at the overall election-related activities of these groups. I then conclude this chapter with a consideration of the goals of these groups and the way in which they have used activism in congressional primaries to carve out a niche for themselves and enhance their national profile.

While the past three chapters presented a somewhat equivocal story about the differences between contemporary primaries and those of years past, this chapter is less ambiguous about what has changed. It shows that a small but growing number of congressional primaries today are far more nationalized, more focused on broader ideological conflict (as opposed to conflict over individual national or local issues), and more vulnerable to the decisions of political actors who reside far from the districts or states in question than was once the case. I present this argument with one significant caveat, however: for the groups and individuals who have abetted this conflict, primaries, particularly primary challenges to incumbents, are not necessarily the only piece of the puzzle. To return to the Sarah Palin example, Palin's target list (as reported by the *Washington Post*) included a large number of candidates who sought to buck the Republican establishment, but many did so in open-seat primaries or in Republican primaries for the right to challenge Democratic incumbents. I have kept the focus of this book narrowly on primary challenges to incumbents, in part out of concern with measuring the nature of the challenge—who is to say with any specificity who the "establishment" candidate is in an open-seat race? The sorts of challenges I emphasize here are one piece of the puzzle for groups or politicians running against the establishment, but they have become a more important piece in recent elections.

Outside Actors in Congressional Primaries

Many of the races discussed thus far in this book prominently featured organized interests. The 2010 race involving Blanche Lambert Lincoln, discussed in chapter 1, likely would have been a far different affair without the involvement of the AFL-CIO and other labor unions or without the fundraising efforts of MoveOn.org. According to the Center for Responsive Politics, a total of over $4 million was spent on independent advocacy against Lincoln (or for Halter), while groups supporting Lincoln spent only $500,000. Although it is difficult to obtain accurate measurements of outside spending for earlier races, there are several other recent primaries where it is evident, from what has been reported, that over $1 million was spent independently to aid primary candidates. Donna Edwards's successful 2008 primary bid was supported by five groups that spent over $100,000: MoveOn, the SEIU, the National Education Association, the National Association of Realtors, and EMILY's List. The SEIU and its affiliates spent a total of over $800,000 on behalf of Edwards. As I noted earlier, accurate bundling numbers are hard to come by, but the data on outside contributions from chapter 3 indicate that many of these groups bundled or inspired a substantial number of contributions in these races.

As I noted already, however, the magnitude of money spent is a poor indicator of the priority that individual interest groups place on elections. Primary elections vary substantially in their cost. The Lincoln race, the Lieberman challenge, the various primary challenges to Arlen Specter in Pennsylvania, and the Donna Edwards race took place in states with large populations or in states or districts with expensive media markets and in places where incumbents were accustomed to raising and spending large amounts of money. An individual interest group looking to make its mark on primary elections may be well served by focusing its efforts on Senate races in smaller states or on districts where an effective campaign can be run without raising large sums of money.

One example of this pattern is the 2002 Alabama primary, discussed in chapter 3, between incumbent Earl Hilliard and challenger Artur Davis. Hilliard raised over $800,000 in 2002, but he had raised only half that amount in his 2000 campaign. Hilliard was an attractive target for the Business Industry PAC (BIPAC) and other business interests, because he had never had to raise very much money to win reelection in his majority-minority district and because the district's media markets, Tuscaloosa and Birmingham, are relatively inexpensive places to advertise. Hilliard's district had also been redrawn in 2002 to include several white neighborhoods in the Birmingham area. Hilliard had won reelection comfortably throughout his tenure in Congress, but he had not campaigned vigorously and was not well known among the district's new voters. Davis wound up raising a substantial amount of money from PACs, but the fact that BIPAC had prominently advocated for his campaign—as BIPAC's Bernadette Budde claimed, the group rarely supported Democrats, let alone Democrats in primaries, but Davis was a candidate who would engage in "dialogue on issues that matter to us"—sent a strong signal to the business community (Hoover 2002). It was the very unconventionality of BIPAC's involvement in the primary process that mattered, not the amount of money BIPAC (a group that rarely spends lavishly on any election) spent.

The 2010 Alaska Republican Primary

More than any other election considered in this book, however, it is the 2010 Alaska Senate primary that represents the "perfect storm" for outside activity in primary elections. In Susan Dunn's history of Franklin Delano Roosevelt's attempted "purge" of the Democratic Party in the 1938 primaries, Roosevelt advisor Jim Farley, who disagreed with Roosevelt's decision to get involved in primaries, decamped for Alaska during the election, saying, "As I surveyed the coming primaries, I wondered if Alaska was far enough" (Dunn 2010, 33). Alaska was, of course, not a state at the time. But since gaining statehood, Alaska has been a state where primary challenges can flourish. Former senator Mike Gravel faced primary challengers in each of his reelection bids; and in 2008, Senator Ted Stevens and the state's lone House member, Don Young, faced primary challengers. Alaska's incumbent senior senator going into the 2010 election, Lisa Murkowski, has been a conventional Alaska Republican in many ways. She has touted her ability to procure federal funds for Alaska, while at the same time siding with Democrats in the Senate on many social issues. Murkowski was, for instance, among the eight Republicans who voted to repeal the military's "Don't Ask, Don't Tell" policy during the 2010 lame-duck session.

Murkowski also came into office under unusual circumstances. She was appointed to the Senate by her father, veteran senator Frank Murkowski, in December of 2002, after her father ran successfully for the state's governorship. Although Lisa Murkowski had served in the Alaska House of Representatives for two terms, her ascension to the Senate was widely seen as a gift from her father. She was challenged in the 2004 Republican primary, winning with 58 percent of the vote. Her father, meanwhile, lost his 2006 primary for reelection to the governorship to political neophyte Sarah Palin, following one term marred by a scandal that touched several other Alaska politicians, including the state's other senator, Ted Stevens. Although Alaska politics has often featured infighting within both parties, the developing split between party regulars such as Murkowski and Stevens and a more conservative reformist faction led by Palin indicated that Murkowski would be vulnerable. The state's small population, low voter turnout, and relatively concentrated population (half of the state's residents live in the Anchorage area) also can make campaigning in Alaska a relatively inexpensive proposition, which may work to the advantage of primary challengers.

Joe Miller, an obscure lawyer from Fairbanks with little prior political experience, mounted a challenge to Murkowski in 2010. Miller raised only $284,000 during the primary, compared with $3.4 million raised by Murkowski. Miller was aided, however, by an independent expenditure of $300,000 by the Club for Growth and by an estimated $600,000 spent by the Tea Party Express on his behalf (Elliott 2010). Miller's challenge to Murkowski was clearly ideological in nature; Miller called for eliminating Medicare, Social Security, the Department of Education, and anything else that he claimed is not "constitutionally authorized" (Tumulty and Rucker 2010). Miller also criticized Murkowski's support for cap and trade legislation (tepid though it was), her pro-choice stance on abortion rights, and even her aggressive effort to procure federal funds for Alaska. Although Miller developed several clever YouTube videos that received national attention, his campaign on the ground in Alaska was largely funded by others. Miller narrowly won the Alaska primary by a 51 to 49 percent margin, a margin of approximately 2,000 of the 110,000 votes cast. Murkowski, who still had $1.9 million on hand after the primary, eventually mounted a write-in campaign and defeated Miller in the general election.

What did outside groups do for Miller? Media reports indicate that the Tea Party Express funded extensive volunteer training exercises, sending volunteers to Alaska to help locals coordinate get-out-the-vote efforts, craft press releases and letters to newspapers editors, and maintain a "war room" on a cruise ship docked in an Alaska harbor (Elliott 2010). Of the money spent by the Tea Party Express, $150,000 was spent on advertisements in the final week of the campaign (Tumulty and Rucker 2010). The fact that Murkowski had led in all of the preprimary polls indicated that this effort must have been effective. The Club for Growth, noting Miller's nearly depleted treasury after the primary election, mounted an aggressive effort after the election to bundle contributions for Miller, who ultimately raised $3.2 million by the end of the general election. The club had made several ad buys for Miller during the primary. It also mounted a campaign to encourage fifteen hundred donors to Murkowski to request refunds after the primary (Club for Growth 2010). The club reported that a similar effort in the wake of Arlen Specter's party switch had cost Specter over $800,000.

During the general election, several other groups would weigh in on Miller's behalf, including the National Republican Senatorial Committee and Senator Jim DeMint's Senate Conservatives Fund. Apart from several small independent expenditures on Murkowski's behalf, however, the field was dominated by the Club for Growth and the Tea Party Express, and the size of these groups' expenditures, although they do stand out, seem less important for their financial clout than simply as signals of these groups' interest in the race.

The other outside actor in this race who may well have mattered was Sarah Palin. Palin endorsed Miller on her Facebook page in June and recorded several robocalls describing Murkowski as "another Democrat in the Senate voting for the Obama agenda which is bankrupting us" (Yardley 2010). This surely came as no surprise to Murkowski—Palin had, after all, run against Murkowski's father for governor and had endorsed Murkowski's primary opponent in 2004—but Murkowski apparently decided that it would be unwise to take Palin on in the race and did not directly criticize her until after the primary. Murkowski sought to separate Miller from Palin and focus instead on Miller's inexperience, while increasing her criticism of the Obama administration and presenting herself as an independent (Horowitz 2010). It is hard to quantify the effect of Palin's involvement in the race, especially since the sorts of numbers available for interest groups are not available for Palin, but her involvement, like that of the Tea Party Express and the Club for Growth, had the effect of making the race more about Lisa Murkowski than about Joe Miller.

The Alaska Republican primary represents a confluence of features we have seen elsewhere in this book. The incumbent was someone who raised the ire of ideological activists. The geography of Alaska was conducive to a well-run campaign on the part of one or two outside groups. The political culture of Alaska is such that the major party organizations are weak, and Alaskans have a history of supporting unconventional politicians. The race was about ideology, but other concerns, about Lisa Murkowski's appointment to the seat and the ethical troubles of her father's gubernatorial administration, ensured that there was more to the race than simply ideology. Miller's lack of a political pedigree may have ultimately made him a problematic general election candidate, and he never fully stepped out of the shadow of the groups supporting him. But his relative anonymity made him a good vehicle for a group-sponsored primary challenge. While the Club for Growth may have been willing to run the risk of sacrificing the seat to the Democrats as a result of their campaign (as arguably happened in the challenges to Lincoln Chafee in 2006 and Wayne Gilchrest in 2008), the relative weakness of the Democrat in the race made it unlikely that this would happen.

In other words, the Alaska race was a good race for conservative groups to use to lay down a marker, and they arguably did this despite Murkowski's ultimate victory. The long-term consequences for Murkowski herself are not clear—her subsequent votes in the Senate do not indicate that she has moved to the right as a result of her narrow escape, and she does not have to face the Alaska voters again until 2016. The Republican Party's decision to support Miller in the general election put her in a situation analogous to that of Joe Lieberman following his 2006 primary defeat. But the rhetoric from the Club for Growth following the election—as well as that of Jim DeMint's group—made it clear that many Republicans up for reelection in 2012 would now have reason to fear similar efforts.

Most of the other strong primary challenges covered here share some of the attributes of the Miller challenge. Many of the most successful interest group interventions have been in states with unusual electoral rules (as was the case in the 2010 Utah Senate race) or in otherwise unusual situations, such as special elections. The 2010 primaries were notable for the relative absence of other liberal challenges after the Lincoln race. The three liberal challengers who garnered the most attention, Bill Halter, Pennsylvania's Joe Sestak (a member of the House of Representatives who ran against Arlen Specter following Specter's party switch), and Colorado's Andrew Romanoff (the speaker of the Colorado House, who challenged appointed senator Michael Bennet) were more seasoned candidates than Miller. Perhaps as a consequence of this (and a consequence of the decision by liberal groups to focus their attention more on defending Democratic seats against Republicans), the message sent by these challenges was not as clear as the Miller challenge. MoveOn.org, for instance, made few references to its support to Halter in its late 2010 reports to members. This may be partly because these candidates insisted on having a role in running their own campaigns; Halter, in particular, did not enthusiastically endorse MoveOn.org's positions and might well have become a more conservative senator than the group would have liked.

On the right, many of the other primaries that featured extensive group activity were primaries for open seats. The Club for Growth and the Tea Party Express both supported Sharron Angle's campaign for the Republican nomination to challenge Harry Reid in Nevada, Ken Buck's bid for the Republican nomination in Colorado, and Marco Rubio's bid for the Republican nomination for the open Senate seat in Florida. The Club for Growth spent heavily on behalf of its former president Pat Toomey, although Toomey ran unopposed for the Republican nomination after Arlen Specter's party switch. In one rather unorthodox primary, the club spent $182,000 to oppose Utah senator Bob Bennett in Utah's convention-based process of candidate selection (Kiely 2010). The Delaware Senate primary, which took place less than a month after the Alaska primary, featured a moderate incumbent House member (the state's only House member) who was ultimately defeated by an insurgent in the mold of Miller, Christine O'Donnell. O'Donnell was running in a small state, albeit a state with more expensive media markets than Alaska, and the Delaware primary had long promised to be a sleepy affair. While the Club for Growth stayed out of the race, perhaps because O'Donnell did not have as strong a focus on fiscal issues as did Miller, the Tea Party Express waged a similar last-minute battle, spending $250,000 on O'Donnell's behalf, and Senator DeMint also endorsed her (Gardner 2010). O'Donnell herself raised only $264,000 during the primary, although she would go on to raise over $7 million by the end of the general election. Her primary opponent, Representative Mike Castle, raised $3.4 million; he went into the last month of the primary with a cash advantage of $2.6 million to O'Donnell's $70,000 (Cillizza 2010c). O'Donnell's low profile may, as was the case for Miller, have made her a good vehicle for anti-incumbent sentiment. Her checkered past, however, ultimately made O'Donnell perhaps an even less suitable general election candidate than Miller in a state that was far less hospitable to conservatives than was Alaska.

Arizona and Massachusetts: When the Big Groups Stay Out

An instructive way to look at the role of interest groups in making or breaking primary challengers is to look at races where groups choose not to intervene. One such race was John McCain's 2010 reelection bid in Arizona. McCain's voting record did not place him on the left flank of his party, but at times during his Senate career, he has sought to position himself as a moderate or at least, as he spoke of himself during his presidential run, a maverick. As noted earlier in this book, defeated presidential candidates have found themselves challenged in their subsequent congressional primary bids. Perhaps the distraction of running for president leads candidates to neglect their home states or districts, or perhaps the positions one must take in running at the national level can put one at odds with some of one's constituents.

Many in the media noted that McCain tacked sharply to the right following his presidential defeat. He disowned an immigration compromise that he had authored in the Senate, and he stepped up his criticism of the Obama administration. Just as important, however, McCain raised $21 million for his primary battle with conservative talk show host and former House member J. D. Hayworth—more than a fivefold increase over McCain's fundraising for his 2004 campaign.[2] McCain also reportedly reached out to the Club for Growth early in 2010 in an effort to keep them on the sideline (Cillizza 2010a). The club, which had previously been active in Arizona House races and had championed the campaigns of Phoenix-area representative Jeff Flake, obliged.[3] McCain also sought to resolve conflicts between Sarah Palin and his 2008 presidential campaign staff (Hagan 2010). While it might have been implausible for Palin to back McCain's opponent, McCain did ensure that Palin endorsed him and campaigned on his behalf.

McCain succeeded in defining Hayworth early in the campaign. He did not debate Hayworth or refer to him by name during his campaign (Steinhauer 2010), but his campaign did release several blistering attack advertisements about Hayworth, mining old clips from Hayworth's radio show and infomercials Hayworth had developed years ago, in order to discredit him. While the Alaska and Delaware primaries were clearly about the incumbents or the political establishment, McCain managed to make Hayworth a known quantity to Arizona voters. Hayworth ultimately secured only minimal interest group support; most national groups stayed out of the race or backed McCain, and the only independent expenditures, summing to only $55,000, came from two small anti-immigration groups, the Minuteman Victory PAC and Americans for Legal Immigration. McCain won the primary with 56 percent of the vote to Hayworth's 32 percent, and he easily coasted to victory in the November general election over a poorly funded Democratic opponent.

Hayworth had announced his candidacy in February of 2010, so McCain had the advantage of knowing early in the year who his opponent would be. In Massachusetts, incumbent Democratic representative Stephen Lynch was in a different situation.[4] Like many of the other incumbents considered here, Lynch had antagonized the party faithful, in this case by voting against the Democratic health care reform bill. Lynch's vote was a bit of a surprise—he had rarely been spoken of as being particularly conservative. He arguably was less secure than were other Massachusetts representatives; he had only held the seat since 2001 and thus had less seniority than most other members of the state delegation. Immediately after Lynch's health care vote, bloggers on the Blue Mass Group site and other liberal blogs began floating the idea of a challenge. The candidate whose name was initially put forward—liberal activist Harmony Wu—deliberated about running but ultimately declined. In a letter to supporters of the "Draft Harmony Wu" movement, she wrote, "Though I will not be running in this election, some important and potentially game-changing results have come out of this process. Most prominently, the support and excitement for my potential candidacy indicates very clearly that it is past time for Mr. Lynch to be held accountable for his decisions as our representative."[5] Wu did express her hope that a challenger would emerge.

The challenger who eventually appeared, New England SEIU political director Mac D'Alessandro, sought support among Massachusetts progressives, but his late start, the fact that Lynch had not previously been on the target lists of progressives, and the fact that Lynch had the support of many other labor unions made this an uphill challenge. Lynch had, in fact, been endorsed earlier in the year by the SEIU, and as the election went on, he reached out to organized labor in an effort to mend fences. Although D'Alessandro received an endorsement from MoveOn.org, the group supplied little money for the race. Lynch's district was solidly Democratic, and he faced only a token Republican challenge in the general election. Lynch spent $1.5 million in the race, most of it in the primary, compared to D'Alessandro's $340,000. The SEIU did spend over $250,000 on D'Alessandro's behalf, but no other groups played a significant role in the race. Lynch adeptly cast D'Alessandro as the labor candidate; while his attacks did not reach the level that McCain's did, it appears that the groups that had been so active in other primary challenges simply did not have the time to mount the sort of attack that would be needed to topple an incumbent in an expensive media market. Lynch won the primary by a margin of 64 percent to 36 percent.

The Arizona and Massachusetts campaigns discussed here demonstrate the role of a very small number of organized interests in the 2010 elections. The incumbents who were challenged are typical of the types of incumbents who faced ideological challenges in previous years. As I demonstrated in chapter 2, there are recurrent themes that explain the occurrence of primary challenges; ideology plays a role, but so does the attention incumbents pay to their state or district and the geography of their state or district. The cases under discussion here also show the strategic calculus of the groups that get involved. Groups such as the Club for Growth or MoveOn.org do not need to win primaries in order to send a message. This does not mean that organized interests do not pick their battles carefully. Some interest groups will be more concerned about access to incumbents than will others, but in all cases, groups must first and foremost be able to use primary challenges in a way that enhances their profile and convinces their members that they are working on their behalf.

The involvement of activist groups in recent primary challenges is a new development. As I shall demonstrate in the next section of this chapter, interest groups have not been entirely absent from past primary elections, but there is something qualitatively different about contemporary interest group involvement, if only because contemporary groups are more effective in using primaries to advance their own goals than were groups in the past. There are no easy quantitative methods of proving this, but looking at the dominant groups of past elections and the history of particular groups' involvement can provide at least suggestive evidence that this is the case. It is to this task that I now turn.

A History of PAC Spending on Primary Challenges to Incumbents

Conventional wisdom suggests that very few PACs will support primary challenges. There are three reasons for this. First, the challenger's chance of victory is low enough that the investment simply will not be worthwhile and will risk antagonizing the incumbent. If groups have an interest in helping candidates during the primaries, they may be wiser to assist primary candidates for open seats or candidates running for the nomination to challenge an incumbent in the general election. Second, many interest groups contribute as a means of ensuring access to incumbents. If the incumbent does lose, groups will have plenty of time after the primary to contribute to the victorious challenger; in the meantime, giving to the challenger does little to advance groups' policy goals. Third, if groups are concerned about issues that split along partisan lines, ensuring that their preferred party's candidates win seats in the general election is a higher concern than unseating some candidates of their preferred party in the primaries.

Most PACs do not support primary challengers, and those that do support primary challengers make a tiny fraction of their overall expenditures in support of them. The data in this chapter show patterns in PACs' willingness to support such candidates: what types of PACs do get involved in primaries and what types of primaries they choose.[6] The following analysis considers records from the Federal Election Commission for all PAC expenditures on behalf of primary challengers from 1980 through 2010. As has been the case in previous chapters, I consider only contributions to primary challengers who received at least 25 percent of the vote. There is no compelling reason to separate out Senate and House candidates here, since the unit of analysis is the group, not the candidate.

A few wrinkles to the data are worth noting. As is the case for individual contributions, FEC data on PAC expenditures provide an individual record for each expenditure, not each candidate. This is of consequence because it is possible to look at the timing of expenditures; where groups spent money throughout the primary and data on whether they provided initial seed money to the candidate or preceded other PACs can be analyzed. The FEC data also include candidate committees[7] and party committees. I have sought to limit my consideration here to interest groups, assuming that the motivations of party committees or candidate committees will be different from those of PACs. Finally, FEC data include both direct contributions to candidates (which are limited to no more than $5,000 per candidate per cycle and are not adjusted for inflation) and independent expenditures (which have no limit). Approximately three-fourths of the expenditures by groups on behalf of primary challengers and two-thirds of the money spent are independent expenditures. In addition, of the 103 independent expenditures in excess of $5,000 (a threshold chosen because it is the size of the maximum permissible direct PAC contribution in each of the elections covered here), all but 16 have been made since 2000, and all but 32 were made in 2006 and 2008. The data here show not only patterns in the types of groups that contribute to primary challengers but also a change in the types of expenditures made by groups.

In considering these data, money is of some importance, but as I mentioned earlier, the types of groups listed in the data may send a stronger signal than do the size of their contributions or independent expenditures. The money spent in these races is, as one reader of this chapter put it, "loose change." Most primary challengers receive little support from PACs, and even for those that do, the amount any individual PAC can give is small enough that it is unlikely to make a difference in the race. If we see PACs that have given money to primary challengers, the signal sent by the PAC's support may be of more value to the challenger than the actual money (the very large independent expenditures of the past decade are a somewhat different matter, which I leave aside for now). For example, a contribution from a business association such as the National Federation of Independent Business or BIPAC may signal to other corporate groups that this is a viable candidate or that the group has serious objections to the incumbent. Of course, the data here will show myriad contributions from all sorts of since there are some races in which the primary challenger is actually expected to win and is a reasonably safe choice for a variety of groups. In the case, for instance, of state representative John Boehner's challenge to Representative Donald "Buz" Lukens in 1990, it was widely believe that, as a result of a sex scandal, Lukens was not likely to retain his seat. In cases such as these, we can infer little from a PAC contribution to Boehner other than that he was expected to win. In the case of contributions to some of the candidates profiled earlier, such as Ned Lamont or Pat Toomey, a group risks a bit more by supporting the challenger, and its contribution can send a signal to other groups that a race is important.

Table 5.1 shows, side by side, the top supporters of all primary challengers and the top contributors to ideological challengers (as defined in the earlier chapters). Here, I have excluded very large independent expenditures (those of over $5,000). I do this partly to avoid placing a small number of groups that were active in only one or two races at the top of the aggregate list and partly because such large expenditures have only been a part of recent elections. The cutoff of $5,000 is somewhat arbitrary, but because it is equivalent to the largest permissible PAC contribution, it places independent expenditures and PAC contributions on an equal footing.

Many of the groups in the left-hand column, of supporters of all types of primary challengers, are there simply because these are among the largest interest groups. Access-oriented, nonideological groups such as the American Medical PAC, the National Automobile Dealers Association, and the National Association of Realtors are on this list simply because they tend to give to most incumbents and to most other candidates who have a good chance of winning. Their activity is generally limited to contributing money. In these cases, these groups have contributed to primary challengers once it became clear that these challengers were winners (as was the case for Boehner). These types of access-oriented groups do not appear in the right-hand column.

The rankings of different types of groups on either side of this table are intriguing. Several different types of issue-related groups appear in this table. These groups' spending almost exclusively takes the form of independent expenditures. Most notably, the National Rifle Association (NRA) is near the top of both lists, and its smaller but arguably more aggressive competitor, Gun Owners of America (GOA), is not far behind. More than one-third of the money spent on primary challengers by the NRA is in support of ideological challengers, and more than one-half of the money spent by GOA goes to support ideological challengers. More than half of

TABLE 5.1. Top PAC Supporters of All Primary Challengers to Incumbents and of Ideological Challengers to Incumbents, 1980–2010 (direct contributions and independent expenditures of less than $5,000)

	Top Supporters of All Primary Challengers			Top Supporters of Ideological Primary Challengers		
PAC	Number of Expenditures	Total ($)		PAC	Number of Expenditures	Total ($)
National Rifle Association	120	215,929		Club for Growth	95	74,650
American Medical PAC	31	109,700		National Rifle Association	28	66,283
Realtors Political Action Committee	35	98,549		Service Employees International Union	11	32,313
Association of Trial Lawyers	26	85,000		League of Conservation Voters	89	32,144
AFSCME	27	83,125		Gun Owners of America	33	30,689
Club for Growth	98	78,248		Stop ERA PAC	18	28,200
United Auto Workers	24	77,625		Machinists	5	25,000
Machinists	23	76,749		United Food & Commercial Workers	6	25,000
AFL-CIO COPE	30	71,453		Right to Life of Michigan	46	23,722
National Education Association	21	70,325		AFL-CIO COPE	7	20,206
Automobile and Truck Dealers	21	70,300		AFSCME	5	20,000
United Food & Commercial Workers	24	63,000		United Auto Workers	5	20,000
Electrical Workers., International Brotherhood of	32	62,150		Electrical Workers, International Brotherhood of	5	18,500
Teamsters, International Brotherhood of	18	61,750		Republican National Coalition for Life	13	18,000
Gun Owners of America	61	59,325		EMILY's List	6	17,808
National Association of Homebuilders	18	57,700		Human Rights Campaign Fund	9	17,805
NARAL	29	56,172		International Ladies Garment Workers Union	9	17,677
American Federation of Teachers	15	55,060		New Jersey Right to Life PAC	16	16,538
League of Conservation Voters	128	51,747		Citizens United Political Victory	4	16,000
Communications Workers of America-COPE	24	48,600		Democracy for America	8	15,659

Source: Author's calculations from Federal Election Commission data.

what the League of Conservation Voters (LCV) spends on primary challengers also goes to ideological candidates. Compare this to the behavior of pro-choice and anti-abortion groups; National Right to Life spent $48,000 in support of primary challengers, but it is not among the top spenders to ideological challengers. Less than one-fourth of its expenditures went to support ideological challengers. Perhaps it is possible to build a primary challenge around an anti-abortion message but not around a message favoring gun rights or an environmentalist message. Candidates who tend to win the approval of the NRA may hold what the organization considers to be the right position on guns, but their campaigns are not *about* guns. The same logic applies to candidates supported by the LCV.

Labor unions are frequent supporters of primary challengers; ten different unions are ranked among the top twenty contributors to primary challengers to incumbents. Eight different unions are present among the list of top contributors to ideological challengers, and the proportion of money spent by labor on these candidates, as compared to its contributions to all primary challengers, is somewhat lower than the totals for issue advocacy groups. This suggests that unions are not reluctant to get involved in primaries and that they do so for many reasons. Their activities are a mix of direct contributions and independent expenditures. This is not particularly surprising; for some time, scholars of campaign finance have noted that unions are less risk-averse and more willing to support general election challengers, even long-shot challengers, than other groups (see, e.g., Sorauf 1992, 109–12).

Only three of the groups on the right-hand side of table 5.1 exist primarily to make a broad ideological statement; the Club for Growth and Citizens United have sought to push for conservative policies, and Democracy for America advocates for liberal policies. Most of the groups that support ideological challengers have a narrower set of issue concerns. The groups on the right in table 5.1 are somewhat similar to those that appear in the right-hand column of table 5.2. This second table compares the top contributors to primary challengers during the 1980s and 1990s and the top contributors during the 2000s. The types of groups that support ideological challengers are well represented among the top contributors overall during the 2000s. We have already seen that ideological challengers are not significantly more frequent than in the past. We may conclude that ideological challengers can count on at least a handful of groups for support today but could not count on this sort of support during the 1980s and 1990s. In those earlier decades, they could not count on any support

TABLE 5.2. Top PAC Supporters of Primary Challengers to Incumbents, by Decade (direct contributions and independent expenditures of $5,000 or less)

| | 1980–98 | | | 2000–2010 | |
PAC	Number of Expenditures	Total ($)	PAC	Number of Expenditures	Total ($)
National Rifle Association	93	156,850	Club for Growth	98	78,248
American Medical PAC	24	83,700	National Rifle Association	27	59,079
Realtors PAC	32	83,549	League of Conservation Voters	87	35,298
AFSCME	24	72,125	United Food & Commercial Workers	10	33,000
United Auto Workers	21	62,625	Electrical Workers, International Brotherhood of	8	30,500
AFL-CIO COPE	28	61,453	Service Employees International Union	11	27,813
National Education Association	19	60,325	American Medical PAC	7	26,000
Association of Trial Lawyers	20	60,000	Automobile and Truck Dealers	6	26,000
Teamsters, International Brotherhood of	16	51,750	Team America PAC	28	25,825
Machinists	18	51,749	American Bankers Association	7	25,000
Automobile and Truck Dealers	15	44,300	Association of Trial Lawyers	6	25,000
National Organization for Women	19	43,789	Machinists	5	25,000
Communications Workers of America-COPE	23	43,600	Stop ERA PAC	17	24,200
National Right to Life	53	41,625	NARAL	9	22,081
American Federation of Teachers	12	40,060	Gun Owners of America	25	22,013
National Association of Homebuilders	13	37,700	Citizens United Political Victory Fund	6	22,000
Gun Owners of America	36	37,312	International Ladies Garment Workers Union	9	21,677
Women's Campaign Fund	18	37,036	The Loose Group	4	20,000
NARAL	20	34,091	National Association of Homebuilders	5	20,000
Electrical Workers, International Brotherhood of	24	31,650	Washington PAC	7	18,000

Source: Author's calculations from Federal Election Commission data.

from groups at all, and they certainly could not approach groups that they had reason to suspect would have an interest in primary challenges.

It must be emphasized that the groups shown in tables 5.1 and 5.2 have not necessarily made it their mission to get involved in congressional primaries. Most of these groups contribute only a small percentage of their funds to primary candidates. All but the Club for Growth have a specific issue focus; in the case of the less familiar organizations in table 5.2, the Washington PAC is a pro-Israel group, the Team America PAC is an anti-immigration group run by former U.S. representative Tom Tancredo, and the Loose Group is an Atlanta-based conservative organization that has generally focused on matters of concern to the Atlanta business community. Although a few access-oriented groups still appear on the list of top contributors during the 2000s, the general constellation of groups here indicates that a number of relatively powerful organizations with little to lose from antagonizing incumbents have become important players in primary challengers. While, again, their individual expenditures do not matter a great deal in dollar terms, the propensity of these groups to get involved does arguably send a message to supporters.

I have not broken out the groups in tables 5.1 and 5.2 by party, in part because some of the groups contributed to primary challengers in both parties. Although the Democrats are traditionally viewed as the party with a larger constellation of interest groups, the groups listed here do not obviously tilt toward the Democratic Party. Although organized labor, generally a supporter of Democrats, is well represented in the tables, gun rights groups, anti-abortion groups, and fiscal conservatives are also represented. Of the groups listed in table 5.1 as supporters of ideological challengers (the only category without bipartisan groups), for instance, eight tend to support Republicans, and twelve tend to support Democrats (i.e., there are more Democratic groups than Republican groups), but this is hardly an overwhelming difference or an indication that a different type of strategic calculus is at work in each party.

As I noted at the beginning of this section, part of the story here is the shift in the types of groups that are active in primary campaigns. Because primaries tend to be relatively low-visibility elections, the fact that groups are involved can be of more consequence than the sums of money spent. The Alaska Senate race provides some evidence of this; there, that a small number of groups got involved in the race was of more consequence than the total expenditure amounts would indicate. Be this as it may, however, the 2000s have seen a surge in very large independent expenditures. Although there were no obvious changes in federal campaign finance law that would have abetted such expenditures (or would have limited them in the past), such expenditures simply were not a feature of congressional primaries prior to about 2008, except in rare instances.[8] It is one thing to say that group spending is not decisive in primaries, but it is another thing to argue that a race featuring expenditures in the hundreds of thousands of dollars is not of interest.

Table 5.3 shows not only that some of the same groups that became important in primaries in the 2000s have been willing to make very large expenditures but that some groups have been expressly formed for this purpose. These independent expenditures were made in a total of twenty-

TABLE 5.3.   Independent Expenditures over $5,000 on Behalf of Primary Challengers to Incumbents, 1980–2010

PAC	Candidates Supported (N)	Total ($)	Year(s)
Service Employees International Union	3	881,634	2006, 2008, 2010
Moveon.Org	3	398,246	2006, 2008
Club for Growth	3	360,836	2004, 2006, 2008
League of Conservation Voters	3	181,063	2000, 2006, 2008
EMILY's List	2	163,748	2006, 2008
American Academy of Orthopaedic Surgeons	1	99,300	2008
Women's Voices Women Vote Action Fund	1	86,473	2008
National Rifle Association	4	82,408	1988, 1992, 1996, 2002
Sierra Club	2	74,044	2006, 2008
Team America Political Action Committee	2	65,480	2004, 2006
NARAL Political Action Committee	2	58,602	1992, 2008
Campaign for Working Families	2	51,178	1998
Minuteman PAC Inc.	1	42,632	2006
Citizens for Progressive Representation	1	32,974	2006
National Right to Life Political Action	2	26,737	1992, 2006
American Airlines	1	16,408	1998
Handgun Control Inc.	1	16,034	2000
American Postal Workers Union	1	15,500	2010
Democracy for America	1	11,890	2010
United Steelworkers	1	10,500	2010
AFL-CIO COPE	2	10,541	1988, 1994
FAIR PAC	1	10,000	2004
United Food & Commercial Workers	1	9,996	2008
Maryland Right to Life Inc.	1	8,263	2006
Progressive Maryland Inc.	1	7,000	2008
Graphic Arts International Union PCC	1	6,000	2001
National Committee to Preserve Social Security	1	6,000	1992
Right to Life of Michigan	1	5,686	2006

Source: Author's calculations from Federal Election Commission data.

nine different House and Senate races. The groups listed in table 5.3 as having made independent expenditures on behalf of a primary challenger between 1988 and 2004 were, in most instances, the only groups active in these races. In 2006 and 2008, however, three races featured ten or more large expenditures: in Michigan in 2006, Timothy Walberg's successful challenge to Representative Joe Schwarz drew ten large expenditures from five different groups; Andy Harris's 2008 race in Maryland drew ten large expenditures, from the Club for Growth and the American Academy of Orthopaedic Surgeons; and the Donna Edwards challenges in 2006 and 2008 drew a combined thirty-three large expenditures from eight groups, for a combined $1.3 million spent.

Furthermore, what matters is not just the fact that large expenditures were made in these races but also the timing of these expenditures. Consider the three races just mentioned, for instance. In the Michigan race, the Club for Growth began spending in November of 2005; no other groups spent money until two different anti-abortion groups contributed in March of 2006, and business groups began to follow in June of 2006. In the Harris challenge, four different PACs representing otolaryngologists and other medical groups provided large direct contributions in June of 2007; the Club for Growth and Citizens United followed directly on their heels. The first Club for Growth expenditure in the race was in August of 2007, long before any other ideological groups, except for Citizens United, had become involved. In the case of Donna Edwards, her unsuccessful 2006 challenge featured several contributions from Democratic groups relatively late in the campaign. For her 2008 challenge, however, groups began spending in September of 2007. By the end of that year, two groups (the League of Conservation Voters and the SEIU) had spent over a combined $100,000, and several other feminist groups, labor unions, and environmental groups began spending soon afterward. Similar dynamics exist in other ideological challenges. The groups that spent a lot on these races tended to spend money early, to try to draw the attention of other groups.

Despite the evident flood of outside activity in the 2010 Alaska Senate primary (described earlier in this chapter), table 5.3 shows fewer large expenditures in that year, and the time trend for large expenditures (shown in figure 5.1) shows a steep decline in 2010 after a surge in 2006 and 2008. This pattern corresponds to the pattern noted in chapter 3. Given the political environment of 2010, outside groups may have channeled more of their resources toward general election candidates and open-seat primaries and less toward primary challenges. Like previous years, however, outside spending was concentrated among a small number of groups (three labor unions and one progressive group, all spending on behalf of Arkansas Senate challenger Bill Halter). The 2010 numbers should also be taken with a grain of salt because of the expanded activities of 501(c)(4) groups (which do not report to the FEC) and the increase in corporate contributions to such groups following the *Citizens United v. FEC* decision. As I previously recounted, we know that outside groups were quite active in the Alaska primary, but none of this spending shows up in FEC records. There certainly was a decline as some of the groups responsible for driving independent expenditures in 2008 turned to other races or other types of spending, but this decline may say more about the opportunities groups had in the general election than about a change in groups' approaches to primary challenges.

These races bring us to the same question we have visited in previous chapters: at what point do we identify something as a trend, as opposed to an anomalous set of races? If one considers the pattern in figure 5.1, we see the same sort of trend we saw in the data on individual contributors. There was a dramatic surge in independent expenditures on behalf of primary challengers, but this surge was driven entirely by a small number of races and by a small number of groups. At what point do we contend that we are witnessing some sort of change in the nature of primary elections? To answer this question, we need to explore not only the types of groups that have driven this change but the changing nature of American interest group politics.

Seeking a Niche in Primary Politics

The Club for Growth

The Club for Growth is not the only conservative group to back ideological challengers over the past few decades. For instance, the Conservative Victory Fund, founded by former congressman John Ashbrook, has supported primary challengers throughout the period covered by the data here—and according to the group's website (www.conservativevictoryfund.org), it has done so since 1969. Citizens United, a relatively obscure conservative group before the Supreme Court case bearing its name, had made contributions of $5,000 to four different primary challengers between 2002 and 2010 and smaller contributions to two others. Paul Weyrich's Committee for the Survival of a Free Congress supported ten differ-

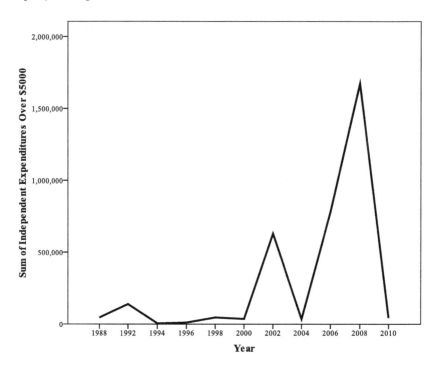

Fig. 5.1. Large (over $5,000) independent expenditures by election cycle. There were no independent expenditures in excess of $5,000 by PACs before 1988. (Author's calculations from Federal Election Commission data.)

ent Republican primary challengers between 1980 and 2002. The National Conservative PAC, or NCPAC, supported a variety of primary challengers during the 1980s.

The Club for Growth differs from these groups, however, in that it has consistently placed a high priority on primary elections, both in instances where it seeks to unseat moderate Republican incumbents and in those in which it seeks to support a favored candidate in an open-seat primary or a primary to take on a Democratic incumbent. While the club has supported incumbents as well—particularly incumbents whom it supported in their initial bid for Congress—it has identified primaries as venues where it can make a difference if it provides early support for candidates. As a consequence, candidates often seek the club's endorsement before beginning their primary campaigns. The club is also distinctive, compared to the groups previously listed, in that it has prioritized bundling and independent expenditures over PAC contributions.

The Club for Growth was formed in 1999 by Stephen Moore, an economist and former staff member at the Heritage Foundation and the Cato Institute.[9] Moore's original idea was to create a short list of business-friendly candidates, to whom a select group of wealthy conservative acquaintances might make contributions. The club sought to be a force, then, by bundling contributions from individuals whose names might mean something to candidates or to other potential donors. Moore would be a sort of broker for these contributors, taking the trouble to vet candidates and ensure their fidelity to conservative principles. The club made a point of prioritizing ideology over electability, but it supported a small enough number of candidates that it could direct substantial amounts of money in their direction. The group has grown substantially over the course of the decade; while it has changed its name and tax status as a result of conflicts with the FEC, the spending of the various arms of the group went quickly from slightly over $100,000 in 2000 to $3 million in 2002 and over $8 million in 2010. The club has outlasted its founder; Moore was ousted from the group in 2005. Since Moore's departure, it has been led by two former members of Congress: Pat Toomey (until his 2010 Senate bid) and former Indiana representative Chris Chocola.

As the tables in this chapter show, the Club for Growth dwarfs all other groups in its consistent support for ideological challengers. By 2010, it also dwarfed all other conservative groups in its total spending. Of the PACs that the Center for Responsive Politics classifies as "Republican/ Conservative"—that is, groups that support conservative policies but without a particular issue of concern—the Club for Growth was by far the biggest spender, spending $3 million, compared to less than $500,000 by the next highest spender. The group's so-called Super PAC, Club for Growth Action, spent an additional $5 million in 2010 . Despite the growth in its spending, however, the Club for Growth supports only a small number of candidates. The club has generally supported at least one and sometimes as many as three or four primary challengers in any given election cycle. In contrast to larger PACs with ties to business groups or with a pro-business agenda, the club has engaged in very little access-related giving, and it does not lobby at all. It supports a relatively small number of candidates; it supported twenty-one candidates in 2008 and twenty-eight candidates in 2010. Ten of the candidates it supported in 2008 were incumbents; this is notably low for a year when many Republican seats were in danger. However, the group supported only two incumbents, Senators Tom Coburn and Jim DeMint, in the 2010 cycle, a much safer election for Republican incumbents. Because neither DeMint nor Coburn were in any danger, the club's support consisted only of directing bundled contributions toward these candidates, not of engaging in independent spending on their behalf.

The Club for Growth has sought, then, to develop candidates and to get behind them early enough that it can play a role in establishing their campaigns, encouraging individual contributions, and potentially scaring other candidates out of the race. This approach has been very successful in primaries that do not feature an incumbent, as the club showed in 2010 in several House races and in helping Sharron Angle upset a more conventional Republican opponent in the Nevada Republican Senate primary. Although the club has scored some successes in challenges to incumbents, they have generally been in unusual circumstances—for instance, it did back Timothy Walberg in his 2006 primary challenge to first-term Senator Joe Schwarz, but, as have seen, Schwarz had only made it through the 2004 Republican primary because of the fractured field and because of support from the left-leaning League of Conservation Voters. It also backed Mike Lee's Utah Senate primary bid in 2010, but this was, again, a challenge at the convention rather than in an election. The club's lone intervention in a Democratic primary took place in 2006, when it backed moderate Democrat Henry Cueller in a challenge to the more liberal incumbent Ciro Rodriguez in a Texas district that had been altered by the state's unusual 2004 redistricting (Kraushaar 2011). The club's support for Andy Harris in Maryland in 2008 was enough to defeat incumbent representative Wayne Gilchrest, but, as noted earlier, Harris went on the lose the 2008 general election.

Not only have the Club for Growth's primary challenges rarely succeeded, but their successes have been due in large part to atypical primaries—races where the sizable incumbency advantage in primaries posited by Ansolabehere, Hansen, et al. (2007) does not apply. In a way, the club's selection of these races speaks to the nationalization of primary competition. These races were clearly chosen in part because of their unusual circumstances—circumstances that policy-driven interest groups or local organizations might not have recognized. A group that makes elections, especially primary elections, a major focus is likely to accumulate information that other organizations will not have.

Some have argued that the Club for Growth's efforts in challenges to incumbents have been less consequential than its efforts in other types of primaries (Kraushaar 2011). It is true that some of the candidates the club supported have eventually made it to Congress: Pat Toomey won the 2010 Pennsylvania Senate race after his unsuccessful challenge to Specter in

2004; in 2010, Harris won the Maryland seat he had failed to win in 2008; and Scott Garrett eventually won an open-seat race in New Jersey. Yet the club could arguably have won an equal or greater number of races for open seats elsewhere had it ignored these three races. So the emphasis on primaries is either a misallocation of resources or is about more than winning elections.

The challenges supported by the Club for Growth become more comprehensible if one considers other unconventional acts by the group. The club ran ads in South Dakota criticizing Senate majority leader Tom Daschle in late 2002, almost two years before Daschle would be up for reelection. These ads sought primarily to amuse and garner attention; they featured bobblehead dolls of Daschle, Hillary Clinton, and Ted Kennedy. The club spent an estimated $600,000 on advertisements calling Republican senators George Voinovich and Olympia Snowe "Franco-Republicans" for their hesitation about supporting President Bush's plan for tax cuts—a hesitation that was labeled as somehow French.[10] The club ran a much-discussed ad in Iowa in December of 2003 describing Democratic presidential aspirant Howard Dean's campaign as a "tax-hiking, government-expanding, latte-drinking, sushi-eating, Volvo-driving, New York Times-reading, Hollywood-loving, left-wing freak show." This ad makes no political sense; a group like the Club for Growth might dislike Dean, but it disliked all of the Democratic presidential aspirants, and many felt that Dean would be a weaker nominee in the general election than other Democratic candidates. The club ad did, however, draw attention to the group.

In terms of immediate electoral goals, in fact, none of these ads made sense—unless, again, one connects them to the defeat of Daschle and Dean or the retirement of Voinovich, connections that are rather tenuous. Club president Stephen Moore (2003) disowned any electoral goals, saying, "My group doesn't want to kick Snowe and Voinovich out of the party. We simply want them to start acting more like Reagan and less like Daschle. Is that asking so much?" But they did help to define the Club for Growth in the public eye, as a group that would take on foes regardless of the political consequences and would push its agenda well outside of election season. Such an approach surely brought about expanded media coverage, and it may well have encouraged individual donors to contribute money to the club—only the group knows whether this is the case. These were, in other words, stunts. If we view primary challenges as stunts, they make more sense. If the goal of these challenges was to define the club as the group that supports primary challenges to moderate Republican incumbents, then they succeeded. The club's efforts in these primary challenges—such as its development of campaigns to encourage donors to Arlen Specter and Lisa Murkowski to ask for their money back—have been similarly unorthodox yet clearly fodder for media coverage. What matters is not even the fact that the club supports primary challengers but what it does to support them.

MoveOn.org

MoveOn.org is roughly the same age as the Club for Growth, but it became interested in primaries much later. It has also generally been less focused on a set of issues than the club. When it was formed in 1998 by Silicon Valley entrepreneurs Wes Boyd and Joan Blades, MoveOn's signature issue was its opposition to the impeachment of President Clinton and its desire for Congress to "move on" to more important political issues. Following the president's impeachment, the group then started a PAC and began bundling contributions aimed at supporting challengers to the Republican impeachment managers. By 2000, MoveOn had developed into a "bottom-up" organization advocating for a variety of progressive causes, but its emphasis was still on bundling small donations. According to one estimate, it raised an estimated $1.85 million for Democratic candidates, from forty-three thousand different donors. In 2002 and 2004, MoveOn retained its emphasis on raising money in smaller donations, but it diversified its activities. According to the group's own estimates, in 2002 it raised $2.3 million, with an average donation of $35, and it raised $4.1 million for candidates in 2004, with an average of about $60, excluding a small number of million-dollar contributions (Boyd 2003). By 2004, MoveOn was airing the second-largest number of advertisements of any group on the left, and it focused its efforts on the presidential race just as much as on congressional elections.

Despite its financial clout, MoveOn has never defined itself primarily as a bundling organization; the vast majority of its members (4.2 million as of 2010) give only token amounts, if anything. MoveOn has sought to coordinate "off-line" gatherings of members, to encourage members to e-mail members of Congress about issues of concern, and to have members cast votes in determining the group's agenda. Yet MoveOn was primarily distinguished from other groups by its leadership in using the Internet to communicate with members and raise money and by the cleverness of many of its activities. The group has sometimes run afoul of Democratic leaders, as in its "General Betray Us" advertisements criticizing David Petraeus (ads that outraged Democratic and Republican leaders alike), but these missteps seem more like amateurish mistakes than a conscious effort to be a thorn in the side of the Democratic Party. They read more like the sorts of stunts that the Club for Growth has developed. Despite its occasional missteps, MoveOn counts among its supporters many prominent party leaders and leaders of other liberal groups.

MoveOn's emphasis on primary elections, then, is less an example of conscious niche filling (as was the case for the Club for Growth) than an offshoot of an organization that always is involved in a large number of projects. The group spent money on only four primary challenges—the challenges to Senators Joe Lieberman and Blanche Lincoln and Donna Edwards's two races against Representative Al Wynn—but it spent well over $100,000 on each of these. MoveOn was not the only contributor in these races, but of the groups that spent money on these campaigns, it was arguably the most willing to explain itself to the public. In its year-end report on the 2008 elections, for instance, the group reported,

> No race was more exciting than helping Donna Edwards win her primary campaign against Al Wynn in February of this year. . . . We're proud to have been a part of electing a progressive champion like Donna to the US House. And the race put other Representatives on notice: fail to listen to your constituents, and you might be next. (MoveOn.org 2008)

The rhetoric, then, is similar to that of other groups that have sponsored primary challenges, but MoveOn listed its expenditures on Edwards's behalf along with eleven other Democrats that the group supported in their general election campaigns.

MoveOn has been behind the biggest ideological challenges to Democrats of the past three election cycles, but it has not played a part in the less viable challenges. While liberal bloggers have touted other campaigns, particularly House races, there is a large gap between the races featuring MoveOn and those that do not. This does not, of course, mean that the group was responsible for these challenges, but its involvement arguably made a difference.

Most important, however, MoveOn has, like the Club for Growth, been responsible for spreading the story about primarying. In appeals such as the one about Edwards and the e-mails about Blanche Lambert Lincoln described in chapter 1, MoveOn has aped the Club for Growth in its claims that centrists should be concerned about primary challenges. While primarying still occurs more on the right than on the left—a sign that MoveOn has not become as much of a threat to Democrats as the Club for Growth is to Republicans—the fact that MoveOn has been able to leverage just four primary challenges (on behalf of three candidates) into a threat that garners some media attention is a sign that it, too, has learned that these efforts can draw attention to the group far beyond what support for an open-seat candidate or a general election candidate might provide.

Other Primary Sponsors

The Club for Growth and MoveOn.org are behind all of the well-funded ideological challenges of the 2000s. Some might argue that I am selecting on the dependent variable here or that these groups did not necessarily bring about ideological challenges but, rather, jumped on the bandwagon after it became clear that these candidates would be viable challengers. I believe the overall track record of these groups and their rhetoric about primaries suggests otherwise. Nonetheless, it is worth considering the motives of other groups that have played a role in these campaigns.

Organized Labor

Labor unions were major participants in several of the Democratic primary challenges, most notably the challenges to Al Wynn and Blanche Lambert Lincoln. As shown in chapter 1, many labor unions saw the Lincoln race as a chance to make the same sort of argument made by groups like the Club for Growth—that they would use primaries as an opportunity to hold centrist politicians accountable. It is difficult to generalize about the motives of all unions, but the data presented earlier in this chapter show that unions have supported ideological challengers in other elections over the past two decades. The amount of money put into the Wynn and Lincoln challenges by some unions, like the SEIU, was unprecedented. Unions had supported other ideological primary challengers in the past, but they tended to do so in heavily unionized areas of the country, such as Pennsylvania or northeastern Ohio.

Issue Groups

As table 5.3 shows, some issue groups have also been active in ideological challenges. The difference here between liberals and conservatives is striking. Liberal groups such as the Sierra Club and NARAL have been involved in the same challenges that MoveOn and organized labor have supported. Most of the independent spending by these groups comes, in fact, in the same races—the Wynn, Lincoln, and Lieberman challenges. Clearly, there is some coordination happening here, either formally or de facto. It is hard to generalize from such a small number of cases, but it is striking to observe that this does not happen for conservative challengers. Conservative issue groups such as the Minutemen PAC (an anti-immigration group) or the National Rifle Association have supported different challengers from those supported by the Club for Growth. There is some overlap in the Walberg race in 2006, but for the most part, one sees individual conservative groups making large independent expenditures without any sort of concerted strategy.

The Tea Party

It is noteworthy that much of the rhetoric and media discussion of the 2010 primaries centered around the Tea Party. As has been well documented, the Tea Party is not a cohesive entity, so it is difficult to be certain that figures for group spending show Tea Party activities. It is worth emphasizing, however, that there are no instances in the 2010 data where the Tea Party was the lead actor in providing the seed money for a conservative challenge to an incumbent. This is not to say that the Tea Party did not play an important role in many races, but it does suggest that it did not play a financial role. The 2010 data was complicated by the fact that many of the strongest insurgent conservative candidates do not quite qualify for this study; Delaware's Christine O'Donnell was running in an open-seat primary, Sharron Angle was running in an out-party primary, Pat Toomey ultimately did not run against Arlen Specter, and the Utah nomination was resolved at the state convention. We may yet see primary challengers propelled by the Tea Party and not by the Club for Growth. But in 2010, despite their activity in other sorts of races, the Tea Party left few financial signs that it was a source of primary challenges to Republican incumbents.

Earlier Groups

Finally, one might go back to the 1980s and 1990s to look for signs that groups like MoveOn or the Club for Growth were active in primaries. PAC contribution data show that some groups were involved in several primary challenges, as I have noted earlier in the case of conservative groups. Groups like NCPAC were involved in several Republican races, but not in ideological challenges. They seem to get involved for pragmatic reasons, in races where the primary challenger appears to have a real chance. Their contributions are sufficiently small that it would be hard to argue that they are seeking to alter the dynamic of the race. In the pre-2000 data, six ideological primary challengers (excluding the anomalous case of Ron Paul) raised more than $20,000 from PACs, enough for one to actually see the contributions as anything other than idiosyncratic behavior. Of these six, five were Democrats, and the Democrats all raised money from labor unions and major advocacy groups (the League of Conservation Voters, Council for a Livable World, etc.); the lone Republican raised money from anti-abortion groups and the National Rifle Association. There is some evidence that the sort of thing that happened in the Donna Edwards–Al Wynn race had happened before at least once; Barbara Kreamer, a former member of the Maryland House of Delegates, challenged incumbent Democrat Roy Dyson in 1990 and received over $40,000 from LCV, Council for a Livable World, the Human Rights Campaign, Handgun Control, and a host of other liberal groups.[11] This race featured a variety of different groups, but it does not seem like a part of a coordinated effort by groups with a particular stake in sending a message through primary challenges. There is no evidence whatsoever of this happening on the Republican side during this time; while some conservative ideological groups show up in primaries, they are almost entirely absent from the list of ideological primary challengers.

The Functional Niche

How important is it that groups such as the Club for Growth and MoveOn .org have identified primaries as a venue for activity? This is subject to debate. If all we are looking at is the decision by a small number of groups to reallocate their campaign dollars toward different types of elections, this hardly seems like an important subject for sustained scholarly inquiry. Such decisions are, however, indicative of a much broader trend among organized interests, a trend that one can trace back to the early 2000s. The trend in question is not one that is exclusively related to primaries, but primaries fit into this story nicely.

Consider again the lists of PAC donors to primary challengers in the 1980s and 2000s. The fact that issue groups are well represented on the first list but less so on the second is not a circumstance solely of primary elections. The lists of major campaign advertisers in the 1990s and 2000s also show a shift among group types, from groups with an identifiable issue niche and track record to groups that raised money and recruited members not so much because of what they cared about but because of their effectiveness in helping get candidates elected or in running particular types of campaigns. This is a trend that first became visible in 2004. In an article on the 2004 and 2006 elections (Boatright 2007), I noted that many of the new 527 groups that sprang up in the years following the implementation of BCRA competed among each other for donors; their appeals revolved around their effectiveness or their campaigning specialty, not their issues of concern. Hence, America Coming Together advertised itself as a get-out-the-vote organization, the Media Fund promoted itself as an advertising group, MoveOn claimed to be a group that would harness the Internet and communicate with younger voters, and so on. This was a pattern that many party operatives had predicted. They had argued that BCRA would weaken parties and spawn "quasi-party" organizations. To an extent, this may have been true; certainly these groups sought to perform functions that benefited the Democratic Party, and in 2004, they were active in some states where the Democratic National Committee was not. But as spending figures for 2004 and 2006 reveal, the party organizations themselves did not decline as some had predicted. By 2010, such groups were acting more as complements to the party than as substitutes.

By 2010, Republican groups had followed suit. If one consults the promotional materials of organizations such as American Crossroads and Americans for Prosperity, these groups provide only vague statements about their concerns. American Crossroads, for instance, stated on its website in 2010 that it was "a new kind of non-profit political organization dedicated to renewing America's commitment to individual liberty, limited government, free enterprise and a strong national defense," a statement that is bland enough to serve as a campaign pitch for just about any Republican candidate.[12] American Crossroads was best known in the election for its leaders—such as Karl Rove—and not for a preoccupation with anything other than helping Republicans. Likewise, Americans for Prosperity, a group funded with the support of David and Charles Koch, provided an even vaguer statement of purpose: it was "committed to educating citizens about economic policy and mobilizing those citizens as advocates in the public policy process."[13] These are groups very much like the Democratic 527s of 2004, albeit with functional niches that are less defined. They are more like these Democratic groups in their function and purpose than they are like any of the dominant interest groups of the 1980s or 1990s.

How do groups that focus on primaries fit in here? They can market themselves the sorts of groups that will get involved in primaries, just as America Coming Together marketed itself as a get-out-the-vote group and American Crossroads promoted itself based on its leadership. To cultivate the image of a group that puts principle above partisanship—that will take on moderates—a group actually has to consistently do this. In other words, the Club for Growth needs to identify a few Republicans to take on in each cycle, and MoveOn must do the same for Democrats. Taking on too many primary challenges will dilute the effectiveness of the group's approach. The important point here is to create a brand for the group and sell the group to prospective donors, not necessarily to take out a large number of incumbents. The Club for Growth has gotten far more attention for its primary challenges than it has for its support of general election candidates. This attention yields contributions, which can, in turn, fund election activities that are less glamorous.

This emphasis on function rather than on group issues is perhaps most understandable if one views interest groups as being akin to business firms. One way to conceptualize the market for products is to assume that firms specialize in particular products—that they seek to develop a comparative advantage by producing a small number of items. Another model of the firm would posit that firms seek to develop a reputation for quality or for a particular sort of expertise and then to apply it in several different areas. This second paradigm corresponds somewhat to Michael Porter's (1985) popular model of competitive advantage. Porter argues that firms seek advantage either on the basis of cost or by differentiating their product. Firms may provide a unique product, which consumers may be willing to purchase even at a high cost, or they may seek to provide the same product as other firms but at lower cost.

What is the product of interest groups? Let us first assume a differentiation strategy. If it is expertise on the environment, some consumers may be willing to purchase membership with little regard to the price and with only secondary regard to the group's success in elections. This would, however, seem like a difficult brand from which to generalize; the audience for such groups is limited by the number of voters concerned about the environment, and groups will face obstacles in expanding the audience. Consider, instead, a group pursuing a cost advantage. If a group is selling its skill in winning elections, helping liberal or conservative candidates, and so on, it is not selling a product so much as it is selling a skill or technique. It has a potentially large audience, but it must show that it is uniquely effective. There are, of course, many groups that seek to help candidates, and citizens could always simply give money to candidates. If groups have a proven track record of helping candidates, however, and if they can provide services for consumers at a reasonable price (e.g., if they can identify good candidates and help connect members with these candidates), the group is, in effect, selling its skills, not any particular product. Such a group must be unique, but the candidates it supports or the issues it uses to advance its cause are less important. The group can establish a brand, and it can then offer a variety of different products (e.g., different ways to become involved in politics and different candidates voters might support), which voters will purchase because they trust the brand.[14]

Traditional theories of interest group entrepreneurship, such as those of Salisbury (1969) and Walker (1983), have emphasized that interest groups succeed to the extent that group entrepreneurs can identify underserved markets or can create demand for organized efforts to address a particular subject. The idea of interest group niches, generally associate with William Browne's work (1988, 1990), is well-established in the literature, although Browne's concerns were with issue niches and lobbying expertise. Many of the classic interest group studies—to name two obvious examples, those of Olson (1971) and Wilson (1973)—made it clear that the same principles that explain interest groups as organizations can be used to explain business organizations, and vice versa. Few examples of groups with a functional niche come to mind, however, when one peruses the foundational interest group literature or considers the dominant groups of the 1960s, 1970s, and 1980s. Groups such as the Club for Growth or MoveOn.org are contemporary examples of Salisbury's paradigm. They have sought to create a demand for groups that will take on centrists, a market that simply did not exist during the 1970s or 1980s. Their functional approach is something that has rarely been captured in the interest group literature, despite the fact that firms of this nature are commonplace in business literature.[15] This approach is part of a package these groups offer. It is not all that they do, but it is crucial to establishing their brand. By creating such a brand (i.e., by showing themselves to be "edgy" through their efforts in primaries), these groups can cultivate favored candidates for higher office (as the Club for Growth does) or turn their attentions to the more crowded marketplace of general elections. Thus they establish their brand through primaries, and once it is established, they can use it to confer credibility on other candidates or other types of group activities, much as established brands in the marketplace may use their reputation in order to expand into other areas. Functional groups thus have greater growth potential than do groups that champion, for instance, gun rights or gun control, niches from which expansion is difficult.

It is far beyond the scope of this book to inquire into the reason why functional groups flourish in contemporary politics. One rather incomplete explanation that might be offered corresponds to much of what we have seen so far in this book. The nationalization of campaigning—both by candidates and by groups—has created a wider audience to whom groups can appeal. As we have seen, this nationalization has corresponded to the growth of Internet campaigning, and it seems clear that the Internet has played a dominant role in the nationalization of campaigns. To use the Internet effectively, groups and candidates must call attention to themselves—through catchy advertisements, clever video clips, or other means of generating traffic. Creating a reputation for unconventional behavior—such as, for instance, backing primary challengers to prominent incumbents—is a way to do this. The loosening of restrictions on independent advocacy brought about by the Supreme Court's decision in *Citizens United v. FEC* will only serve to strengthen groups that can establish such a brand—even as their appeal is geared not toward big spenders but toward the mass public.

Functional Niches and the Party Organizations

The success of some interest groups in creating a niche in the primary process also presents an interesting (and, to some, troublesome) development in the ongoing debate over the health of the political parties. The standard story that political scientists have told about the Democratic and Republican party organizations is that they entered a period of decline in the 1970s but recovered in the 1990s. The homogeneity within the parties' congressional delegations and the polarization between the two parties are often held up as a sign that we now have, for better or worse, a party system that resembles the "more responsible" two-party system envisioned by the 1950 American Political Science Report (Committee on Political Parties 1950). However, the passage of BCRA and its imposition of fund-raising restrictions for the parties, was also predicted to be detrimental to the parties. Many party functions, some feared, would be taken over by unaccountable nonparty groups. This concern has been heightened by the *Citizens United v. FEC* decision and the subsequent formation of so-called Super PACs, groups that can raise unlimited amounts of money from corporate donors for the purpose of direct political advocacy. We are, then, in a period of heightened partisanship, yet there are signs that the formal party organizations are in some trouble.

Contemporary scholars such as Herrnson (2009) have sought to expand our definitions of the parties to include sympathetic groups as "party allies." Others, such as Skinner, Masket, and Dulio (2012), have emphasized a conception of the party as a network of politicians, unelected political elites, and nonparty organizations. In one sense, niche groups are clearly part of this expanded definition of the party as network. All of the organizations involved in primaries take an interest only in one of the two major parties' primaries, and there is little doubt of the partisan leanings of members of Club for Growth and MoveOn.org. Yet these groups' actions tend to run afoul of the goals of the party committees; they threaten to unseat powerful Democratic and Republican incumbents and have sometimes threatened to throw safe party seats to the other party by bringing about the nomination of candidates who may be unelectable in the general election. Even where this does not happen in the short term, there is a possibility that these groups will push legislators and their parties away from the center—by seeking to establish their preferred candidates not merely as Republicans but as Club for Growth Republicans or Tea Party Republicans (and likewise for Democrats). This can certainly weaken the parties in the long run, as perhaps is shown by the difficulties the Republican House leadership has had in the 112th Congress in reining in newly elected Tea Party candidates. In addition, researchers have generally concluded that increased party support by legislators can hurt at the ballot box (Canes-Wrone, Brady, and Cogan 2002; Lebo, McGlynn, and Koger 2007; Carson et al. 2010). Groups with a functional niche are a part of the party network, but they are not necessarily a welcome part.

The preceding discussion casts doubt on the notion that changing campaign finance laws have brought about the development of such groups. It may well be that BCRA and *Citizens United v. FEC* were beneficial to such groups. Yet the functional groups that raised the most money in the wake of BCRA (America Votes) and *Citizens United* (American Crossroads) were not groups that took an interest in primarying, and the most active primarying groups were formed before these changes. Both MoveOn.org and the Club for Growth capitalized on the development of the Internet and on the ability it provided to link partisan ideologues across the country. The Tea Party has not been cast as an innovator in the use of the Internet, but its spread was clearly abetted as well by social networking sites and similar means of communication (Bullock 2012). These developments have little to do with changes in campaign finance law. This change, of course, means that it is not clear what parties might do if they seek to limit these groups' influence. In a decade where control of Congress has been at stake in nearly every election, there is certainly a place for groups that seek to threaten a party's prospects for winning majorities, and primarying groups may play an outsized role right now because of this implicit threat.

Conclusions

In the introduction to this book, I listed three different claims about congressional primary challenges: that they have increased in number, that stronger challengers have emerged, and that they have a greater effect on Congress now than they once did. The first claim, as I showed in chapter 2, is dubious. The second and third suffer from a lack of conclusive evidence. It appears that challengers today garner more attention, and a select number of them do raise more money than has been the case in the past, but that they are stronger is a claim that ultimately cannot be proven, and there are simply too many unmeasurable consequences of challenges for one to have confidence in the third claim.

We can, however, measure changes in the attention primary challenges receive from different types of groups. As I have sought to show here, the types of groups that support primary challengers today are different than those that did so in the past. This is the case not only because different groups have taken an interest in these races but because new types of interest groups have formed over the past decade. Supporting primary challengers simply did not make sense for very many groups in the context of American politics in the 1970s and 1980s. Doing so makes quite a bit of sense for the sorts of groups that have been created to take advantage of the new technological, political, and legal environment of the 2000s. While traditional, candidate-centered analyses of elections may posit that groups exist to support candidates or political causes, the developments documented in this chapter indicate that it may be more accurate today to say that challenges such as those discussed in this book exist in order to benefit new types of political groups.

6 | Conclusions

It scarcely took a week for the dust to settle on the 2010 election results before talk of primary threats to incumbent members of Congress began again. A November 10 *Politico* article reported that Republican senators Scott Brown, Orrin Hatch, Olympia Snowe, John Ensign, Kay Bailey Hutchison, and Richard Lugar all potentially faced primary competition (Toeplitz 2010). Ensign had spent much of his term embroiled in a complicated sex scandal, and Hutchison had lost badly in the primary for Texas governor in 2010. Ensign, Hutchison, and Snowe subsequently decided not to run again, and Ensign resigned altogether. Talk of opposition to the other three, however, was rooted in nothing other than ideology.

Brown had been the darling of conservative activists during his upset victory in a special election for Ted Kennedy's old Massachusetts seat in early 2010, but he had quickly disappointed them once he reached the Senate, by siding with Democrats on a number of economic bills and on repeal of the "Don't Ask, Don't Tell" law. Lugar and Hatch were generally not considered centrists, however, and while their voting records showed occasional breaks with the party, their reputation for failing to be sufficiently conservative may have had more to do with their collegiality with Democrats than with their politics.

By November 18, Senator Jim DeMint had gone so far as to say that he currently had no plans to support challengers to any of his colleagues (Raju 2010). Lugar, who had broken with the party to support immigration reform and had voted to confirm both of President Obama's Supreme Court nominees, had a stormy meeting with Indiana Tea Party members. According to one attendee at the meeting,

> We obviously would beg to differ that he is conservative, and our experience is that he won't get the support of any Tea Party group across the state. This is something that has really been building for

years. A lot of Tea Party people have said, "Who is this guy? He
might as well have a 'D' in front of his name." (Hamby 2011)

A group named Hoosiers for a Conservative Senate announced that it
would host a "Road to Retirement" event on January 22, 2011, in order to
begin its campaign against Lugar and to start to search for a candidate to
oppose him.[1] Lugar would go on to lose the 2012 primary to Indiana Trea-
surer Richard Mourdock, receiving only 39 percent of the vote. Hatch
faced a primary challenger but defeated him easily, and Brown ran unopposed.

There is clearly an audience for election-related political coverage even
during the months when an election is far away. Speculation about who
will get primaried is a good fit for these months. In subsequent elections,
we will likely have more politicians in the shoes of Joe Lieberman, Blanche
Lincoln, or Lisa Murkowski. In the introduction, I framed this book as a
response to three different claims that are frequently made about primary
challenges: that they are becoming more common, that they are becoming
more consequential, and that they affect the behavior of members of Congress. As I have sought to demonstrate, there is little evidence to support
the first and third of these claims; the evidence we can muster regarding
primaries indicates that these claims are either untrue or exaggerated. In
this concluding chapter, I step back to ask how it is that primary challenges have assumed such an outsized role on analyses of congressional
elections and whether we should care about the inflated claims that are
made about primaries.

The Real Consequences of Congressional
Primary Challenges

The first of the questions addressed in this chapter is in some ways easy to
answer—but, as I hope I have shown here, the situation is not as simple as
it might appear. Congressional primaries have traditionally received scant
attention from the national media, from the political establishment, and
from political scientists. When they have received attention, it has been
because the occurrence of primary elections said something about the political culture and political party system of the region of the country in
which they took place. This has changed; as the data in this book show,
primary challenges—especially ideological challenges—can happen in
any part of the country.

The attention I have paid to primary challenges in this book shows that contemporary primaries look very much like the primaries of years past in many ways. There are no more primaries today than there were in the past, although there are more than there were during the late 1990s. The number of primary challenges per year waxes and wanes with the overall competitiveness of each year's congressional elections; cycles with high-turnover general elections tend to have a large number of competitive primary elections. Primary elections are also not more consequential today than they were in previous decades. There has not been an increase in the number of incumbents defeated or seriously challenged, and the incumbents who have defeated primary challengers do not appear to change their behavior when they return to Congress.

The biggest change in American congressional primary elections is that a small number of primaries have been nationalized. The best-known primary challengers of the past decade have drawn on a national fundraising base and have had the assistance of a small but influential coterie of interest groups. This was not the case in the 1970s, 1980s, or 1990s, and it is a result of changes in the political media—in the way that groups communicate with their supporters, in the way that liberal and conservative blogs draw attention to different parts of the country, and in the way that political news sites provide sustained coverage of individual congressional races. In the months after the 2010 congressional elections, politically aware Americans living far from Alaska and Arkansas could probably describe those states' Senate primaries. I cannot prove that this was *not* the case in 1980, but it seems unlikely.

There is a lot that we cannot measure about congressional primaries. My aim in this book has been to explore what we *can* measure; and the things we can measure show that the received wisdom about congressional primaries has been somewhat exaggerated. Moreover, they show that there are clear reasons why these exaggerations have taken place: the groups that sponsor primary challenges benefit from parlaying two or three challenges into a broader perception that these challenges are a threat to all incumbents.

What does all of this mean? What is the lingering effect on American politics from the apparent likelihood that we will have two or three such races in each election cycle for the foreseeable future? It is easy to do as Thomas Mann (2006) has done and include primaries with campaign finance and gerrymandering as institutional sources of polarization in contemporary politics. The problem, however, lies in developing normative arguments about primaries. To allegations that the campaign finance system is "broken," one can respond by developing proposals to fix it—to craft public financing mechanisms or to prohibit certain types of advertisements and certain types of contributions or expenditures. Likewise, one could explore the myriad proposals for fixing the redistricting process, such as nonpartisan state commissions. But what can one really recommend be done about primaries? Limiting competition does not seem like an attractive option for reformers, and distinguishing between legitimate and illegitimate primary challenges seems a problematic and controversial endeavor. One could, perhaps, seek greater transparency in these elections—for instance, one might advocate informing the voters of Alaska and Alabama about how much of the primary challengers' money is coming from out of state. But, especially because we have seen that money is not necessarily decisive, this also seems like a fruitless tactic.

Besides, as any treatment of congressional elections will emphasize, the deck is so stacked in favor of incumbent members of Congress that decrying primary competition seems particularly unreasonable, both from an academic perspective and, it seems evident, from the perspective of the average citizen (congressional approval is, as I write this, barely over 10 percent). The argument generally made about the relationship between primaries and polarization tends to go something like this: congressional districts tend to be so safe for one party or the other that incumbents have more to fear from primaries than from the general election. I am not sure this argument is true, but even if it were, it would seem illogical to then argue that there should be fewer primary challenges—unless the decline were a result of drawing districts that were more competitive in the general election. Even then, the logical consequence would be not fewer primary challenges but more general election challenges, and the "threat" factor would tilt more toward the general election. As the data in this book make clear, there are not more competitive primary challenges in districts with less competitive general elections.

So, instead of diving into what I would consider a relatively obscure discussion of the normative consequences for the American public of congressional primary challenges, let us instead look a bit more at their consequences at the microlevel—for the pivotal players actually involved in the challenge. In this book, I have discussed some of the potential causes of challenges—troubles on the part of the incumbent, policy disagreements between incumbent and challenger, and so forth—but to some extent, these are rather unsatisfying causal mechanisms. I have limited my inquiry here to what we can observe about elections, but we cannot observe motives. One might argue, for instance, that John Kerry ran against

George W. Bush in 2004 because he disagreed with Bush's policies as president. It would be easy to catalog disagreements between Kerry and Bush on matters of policy and on matters of the president's competence. But no one seriously believes that this is why Kerry ran; instead, most discussions of why he ran would focus on the nature of Kerry's political ambition, the trajectory of his political career and the logic of seeing the White House as a reasonable next step, and his sense of timing—why it made sense to run in 2004 instead of waiting for four or eight years. Many of these sorts of factors are difficult to generalize, much less to quantify, but in this closing chapter, let us look a bit at the incentives of the various participants in congressional primaries: incumbents, challengers, and the challengers' sponsors.

The Incumbent's Point of View

In one sense, the incentives for incumbents regarding primaries are quite simple. Incumbent members of Congress certainly would prefer to avoid primary competition. As we saw in chapter 4, the most common reasons for primary challenges are mistakes on the part of the opponent—ethical transgressions, inattentiveness to the district, or other failings—so it is tempting to simply state that incumbents can best avoid primary opposition by staying out of trouble. Alternately, if one wishes to say anything prescriptive or normative about the primarying phenomenon, one might simply say that if incumbents are doing their jobs, they either will not face primary opposition or will comfortably defeat any challengers who do emerge.

There is more to the issue than this, however. The most common treatments of the incentives of members of Congress, from David Mayhew's (1974) paradigm of the "single-minded seeker of reelection" to Richard Fenno's notion of concentric circles of representation, all emphasize the importance of satisfying the incumbent's primary constituency. The increased clout of national interest groups in the primaries and the rhetoric regarding primarying indicate, however, that members of Congress must now pay more attention to partisanship than before. Fenno's notion of the "primary constituency" makes it clear that he is considering only those who actually vote in the primary; this constituency is a subset of the reelection constituency (Fenno 1978, 18–24). Hibbing (1991, 130–31), among others, notes the importance of the link between constituency service and renomination or reelection. The problem with assuming that this connection is enough, however, is that primary turnout is so low. As we have seen in a number of the high-profile ideological challenges considered in this book, constituency service had little or nothing to do with the occurrence of the challenge or the success of the challenger. Fenno describes a representative's primary constituency as his or her strongest supporters. While an incumbent's strongest supporters may well turn out to vote in the primary out of loyalty, it is debatable whether primary voters, in the aggregate, are likely to be strong supporters of the incumbent, as opposed to habitual voters or voters who turn out for some other reason. Ideology matters far more to primary voters than to general election voters (Ezra 2001; Burden 2001; but see Abramowitz 2008). This would seem to indicate that the strategies incumbents cultivate to ensure general election success may not work in primaries.

The other relevant feature of Fenno's description of constituencies is that his discussion begins with geographic constituencies—the people who will actually vote for or against an incumbent. While some ideological challenges begin in the district, the fact that they are sometimes encouraged by groups outside the district indicates that even assiduous attention to the constituency is not sufficient to ward off well-funded challengers. Some have alleged that congressional elections are far more nationalized today than they were at the time Fenno and Mayhew were writing (e.g., Gelman and Huang 2008; Gelman 2011). If this claim is true, there is surely a corresponding possibility that primary elections have also effectively been nationalized.

It is clearly in the interest of incumbents to avoid primary challenges where possible. Even if there is little evidence that these challenges hurt incumbents in the general election, they at least sap resources that could otherwise be used in the general election. At a minimum, they are a nuisance that incumbents would wish to avoid. The frequency of challenges in particular districts or states, however, seems to indicate that they are an unavoidable feature of some swing districts or heterogeneous districts. Maryland, for instance, contains four different districts that have had particularly competitive primaries in the past two decades; during this time, three of these districts have been represented by moderates and have switched party hands at least once. For districts such as these, moderation may be a winning strategy for the general election, but the cost of this moderation may be a primary challenge. In other districts, long-standing divisions that are far more complicated than simple partisanship may lead to frequent challenges. As the 2010 Alaska Senate primary showed, primary challenges may epitomize intraparty divisions that go beyond simple measures of ideology.

Despite the very slight differences in the frequency of House and Senate challenges, an argument could be made that Senate primary challenges ought to be more difficult for incumbents to avoid than House primaries. Many studies of general elections have noted that part of the reason Senate general election races are more competitive than House races is that Senate constituencies are more heterogeneous than House districts (see, e.g., Krasno 1994). Other comparisons have emphasized the limited role of constituency service in Senate races. To this, one might add that the value of knocking off a Senate incumbent is much more valuable to interest groups, that the Senate is more attractive than the House to many prospective candidates, and that Senate races are already easier to nationalize than House races. One might further add that senators may experience a greater disjunction between legislative prowess and appeal to voters at home; the defeat of Senator Bob Bennett in Utah in 2010 is one example of the consequences of such a disjunction.[2] Part of the newsworthiness of Senate primary stories is certainly that there is something poignant in reading about the pleas to Tea Party activists from a veteran senator like Richard Lugar or in reading the sober commentary of someone like Bennett on today's Senate (see Green 2011) and realizing that Bennett was unable to even get his name onto the primary ballot.

One of the reasons why books such as Mayhew's and Fenno's were so important during the 1970s was that they provided a frame of reference for understanding what drove incumbents' behavior in an era of congressional politics when the average member's tenure was lengthening, the incumbency advantage was growing, partisanship was becoming a less important predictor of electoral success, and members were accruing substantial bases of individual power within Congress. Their arguments have continued to hold true even as partisanship has increased and as the power of seniority has declined in the past two decades. There is no corresponding theory of primaries, though, in part because primaries have generally been accorded so little attention. Studies such as those of Ansolabehere, Hansen, et al. (2007) demonstrate that primaries were more common in the first half of the twentieth century than they are today. These primaries occurred in an era when incumbents had very different career paths ahead of them than do today's incumbents. Members continue to have the same incentives to avoid primaries that they had in the 1970s and 1980s, but their abilities have declined as congressional careers have become more subject to national politics, partisanship, and the activities of organized interests.

What do primary challenges mean for incumbents, then? It is tempting to say that incumbents will respond by changing their style, not their substance. Hence, shortly after rumors of primary challenges began to circulate in 2010, Olympia Snowe secured the support of Tea Party-supported Maine governor Paul LePage (Travis 2011), and Orrin Hatch increased his criticism of Barack Obama (Catanese 2011). As I have shown, evidence of enduring changes in congressional voting behavior is mixed, but it does seem likely that incumbents will cater to the views of party loyalists in their primaries. This is nothing new.

The Challenger's Point of View

This book has paid more attention to primary challenges than to primary challengers. I have sought to understand why challenges happen, how they have changed, and how they affect the political system. One question, however, might linger in the mind of the reader: who are the people behind these challenges?

In the small but vital literature on political ambition, there is a general consensus on two characteristics of nonincumbent congressional candidates: first, that the stronger candidates tend to be those that wait their turn, who wait patiently to run when a seat opens up or when they are in the position to catch the incumbent at a weak moment; and second, that the strongest congressional candidates are those who have prior electoral experience. These two characteristics are the hallmark of the theory of progressive ambition, a theory that holds that strategic congressional candidates look to move up the political ladder when the moment is right.[3] But as I have noted earlier in this book, ambition theory does not explain primary challenges to incumbents particularly well.

Some studies of congressional primaries have sought to categorize challengers according to their prior political experience (see Gaddie and Bullock 2000; Pearson and Lawless 2008). In my opinion, the value of using these categories in looking at primary challenges to incumbents is limited, and therefore I have not used such measurements in my analysis. In instances where an incumbent is particularly weak, a seasoned politician may step up to run in the primary. In a few instances, politically experienced candidates may see an ideological challenge as a possible path to victory, as in the case of Bill Halter's race against Blanche Lambert Lincoln. As I have sought to show, however, successful primary challenges are rare enough that surely the majority of primary challengers must know that they are embarking on a rather hopeless endeavor.

Thus the point of the challenge is not necessarily to win. This makes a challenge a particularly risky endeavor for a strategic politician. A primary challenger can expect to make enemies not only of the incumbent but of local party leaders, who may worry that the challenge will weaken the incumbent. While some candidates for open seats or in general election bids may seek to burnish their credentials for runs for other offices (see Maisel 1986; Boatright 2004), a primary race against the incumbent seems unlikely to accomplish this. A few of the primary challengers here have gone on to win open seats (or at least their party's nomination) in subsequent elections, but this hardly seems like something a challenger can count on.

What makes primary challengers run, then? One can point to three factors. First, the promise of support and the sense of being part of a movement may appeal to some candidates. Consider the emergence of the primary challenger to Massachusetts Democrat Stephen Lynch, described in chapter 5. Groups unhappy with Lynch's vote on the health care reform bill cast around for a challenger. Lynch's eventual challenger, Mac D'Alessandro, was not the first potential candidate these groups discussed, but there is no doubt that part of the reason he ran is because he was asked. Particularly in contemporary races where ideology is a factor, the buzz generated by ideological groups about the need to challenge some incumbents serves as an invitation to some candidates.

Second, David Canon's theory of political amateurs, discussed in chapter 1, captures many of the apparent motives of the primary challengers I have discussed in this book. In an update to his 1990 book, written after the 2010 election and presumably prompted by the role of the Tea Party in that election, Canon spends some time discussing whether amateur candidates are good candidates. The evidence on this, he argues, is mixed, but he does contend that in what he calls "high-opportunity" or landslide elections, amateurism can be a positive attribute: amateurs can make the claim that they are not part of the political class, and their status as outsiders will appeal to voters who are dissatisfied with conventional politicians. If amateurs are more willing than strategic candidates to consider primary challenges, it makes sense that surges in primary challenges coincide with competitive general elections, a phenomenon I noted in chapter 3.

Third, the correlation between primary challenges and general election turnover indicates that primary challenges are more frequent in elections where there is more widespread dissatisfaction with the party in power. One common link between the elections of 1974, 1992–94, and 2006–10 is that they were marked just as much by a hostility toward incumbent politicians as by a hostility toward one particular party. In an election where incumbency can be turned into a liability, a primary challenger may stand as much of a chance of benefiting from anti-incumbent sentiment as does a general election challenger. Gaddie and Bullock (2000, 66, 74, 80) have shown that in 1994, political amateurs defeated seasoned politicians in a much larger percentage of open-seat primaries than is the norm. Likewise, the 2010 election featured several out-party primaries or open-seat primaries where veteran state legislators or other elected politicians were up-ended by political neophytes. The same logic may propel some amateurs in challenges to incumbents. In short, being an amateur is less of a liability in wave election years than it would be in others; challenging an incumbent in a primary in a wave election year may, in fact, be a more strategic move for someone with no political experience but strong ideological beliefs than would waiting for the next open-seat primary in a potentially more sedate year.[4]

What are the consequences of a primary challenge, then, for the challenger? For a very small number, the consequence is a seat in Congress. For most, however, the consequence is that they have done their duty to let the incumbent know that a segment of the incumbent's fellow partisans is dissatisfied with his or her performance. In chapter 4, I outlined the ways in which we might measure the effect of the challenge on the incumbent's legislative or electoral fortunes; perhaps the challenger cares about these matters. For the most part, however, the easiest way to look at the challenger's motivation is to view the run as an exercise in political participation. E-mails that Moveon.org sent out about Blanche Lambert Lincoln, which I described in chapter 1, exhorted members by saying, "Let's send a message." The challengers who step forward in such races may merely be people trying to send a message and may take pride in having done so. Viewed through this lens, it is hard to say anything normative about primary challenges. What is wrong with sending a message?

The Sponsors' Point of View

As I sought to demonstrate in chapter 5, many contemporary primaries are not really about the candidates. If they were, there would be more consistency in the types of incumbents who are challenged and the types of states and districts where challenges emerge, and we might expect to find higher-quality challengers. To the extent that messages are sent in primary challenges, there is one message from groups to members of Congress ("Watch out, because we will support a primary challenge") and one message from groups to the public ("We are the sort of group that will support primary challengers").

For reasons I have already outlined, contemporary interest groups are well positioned to take on the risks involved in primary challenges. Groups that do this are analogous to business firms seeking to create a brand, and such a brand can only be maintained if the group's claims about itself have a semblance of credibility. Groups support primary challengers, then, because they need to show that they can. They do not need to support a large number of challengers or even to win the primaries in which they invest, but they must make a credible showing. Their role in primaries largely accords with the scenario described by Justin Buchler in his 2011 book *Hiring and Firing Public Officials*. Buchler argues that competition is not actually required for politicians to be held accountable; instead, it is the threat of competition that matters. As long as incumbents have a clear understanding of what is expected of them by their constituents, they will perform their tasks responsibly. The problem with the heightened role of interest groups accords with Buchler's concerns about the distorting role of party soft money: if incumbents are concerned about the threat posed by organized interests, they are likely to be cross-pressured, acting with one eye toward what the voters want and another toward the demands of wealthy interest groups.

Engaging in primary competition carries risks for most interest groups, however. Just as established access-seeking groups will find it risky to antagonize incumbents or to risk weakening incumbents in the primaries to the extent that their party loses the general election, so even the groups that profess not to care about these sorts of things risk being accused of being spoilers, of presenting unfair litmus tests to incumbents, or of supporting low-quality candidates. If a group wishes to burnish its reputation by becoming involved in primaries, it is essentially trusting political neophytes and amateurs to help raise the group's profile. Consider the damage that Christine O'Donnell or Sharron Angle did to the Tea Party's reputation in 2010; any interest group that supports similar candidates runs the risk of being deemed not just a spoiler but a group that is not serious about choosing candidates who can govern. This is the case not only if the group's candidates flame out—as did Angle, O'Donnell, or Joe Miller—but also if the candidates win but ultimately prove to be ineffective in office. Even if there is little that the parties can do to penalize the sponsors of these challenges, these groups may ultimately lose credibility with the public or with their own supporters. The barriers to membership in a group like MoveOn .org may be low, but so are the barriers to exit for disgruntled contributors.

It is worth considering how all of this played out during the last well-publicized era of primarying, the elections of 1938. As many works that talk about congressional primaries have noted, Franklin Delano Roosevelt is the only president who sought to play a direct role in pursuing the primary defeats of members of Congress who he felt were standing in the way of his objectives. As recounted by Susan Dunn in *Roosevelt's Purge* (2010), Roosevelt's efforts shared some of the traits of today's primaries: they were coordinated by a so-called elimination committee comprised of Roosevelt's strategists and confidants, and they were labeled a "purge" by journalists, although not by Roosevelt. In a fashion reminiscent of his court-packing scheme, Roosevelt lost the battle—or at least the majority of primary battles into which he inserted himself—but he may well have won the war, by rendering those whom he sought to purge more amenable to his goals in subsequent years. Dunn attributes the failure of Roosevelt's purge to weak candidates, the lack of a grassroots effort, and the fact that Roosevelt's elimination committee was composed primarily of Washington insiders, men who knew little of the politics of the locales in which they sought to purge incumbents.

The parallels here are evident. What is different, however, is that Roosevelt ultimately abandoned his efforts to purge disloyal Democrats, because he was concerned about damage to his own reputation and because he recognized that the Democratic Party needed to maintain an ideologically and geographically broad coalition. Roosevelt had to govern; today's primary challenge sponsors do not. Roosevelt had a reputation to protect; the sponsors of today's challenges have reputations that are staked on their willingness to insert themselves into primaries. Today's primaries take place, of course, within political parties far more polarized than those of Roosevelt's day. Roosevelt's purge, like most earlier primary challenges, also took place in an era when the distance between Washington-based elites and the electorate was far larger than that of today. The rise of Internet-based campaigning has made it easier for elites to communicate with the public and to raise money from the public. This does not necessarily mean that there will be more primary challenges, but it does mean that we will see primary challenges that are qualitatively different today than in the past. They mean different things in an era where a challenge to a sitting representative or senator becomes a national story.

The Future of Primarying

So, in the end, do congressional primary challenges matter? They do, but they matter largely because politicians and those who follow politics have been told repeatedly that they do. They are an instance of belief becoming reality. They are not more numerous than they were in the past, but they draw more national attention and more money. There are no easily measurable effects on incumbents' voting, but it is certainly plausible that they affect the behavior of incumbents who are not ultimately challenged—that the fear of being primaried is a crucial source of party discipline. There is always the possibility that the *belief* that primary challenges are becoming more frequent and that centrist incumbents are becoming more vulnerable will prompt potential candidates to come out of the woodwork, so that we will see more challenges in the future. Perhaps this began to happen in 2010. It is hard to argue that more competition would be bad for democracy, but it is certainly a concern for advocates of bipartisanship, centrism, civility, and so forth in Congress.

It seems unlikely that the behavior of elected legislators is really a cause of increased attention to primaries. There is little evidence that the conduct of Congress has very much to do with primary challenges, and thus there is little that incumbents can do to ward off such challenges. Instead, the fault may well lie in two developments outside of Congress. One of these developments is the shift of American interest groups from seeking policy niches to seeking functional niches. In other words, the major political interest groups are increasingly seeking to define themselves according to what they can do, not what they stand for. A second development is the rise of a year-round political media, of both traditional professional media provenance and online amateur provenance. For those who wish to discuss elections all year, not just during campaign season, the whispers about who will be primaried fill the periods of time when no real campaign developments are taking place. These two trends are complementary: the media may seek political conflict in order to entertain its readers, and groups are happy to provide this conflict as a means of increasing their own visibility.

Primarying is not the only political phenomenon of the past decade in which a belief on the part of political insiders created its own reality. In the early 2000s, prompted by a spate of research showing that grassroots organizing and direct voter contact were the best means of winning elections, many groups increased their spending on personal contact with voters. Many of these groups did so not because what they had heard was true but because they simply found the story behind it convincing. Grassroots campaigning became an effective part of the 2004 and 2006 campaigns partly because effective political groups did more of it.[5] During 2010, following the Supreme Court's *Citizens United v. Federal Election Commission* ruling removing restrictions on corporate political advocacy, many corporations began to spend more on advocacy—including advocacy techniques that were legal before *Citizens United v. FEC*. As one expert on campaign finance noted,[6] there is little evidence that the court's decision had any effect on the amount of spending in 2010, but the decision may have changed the way corporations thought about politics: they now believed they had a role to play. In both of these instances, political actors' beliefs about the political landscape were more important than the actual facts about politics, and as these actors' beliefs about what was going on changed, they began to act in ways that brought about the sorts of changes they believed they had already seen.

So primaries matter not so much because they are more frequent or more likely to succeed than they were in the days when less was written about them but because they are said to matter by political elites. The public, of course, has no collective means of disregarding such claims. To return to a point made in the introduction to this book, the fact that we now have a convenient shorthand verb to describe the act of challenging an overly moderate incumbent may say more about the state of political discourse and political polarization in America today than do the details of these challenges.

What does this development hold for the future? What prescriptions might one make about primarying? It would certainly be too facile to recommend that the public, let alone elected officials, simply ignore primary challenges. The data presented in this book suggest that there is somewhat of a cycle to primary challenges; they will likely wane in elections where control of Congress is not truly at stake. We are currently in a climate where there is at least the potential for wild seat swings in the House of Representatives, and effective control of the Senate requires that the majority party hold enough seats to withstand a filibuster. In short, the dynamics of congressional elections are likely to encourage primary challenges for some time to come. There are no obvious institutional changes that will reduce the level of primarying; as I have argued in the first and third chapters of this book, it is not at all clear that changes in campaign finance law had much to do with the instances of primarying in the 2000s, so any further changes in campaign finance law will also likely not make a difference.

It is tempting to end this book with an exhortation not to worry so much about primary challenges—an ending that would indeed be odd for a book devoted to that subject. I do believe they are important, however, and the historical account of primary challenges I have presented here is intended to shed some light on them—to show that they always have been an important part of American elections—and to begin the process of developing theories about them. It seems clear to me, though, that politicians should not worry about them without thinking about the broader context that has made contemporary challenges possible. It would indeed be unfortunate if both parties were composed of the legislators Barney Frank described in the introductory chapter—a combination of extremists and more pragmatic legislators who live in fear of challenges from extremists. It is too early to tell whether the sorts of groups that sponsor primary challenges have adequate staying power or how the party organizations will adapt to the presence of these groups. It is clear, however, that primary challenges are less about incumbent members of Congress than about efforts by outside groups to promote themselves. Instead of ignoring them, then, a more appropriate conclusion would be to say that a full accounting of when primary challenges occur and how they have changed over time will remove some of the novelty from them and will help to dial down some of the incendiary and apocalyptic rhetoric that accompanies them. This book has been my contribution toward that end, but there is much more research to be done on the subject.

Notes

INTRODUCTION

1. The closest we come to a dissent from this perspective is Alan Abramowitz's claim (2010, 11, without supporting data) that primary competition is actually *decreasing*:

> Growing ideological homogeneity within both major parties has contributed to a decline in primary competition, especially in races involving incumbents. In the absence of a scandal or some other personal problem, an incumbent whose policy positions fall within the ideological mainstream of his or her party is unlikely to experience a serious primary challenge. Even in nomination contests without an incumbent, such as the 2008 Democratic and Republican presidential races, policy differences among primary candidates are generally minimal. As a result, primary voters tend to choose candidates on the basis of their personal qualities or perceived electability.

2. In the same interview, Frank had similar, although less caustic, things to say about liberal activists.

CHAPTER 1

1. The House banking scandal arose following the revelation in a 1991 auditor's report that over four hundred current and former members of the House of Representatives had been given free overdraft protection by the bank of the House of Representatives. Names of the members who had availed themselves of this protection—the equivalent, for citizens, of bouncing a check—were released in early 1992. The House Ethics Committee subsequently reprimanded twenty-two sitting members, including Bill Alexander. For good summaries of the scandal and its consequences, see Jacobson and Dimock 1994; Stewart 1994.
2. This excludes incumbents who were forced by redistricting to run against other incumbents in their primaries.
3. I provide the Worcester example because this is the e-mail I received; no doubt, residents of other cities received similarly personalized types of messages.
4. This outcome was somewhat of a surprise to observers. Some polls had shown Halter leading shortly before the primary; following the race, there was some concern that polling results had been altered to provide momentum for Halter (Catenese 2010b).

5. For analysis of the election itself, see Uslaner and Conway 1985; Jacobson and Kernell 1986. For discussion of its consequences, see, among others, Uslaner 1997, 59; Loomis 1988; Jacobson 2007.

6. Cellar's defeat is discussed at length in Hibbing 1991, 1–24.

7. Statewide polling in Massachusetts showed a substantial decrease in Kerry's popularity in Massachusetts following his presidential bid—see the 2005 Bay State Poll results, available at http://kahuna.merrimack.edu/polling/data.html.

8. I use first-dimension DW-NOMINATE scores as reference points here.

9. Not all of these states used direct primaries for all offices, and there were a few instances in which direct primary legislation was subsequently repealed.

10. This point was frequently made in news accounts of one of the few contemporary instances where White House officials (but not necessarily the president) backed a primary challenger, the 2002 New Hampshire primary between incumbent Senator Bob Smith and challenger John Sununu (see Belluck 2002). Given Smith's decision to leave the party briefly during his 2000 presidential campaign, accompanied by his harsh criticism of the party during this time, this is a somewhat unusual case. Some accounts suggest that other presidents have tacitly encouraged primary challenges as well. Woodrow Wilson has been said to have done this in 1918 (Herring 1965, 219–20), and Richard Nixon and Vice President Spiro Agnew allegedly became involved in the New York Republican primary in 1970 (Perlstein 2008, 529).

11. On changes in delegate selection, see Polsby 1983; Klinkner 1995, 160–76. On the interaction between the Federal Election Campaign Act's public financing rules, the effects of inflation on contribution and spending limits, and primary front-loading, see Campaign Finance Institute Task Force on Presidential Nomination Financing 2003.

12. One such summary is presented in Rozell, Wilcox, and Madland 2006, 113–50.

13. Data from the Center for Responsive Politics, http://www.opensecrets .org/527s/527cmtes2.php?ein=&cycle=2004&tname=America+Coming+Together, accessed December 5, 2011.

14. A Super PAC is an organization that limits its activities to independent expenditures and does not contribute money to candidates. These are groups created following the Supreme Court's *Citizens United v. Federal Election Commission* decision (558 U.S. 50 (2010)), which lifted restrictions on advocacy spending by corporations and labor unions.

15. On this subject, see also McCarty, Poole, and Rosenthal 2006, 68–70.

16. This conclusion may seem a bit confusing; assume, however, that a Democratic incumbent is within the mainstream of the party, somewhat left of center but not overly so. In an open primary, this candidate would be more likely (than in a closed one) to lose vote share to a candidate to his or her right *and* to single-issue candidates.

17. California voters approved a referendum creating such a primary system in 1996, but the results were struck down by the Supreme Court (see Fiorina 2009, 166–68). In 2010, voters approved a constitutional amendment with this purpose, to take effect in the 2012 elections.

CHAPTER 2

1. For those unfamiliar with them, *Politics in America,* published by CQ Press, and the *Almanac of American Politics* are the two standard compendia of biographies of members of Congress.

2. Candidates who raise or spend in excess of five thousand dollars are required to file with the FEC.

3. For a listing of these states, see chapter 1.

4. For a study that does draw distinctions between single-challenger and multiple-challenger primaries, see Canon 1990, 81–85.

5. Perhaps the best-known multiple-challenger race considered here is the reelection campaign of Republican Donald "Buz" Lukens in Ohio in 1990. Lukens had been accused of having sex with a minor and won only 17 percent of the vote in the primary. He faced two opponents, the district's former representative Thomas Kindness and state representative John Boehner. While Boehner and Kindness ran quite different campaigns, they clearly got into the race because of Lukens's weakness and the scandal that caused it. By most accounts, Boehner and Kindness campaigned against each other, ignoring Lukens altogether. The *Almanac* description is clear on the reason for these challengers' emergence, however, and thus the reason in this race remains the incumbent. The few other races with two or more strong challengers fit a similar pattern.

6. Incumbents who received less than 50 percent of the vote were not necessarily defeated; many such incumbents ran against multiple challengers and won the primary with less than a majority of the vote.

7. Because of the off-cycle Texas redistricting in 2004, each of these periods includes at least two incumbent-versus-incumbent primaries.

8. This may have something to do with the coding method. Cannon had been challenged in the two previous elections, but the coverage of these elections had focused on immigration issues. Inglis's categorization as the subject of an ideological challenge must also be considered in the context of three other primary challenges in the Carolinas (those against Republican representatives Walter Jones and Patrick McHenry and Senator Lindsay Graham, all of whose opponents ran single-issue campaigns).

9. This is an admittedly imprecise measure of political volatility; one might hypothesize other measures of competitiveness, although some such measures would be difficult to objectively gauge across election cycles. I did run correlations between the number of primaries and the number of incumbents held below 60 percent of the vote; the relationships are substantially the same.

10. One would expect redistricting to increase the number of primary challenges in 2012 as well.

11. Although I consider the 2004–8 cycles as a unit in table 2.2, I include 2002 as well as 2010 here, to show the consistency of the pattern in Republican challenges over this period. Removing 2002 from the sequence does not dramatically change results.

12. The lone Democrat primaried undeservingly was New York's James Delaney in 1972.

13. Canon (1990, 83) finds similarly puzzling party differences in the success of politically experienced primary challengers.

14. This is admittedly a somewhat dated set of codes; as one reviewer of an earlier draft of this book argued, the Mayhew codes do not always correspond to other measures of party strength. I use them here because they are the most commonly used state-by-state party organization measures; see, e.g., Ansolabehere, Hansen, et al. 2007.

15. This finding corresponds to McGhee et al.'s (2011) conclusions about the lack of a relationship between primary types and competition in state legislative primaries. The authors of this piece speculate that the influence of party activists and donors may outweigh the consequences of different primary systems.

16. The percentages here are taken from the number of all districts in multidistrict states in redistricting years—generally including years ending in "2," but also including districts redrawn outside the normal redistricting cycle, as in Texas in 2004 or by court order in other states. Not all of these districts were substantially redrawn, but they are at least districts that were or could have been adjusted slightly. The percentage of districts not redrawn is taken from races in nonredistricting years and from single-district states in all election years. One might develop measures of the degree to which districts are redrawn, so that those measures might be used for analysis, but I do not do that here.

17. To do this, one would have to identify all scandals, ethical transgressions, instances of incompetence, older incumbents, and so on—for the most part, an impossibly subjective task. Some studies have used House Ethics Committee inquiries to code House scandals (see, e.g., Brown 2006; Praino, Stockemer, and Moscardelli 2011) and might be of use in this regard, but the measurement is ultimately at the discretion of the challenger. A perceived scandal or ethical failure can be grounds for a challenge, regardless of whether outside observers see it that way or whether it is of sufficient importance that an inquiry by the Ethics Committee has been opened.

18. More discussion of the difference in competitiveness thresholds is available in a file of supplementary material for this book, available at the author's website, wordpress .clarku.edu/rboatright/books/congressional-primaries-2/.

19. See also Canon 1990, 83–92.

20. This Charles Wilson should not be confused with a better-known representative of the same name, Texas's Charlie Wilson.

21. Abramowitz and Segal (1992, 83) find that a majority (four of six) of the defeated incumbents from 1974 through 1990 were more liberal than their state or their successor. These defeated incumbents include Democrats and Republicans, however, so not all of these incumbents were "primaried" in the sense that I use that term here. The authors admit, however, that ideology was not actually a major issue in all of these campaigns; it is not clear which races other than the Dixon challenge are indisputably instances of primarying.

CHAPTER 3

1. This was posted during 2008 at the Working for Us PAC website, http://www .workingforuspac.org; although the website is still functional, this quote has since been removed.

2. This is somewhat problematic, in that candidates' preprimary reports, filed seven days before the primary, exclude some contributions received in the final week. Where possible, I have used the latest report by candidates that lists fundraising for the primary; in some instances, these reports were filed weeks or even months after the primary. For candidates since 2002, I have used the FEC's online database of reports; for earlier candidates, I have used the FEC's microfiches of candidate reports.

3. Some analyses of fundraising (including those of the Center for Responsive Politics and the Campaign Finance Institute) aggregate by donor. I do not do this here, partly because such an effort would lead to few differences in the data presentation and partly because I am concerned with candidates' fundraising efforts—I focus here on the

candidates' efforts (or the efforts of others on their behalf) to raise small contributions, regardless of whether the donor has previously contributed.

4. Reports of fundraising in and out of the candidate's state can, as I show later in this chapter, give some evidence of whether the candidate has a national fundraising base. They should be treated with some caution; after all, not all residents of the candidate's state will be constituents (depending on the size of the state). In addition, some donors may reside in one state, work in another, and use their business address when contributing. For instance, it is difficult to know how to treat contributions from Washington, DC, to candidates running in a district in its Maryland or Virginia suburbs (both of which are included in the data set here). As I show later in this chapter, however, the differences between candidates in terms of in-state and out-of-state fundraising are stark enough that simply using this measure provides strong evidence of changes in the nature of fundraising over the past few election cycles, despite the imperfections of the data.

5. Huffington raised over $3.5 million, $3.4 million of which was his own money, to defeat longtime incumbent Robert Lagomarsino; Campbell raised $1.45 million (none of which was his own money) to defeat scandal-tainted incumbent Ernest Konnyu. I exclude these campaigns simply because their depiction obscures general trends in the data, not because of any judgment on the nature of the campaigns themselves. They are included in other analyses in this book.

6. These figures are not adjusted for inflation. To give a sense of how the increase here looks, the $96,472 average for primary challengers in 1980 is equivalent to $153,020 in 1990 dollars and $255,295 in 2010 dollars; that is, when adjusting for inflation, the average sum raised by primary challengers in 2010 was actually less than that raised by 1980 candidates.

7. I classify this as an ideological challenge following the description of Paul's campaign in the *Almanac of American Politics* (Barone et al. 1997, 1401), but this is not a typical ideological challenge, because of Paul's background.

8. This is not a problem in the individual contributor files, so I have used 1980 and 1982 data on individual contributors where possible in this chapter. The 1980 and 1982 files do include PAC, party, and candidate contributions.

9. The reader may ask why the percentages for both types are so high for 1984. That year appears to feature a large number of poorly financed primary challengers; the percentage of funds from small donors is high, but only four of twenty candidates raised over $100,000. This could also be a glitch in FEC data; as noted, 1980 and 1982 data are problematic for several reasons; candidates may simply not have itemized contributions as diligently as they should have in 1984.

10. Because contributions of less than $200 are not listed in the FEC records, we have no way to know where these contributors reside.

11. McKinney was defeated by Majette in 2002 but reclaimed the seat in 2004, when Majette left to run, unsuccessfully, for the Senate.

12. I code Parnell's challenge as being about scandal, although Parnell is a part of the same faction of the Alaska Republican Party as Sarah Palin and Joe Miller, a faction that has criticized Alaska's long-serving Republican House and Senate members for being insufficiently conservative and too willing to pursue government funds. Parnell is now the governor of Alaska.

13. As with the case for the House data, I am concerned only with candidates who

received at least 25 percent, and I consider only voting percentages in primary elections, not in runoffs. As a result, I exclude one of the highest spending primary challengers over this period. Incumbent Georgia Senator Herman Talmadge faced three challengers in 1980; the strongest of these challengers was Zell Miller, then the state's lieutenant governor. Miller received 24 percent of the primary vote (that is, just below my cutoff). Talmadge was held to 37 percent of the primary vote and defeated Miller by a 59 to 41 percent margin in the subsequent runoff election. Miller raised $468,109 in the primary, more than any other primary challenger during the 1980s. Miller would go on to serve two terms as governor and one term as senator.

14. In instances where the percentages of individual, PAC, and candidate contributions do not sum to 100, the difference is accounted for primarily from these transfers. A very small amount of this money also is from party contributions.

15. See, e.g., http://www.opensecrets.org/bigpicture/bundles.php (accessed December 19, 2011).

CHAPTER 4

1. See Grose and Yoshinaka 2003 for a more detailed look at the consequences of party switching.

2. See, for instance, Abramowitz and Stone 1984, 56–96; Bartels 1988, 219–38; Butler 2004, 138–41, 161–64; Kamarck 2009, 137–40; Mayer 2009. As the authors of these studies would likely be the first to point out, arguments about the relationship between ideology and success in presidential primaries depend on a number of factors that are hard to translate into the context of congressional primaries, including the number of candidates running, "front-loading" and the sequencing of primaries, the role of momentum, perceptions of electability, and candidates' fundraising success. One could debate whether ideology is more or less important in the congressional context than in the presidential context. The lower visibility of congressional campaigns, however, suggests that congressional incumbents will be less likely than presidential candidates to be penalized for ideological inconsistency during their campaigns (see Burden 2001). Whereas arguments about ideology in presidential races are often based on the tenor of candidates' campaigns, I would argue that the focus here, on what candidates actually do in office to ward off future primary challengers, is more easily measurable.

3. Any challenger can accuse an incumbent of being corrupt without this actually being the case; the Welch and Hibbing data (1997; see also Praino, Stockemer, and Moscardelli 2011) use measures where there demonstrably has been some corruption or a formal investigation.

4. These assertions are, as the authors note, complicated by the fact that during the years considered in these works, the most senior incumbents were often Southern Democrats, at a time when there was little two-party competition in the South.

5. Rigorously defining district homogeneity or heterogeneity is beyond the scope of this chapter; for an example of an effort to relate such factors to electoral competition, see Ensley, Tofias, and de Marchi 2009.

6. Some readers of this chapter have argued that an incumbent in such a district might even be helped by having a primary challenger. The logic here is that a moderate Democrat who is criticized from the left might gain credibility among moderate or even

conservative voters, who may think that a candidate liberals do not care for may be conservative enough for them. This may well have happened in some races—in 36 of 65 cases, incumbents who faced ideological challengers in the primary actually increased their general election vote from the election two years before the primary to the year of the primary. For the most part, however, these increases are small, and it is impossible to know whether the increases are, in fact, due to other factors. (Recall that there were a total of 101 instances of primarying; the remaining 36 instances of primarying either took place in a dyad that included a redistricting year or featured incumbents who had served only one term.)

7. I here mean measures of polarization within the district itself, not between districts or between candidates or members of Congress.

8. I discuss these briefly later in this chapter, but I mostly exclude challenges inspired by redistricting from this analysis.

9. This is so in part because many of the redrawn majority-minority districts, particularly in 1992, were so obviously drawn to elect minority candidates that white incumbents retired or opted to run in neighboring districts. In the few cases where candidates of different races opposed each other in these redrawn districts' primaries (e.g., in several of the New York City districts in 1992), the rhetoric of the challenger tended to deal more with the new district than specifically with race.

10. I exclude incumbent-versus-incumbent primaries here.

11. Again, I exclude incumbent-versus-incumbent primaries from these calculations.

12. I do not take into account here the possibility that an incumbent challenged in one election may also have a challenger in the subsequent election. It would be interesting to consider the cumulative effects of a string of challenges, but excluding incumbents who were challenged in both elections would censor the set of cases here.

13. The numbers in this table are smaller than those in earlier tables, because I am considering not individual challenges but incumbents, some of whom were challenged more than once.

14. This is not precisely a measure of moderation. It does not measure whether representatives have staked out a position in the political center. Nor does it measure voting with reference to the district's level of partisanship, as I sought to do in the scatter plots in chapter 2. It is, however, a measure of movement. It is thus, I would argue, the simplest way to see whether incumbents have responded to being challenged.

15. Liberal groups have not developed a moniker for conservative Democrats that is as catchy as "RINOs."

16. McCain received the lowest ADA score of his career (a zero) and the lowest DW-NOMINATE score of his career in 2010.

CHAPTER 5

1. See the *Washington Post* trackers for both of these at http://www.washingtonpost.com/wp-srv/special/politics/palin_tracker/ and http://www.washingtonpost.com/wp-srv/special/politics/tea-party-endorsement-results/ (both accessed December 21, 2011).

2. Approximately $16 million of this money was left over from his 2008 presidential campaign.

3. When Arizona's other senator, John Kyl, announced that he would not seek re-election in 2012, the club instantly endorsed Flake's bid for that seat.

4. Much of the information on the Massachusetts race is drawn from my own observations; for an article summarizing some of these events, see Miller 2010.

5. http://massbeacon.com/2010/04/07/harmony-wu-will-not-challenge-congress man-lynch-in-primary (accessed December 21, 2011).

6. I do not provide direct comparisons between overall PAC size or total contributions and PAC contributions to and expenditures on behalf of primary challengers. Readers interested in making this comparison should consult the Center for Responsive Politics website or one of several books that consider PAC spending, including Sorauf 1992, Sabato 1984, and Rozell, Wilcox, and Madland 2005.

7. The data is on authorized campaign committees for individual candidates. These committees may give up to $2,000 (not inflation indexed) to other candidates and an unlimited amount of money to party committees.

8. The Bipartisan Campaign Reform Act contained a provision prohibiting interest groups from running so-called issue advocacy advertisements during the thirty days preceding a primary election and the sixty days preceding a general election unless the group was using PAC money. This provision could be said to have encouraged groups to make independent expenditures where they once might have used treasury funds to purchase such advertisements. However, by 2008, the decision in *Federal Election Commission v. Wisconsin Right to Life* (551 U.S. 449 (2007)) had largely invalidated this portion of BCRA, and it would be repealed entirely in *Citizens United v. Federal Election Commission* in 2010 (558 U.S. 50). We might thus expect independent expenditures to have been encouraged in 2004 and 2006, but this does not correspond to any marked change in figure 5.1, presented later in this section.

9. The group succeeded a less formal organization called the Political Club for Growth, organized by Richard Gilder in the 1980s. The Political Club for Growth was oriented more toward advocating for the policy views of a small number of investors convened by Gilder (for discussion, see Kraushaar 2011).

10. These ads appeared during the Iraq War, at a time when some criticized the French government for failing to support the American war effort, so the implications of the ad were more evident to viewers at the time than they may be today. The ads ran in April of 2003, one month after Representatives Robert Ney and Walter Jones succeeded in changing the name of the french fries served in the House of Representatives cafeteria to "freedom fries."

11. Kreamer did not win her race, but, interestingly, Dyson lost in the general election to Wayne Gilchrest, who had his own primary troubles in subsequent elections. Perhaps this pattern indicates something unusual about this district or about Maryland politics. Maryland is a state that, according to Mayhew's (1986) discussion of state party systems, is riven by intraparty conflict.

12. http://www.americancrossroads.org/about/ (accessed December 21, 2011).

13. http://americansforprosperity.org/about/ (accessed December 21, 2011).

14. This goes somewhat beyond the Porter analogy. Porter is concerned that firms seeking a cost advantage will become known for making cheap, low-quality products. The very thing that provides them an advantage makes their product suspect. The interest group analogy here does not quite fit, as the product, the winning of elections, seems like something that has nothing to do with Porter's "quality" concerns. A more apt anal-

ogy is to a firm that becomes known for producing a high-quality product but at lower cost than its competitors. Examples of efforts to do this are the establishment of "house brands" and instances where supermarkets, department stores, and so on license lower-cost products by established brands.

15. The Porter approach has, however, been used extensively in analyses of nongovernmental organizations. See, e.g., Rothenberg 2010.

CHAPTER 6

1. http://theseymourpundit.blogspot.com/2010/12/hoosiers-for-conservative-senate.html (accessed January 7, 2011).

2. As I noted in the introduction, Bennett was denied renomination at the Utah Republican convention in 2010; he thus is, for all practical purposes, an incumbent defeated in the primary, but the circumstances here are unusual enough that I have excluded him from the book's data analysis.

3. On political ambition, see Fowler and McClure 1989; Kazee 1994; Schlesinger 1966, 1994. On candidates' prior experience, see Gaddie and Bullock 2000; Jacobson 1989.

4. For a discussion of the role of ideology in the 2010 set of primary challenges, see King, Orlando, and Sparks 2011.

5. On this point, see Boatright et al. 2006.

6. The expert in question is former Federal Election Commissioner Trevor Potter; see Luo 2010.

Bibliography

Abramowitz, Alan I. 2008. "Don't Blame Primary Voters for Polarization." *Forum* 5 (4): article 4.

Abramowitz, Alan I. 2010. *The Disappearing Center: Engaged Citizens, Polarization, and American Democracy*. New Haven: Yale University Press.

Abramowitz, Alan I., and Jeffrey A. Segal. 1992. *Senate Elections*. Ann Arbor: University of Michigan Press.

Abramowitz, Alan I., and Walter J. Stone. 1984. *Nomination Politics: Party Activists and Presidential Choice*. Westport, CT: Praeger.

America Votes. 1972–2012. Vols. 9–29. Washington, DC: CQ Press.

Ansolabehere, Stephen, and Alan Gerber. 1996. "The Effects of Filing Fees and Petition Requirements on U.S. House Elections." *Legislative Studies Quarterly* 21 (2): 249–64.

Ansolabehere, Stephen, John Mark Hansen, Shigeo Hirano, and James M. Snyder Jr. 2006. "The Decline of Competition in U.S. Primary Elections, 1908–2004." In *The Marketplace of Democracy: Electoral Competition and American Politics*, ed. Michael P. McDonald and John Samples, 74–101. Washington, DC: Brookings Institution and Cato Institute.

Ansolabehere, Stephen, John Mark Hansen, Shigeo Hirano, and James M. Snyder Jr. 2007. "The Incumbency Advantage in U.S. Primary Elections." *Electoral Studies* 26 (3): 660–68.

Ansolabehere, Stephen, John Mark Hansen, Shigeo Hirano, and James M. Snyder Jr. 2010. "More Democracy: The Direct Primary and Competition in U.S. House Elections." *Studies in American Political Development* 24 (2): 190–205.

Ansolabehere, Stephen, James M. Snyder, and Charles Stewart. 2001. "Candidate Positioning in U.S. House Elections." *American Journal of Political Science* 45 (1): 136–59.

Aynesworth, Hugh. 1992. "Redistricting, Checks Heat Congressional Races; 2 in Arkansas Could Bounce." *Washington Times*, May 25, A1.

Bai, Matt. 2003. "Fight Club." *New York Times*, August 10.

Baker, Ross K. 1989. "The Congressional Elections." In *The Election of 1988: Reports and Interpretations*, 153–76. Chatham, NJ: Chatham House.

Barnes, James A. 2010a. "Labor's Lost Love." *National Journal*, January 30, 54.

Barnes, James A. 2010b. "They Regret Nothing." *National Journal*, June 12, 53.

Barone, Michael. 2010. "More Anti-Democrat than Anti-Incumbent." *American*, May 28. http://www.american.com/archive/2010/may/more-anti-democrat-than-anti-incumbent.

Barone, Michael, et al. 1971–2011. *Almanac of American Politics*. Various publishers.

Bartels, Larry M. 1988. *Presidential Primaries and the Dynamics of Public Choice*. Princeton: Princeton University Press.

Bedlington, Anne H., and Michael J. Malbin. 2003. "The Party as Extended Network: Members Giving to Each Other and Their Parties." In *Life after Reform: When the Bipartisan Campaign Reform Act Meets Politics*, ed. Michael J. Malbin, 121–40. Lanham, MD: Rowman and Littlefield.

Belluck, Pam. 2002. "A G.O.P. Primary Strains Party Ties and Bush Loyalties." *New York Times*, July 7.

Bernstein, Robert A. 1977. "Divisive Primaries Do Hurt: U.S. Senate Races, 1956–1972." *American Political Science Review* 71 (2): 540–45.

Berry, Jeffrey M. 1999. *The New Liberalism: The Rising Power of Citizen Groups*. Washington, DC: Brookings Institution.

Biddle, Larry. 2008. "Fund-Raising: Hitting Home Runs On and Off the Internet." In *Mousepads, Shoe Leather, and Hope: Lessons from the Howard Dean Campaign for the Future of Internet Politics*, ed. Zephyr Teachout and Thomas Streeter, 166–78. Boulder, CO: Paradigm.

Boatright, Robert G. 2004. *Expressive Politics: Issue Strategies of Congressional Challengers*. Columbus: Ohio State University Press.

Boatright, Robert G. 2007. "Situating the New 527 Groups in Interest Group Theory." *Forum* 5 (2): article 5.

Boatright, Robert G., Michael J. Malbin, Mark J. Rozell, and Clyde Wilcox. 2006. "Interest Groups and Advocacy Organizations after BCRA." In *The Election after Reform: Money, Politics, and the Bipartisan Campaign Reform Act*, ed. Michael J. Malbin, 112–40. Lanham, MD: Rowman and Littlefield.

Born, Richard. 1981. "The Influence of House Primary Election Divisiveness on General Election Margins, 1962–1976." *Journal of Politics* 43 (3): 640–61.

Boyd, Wes. 2003. Comments at the *Take Back America* Conference. Washington, DC, June 4.

Brady, David W., Kara Z. Buckley, and Douglas Rivers. 1999. "The Roots of Careerism in the U.S. House of Representatives." *Legislative Studies Quarterly* 24 (4): 489–510.

Brady, David W., Hahrie Han, and Jeremy C. Pope. 2007. "Primary Elections and Candidate Ideology: Out of Step with the Primary Electorate?" *Legislative Studies Quarterly* 32 (1): 79–105.

Brown, Lara M. 2006. "Revisiting the Character of Congress: Scandals in the U.S. House of Representatives, 1966–2002." *Journal of Political Marketing* 5 (1/2): 149–72.

Browne, William P. 1988. *Private Interests, Public Policy, and American Agriculture*. Lawrence: University Press of Kansas.

Browne, William P. 1990. "Organized Interests and Their Issue Niches: A Search for Pluralism in a Policy Domain." *Journal of Politics* 52 (3): 477–509.

Brownstein, Ronald. 2009. "The Parliamentary Challenge: Legislators Face Enveloping Pressure to Stand with Their Side on Every Major Issue." *National Journal*, September 12.

Brownstein, Ronald. 2010a. "Behind Enemy Lines." *National Journal*, April 24.

Brownstein, Ronald. 2010b. "Why Senators Are Falling." *National Journal*, September 18, 58–60.

Buchler, Justin. 2011. *Hiring and Firing Public Officials: Rethinking the Purpose of Elections*. New York: Oxford University Press.

Bullock, Charles S. 1972. "House Careerists: Changing Patterns of Longevity and Attrition." *American Political Science Review* 66 (4): 1295–1300.

Bullock, Charles S. 2012. "Evaluating Palin, the Tea Party, and DeMint Influences." In *Key States, High Stakes: Sarah Palin, the Tea Party, and the 2010 Elections,* ed. Charles S. Bullock, 211–26. Lanham, MD: Rowman and Littlefield.

Burden, Barry C. 2001. "The Polarizing Effects of Congressional Primaries." In *Congressional Primaries and the Politics of Representation,* ed. Peter F. Galderisi, Marni Ezra, and Michael Lyons, 95–115. Lanham, MD: Rowman and Littlefield.

Burden, Barry C. 2004. "Candidate Positioning in US Congressional Elections." *British Journal of Political Science* 34 (2): 211–27.

Butler, R. Lawrence. 2004. *Claiming the Mantle: How Presidential Nominations are Won and Lost before the Votes Are Cast.* Boulder, CO: Westview.

Calmes, Jackie. 2009. "Congressional Memo: GOP Senator Draws Critics in Both Parties." *New York Times,* September 22.

Campaign Finance Institute Task Force on Presidential Nomination Financing. 2003. "Participation, Competition, Engagement: How to Revive and Improve Public Funding for Presidential Nomination Politics." Washington, DC: Campaign Finance Institute. http://www.cfinst.org/pdf/federal/president/TaskForce1_Fullreport.pdf.

Canes-Wrone, Brandice, David W. Brady, and John F. Cogan. 2002. "Out of Step, Out of Office: Electoral Accountability and House Members' Voting." *American Political Science Review* 96 (1): 127–40.

Canon, David T. 1990. *Actors, Athletes, and Astronauts: Political Amateurs in the United States Congress.* Chicago: University of Chicago Press.

Canon, David T. 2010. "The Year of the Outsider: Political Amateurs in the U.S. Congress." *Forum* 8 (4): article 6.

Carson, Jamie L., Gregory Koger, Matthew J. Lebo, and Everett Young. 2010. "The Electoral Costs of Party Loyalty in Congress." *American Journal of Political Science* 54 (3): 598–616.

Catanese, David. 2010a. "Castle Won't Endorse O'Donnell." *Politico,* September 15.

Catanese, David. 2010b. "Poll Scandal Shocks Campaigns." *Politico,* July 1.

Catanese, David. 2011. "A Tale of Two Tea Party Strategies." *Politico,* February 23.

Cillizza, Chris. 2005. "Out of the Club: Why a Conservative Powerhouse Booted Its Founder." *Washington Monthly,* May.

Cillizza, Chris. 2010a. "John McCain's $21 Million Campaign." *Washington Post,* August 24.

Cillizza, Chris. 2010b. "Lindsey Graham's Vote on Elena Kagan Ensures a Primary Challenge." *Washington Post,* July 21.

Cillizza, Chris. 2010c. "Republicans Fear Echoes of Alaska in Delaware Primary." *Washington Post,* September 5.

Club for Growth. 2010. "Club for Growth PAC Launches Murkowski Refund Campaign." Washington, DC: Club for Growth. http://www.clubforgrowth.org/perm/?postID=14271.

Committee on Political Parties. American Political Science Association. 1950. "Toward a More Responsible Two Party System." *American Political Science Review* 44, supplement.

Cook, Charlie. 2010. "Twin Furies." *National Journal,* May 15, 68.

Cook, Rhodes. 2010. "2010 Primaries: Gauging Anti-Incumbent Sentiment." *Sabato's Crystal Ball,* March 4. http://www.centerforpolitics.org/crystalball/articles/frc2010030401/.

Corrado, Anthony. 2006. "Party Finance in the Wake of BCRA: An Overview." In *The Election after Reform: Money, Politics, and the Bipartisan Campaign Reform Act,* ed. Michael J. Malbin, 19–37. Lanham, MD: Rowman and Littlefield.

Curran, Tim, and Susan B. Glasser. 1992. "The House Check Flap's Most Unlikely Victims." *Roll Call,* March 19.

Currinder, Marian. 2008. *Money in the House: Campaign Funds and Congressional Party Politics.* Boulder, CO: Westview.

Downs, Anthony. 1957. *An Economic Theory of Democracy.* New York: HarperCollins.

Dunn, Susan. 2010. *Roosevelt's Purge.* Cambridge, MA: Harvard University Press.

Dwyre, Diana, and Robin Kolodny. 2006. "The Parties' Congressional Campaign Committees in 2004." In *The Election after Reform: Money, Politics, and the Bipartisan Campaign Reform Act,* ed. Michael J. Malbin, 38–56. Lanham, MD: Rowman and Littlefield.

Elliott, Justin. 2010. "Tea Party's Secret Campaign Weapon: Lavish Alaska Cruise." *Salon,* September 17.

Ensley, Michael J., Michael W. Tofias, and Scott de Marchi. 2009. "District Complexity as an Advantage in Congressional Elections." *American Journal of Political Science* 53 (4): 990–1005.

Ezra, Marni. 2001. "The Benefits and Burdens of Congressional Primary Elections." In *Congressional Primaries and the Politics of Representation,* ed. Peter F. Galderisi, Marni Ezra, and Michael Lyons, 29–47. Lanham, MD: Rowman and Littlefield.

Ezra, Marni. 2005. "Nomination Politics: Primary Laws and Party Rules." In *Guide to Political Campaigns in America,* ed. Paul S. Herrnson, 70–83. Washington, DC: CQ Press.

Fenno, Richard F. 1978. *Home Style: House Members in Their Districts.* Boston: Little, Brown.

Fiorina, Morris. 2009. *Disconnect: The Breakdown of Representation in American Politics.* Norman: University of Oklahoma Press.

Fishel, Jeff. 1973. *Party and Opposition: Congressional Challengers in American Politics.* Philadelphia: McKay.

Fisher, Marc. 2008. "Counting on Change Back from the Campaign." *Washington Post,* February 13.

Fowler, Linda L., and Robert D. McClure. 1989. *Political Ambition: Who Decides to Run for Congress.* New Haven: Yale University Press.

Francia, Peter, Paul S. Herrnson, John C. Green, Lynda W. Powell, and Clyde Wilcox. 2003. *The Financiers of Congressional Elections.* New York: Columbia University Press.

Freeman, Jo. 1986. "The Political Culture of the Democratic and Republican Parties." *Political Science Quarterly* 101 (3): 327–56.

Fritze, John. 2010. "House, Senate Candidate Pool Grows from Sour Mood." *USA Today,* June 2.

Gaddie, Ronald Keith, and Charles S. Bullock III. 2000. *Elections to Open Seats in the U.S. House: Where the Action Is.* Lanham, MD: Rowman and Littlefield.

Galderisi, Peter F., and Marni Ezra. 2001. "Congressional Primaries in Historical and Theoretical Context." In *Congressional Primaries and the Politics of Representation,* ed. Peter F. Galderisi, Marni Ezra, and Michael Lyons, 11–28. Lanham, MD: Rowman and Littlefield.

Galston, William A., and Pietro S. Nivola. 2006. "Delineating the Problem." In *Red and Blue Nation?*, ed. Pietro S. Nivola and David W. Brady, 1:1–48. Washington, DC: Brookings Institution.

Gardner, Amy. 2010. "In Delaware, GOP Comes out Swinging against Tea Party." *Washington Post,* September 13.

Gelman, Andrew. 2011. "All Politics Is Local? The Debate and the Graphs." *FiveThirtyEight, January 3.* http://fivethirtyeight.blogs.nytimes.com/2011/01/03/all-politics-is-local-the-debate-and-the-graphs/.

Gelman, Andrew, and Zaiyang Huang. 2008. "Estimating Incumbency Advantage and Its Variation, as an Example of a Before-After Study." *Journal of the American Statistical Association* 103 (482): 437–51.

Gerber, Elizabeth R., and Rebecca B. Morton. 1998. "Primary Election Systems and Representation." *Journal of Law, Economics, and Organization* 14 (2): 304–24.

Goodliffe, Jay, and David B. Magleby. 2001. "Campaign Finance in U.S. House Primary and General Elections." In *Congressional Primaries and the Politics of Representation,* ed. Peter F. Galderisi, Marni Ezra, and Michael Lyons, 62–76. Lanham, MD: Rowman and Littlefield.

Green, Joshua. 2011. "Strict Obstructionist." *Atlantic Monthly,* January/February.

Grose, Christian R., and Antoine Yoshinaka. 2003. "The Electoral Consequences of Party Switching by Incumbent Members of Congress, 1947–2000." *Legislative Studies Quarterly* 28 (1): 55–75.

Hacker, Andrew. 1965. "Does a 'Divisive' Primary Harm a Candidate's Chances?" *American Political Science Review* 59 (1): 105–10.

Hacker, Jacob S., and Paul Pierson. 2005. *Off Center: The Republican Revolution and the Erosion of American Democracy.* New Haven, CT: Yale University Press.

Hagan, Joe. 2010. "What Would a Maverick Do?" *New York,* July 11.

Hamby, Peter. 2011. "Tea Party Leaders Not Swayed by Lugar Meeting." *CNN Political Ticker,* January 5. http://politicalticker.blogs.cnn.com/2011/01/05/tea-party-leaders-not-swayed-by-lugar-meeting/.

Hamm, Keith E., and Robert E. Hogan. 2008. "Campaign Finance Laws and Candidacy Decisions in State Legislative Elections." *Political Research Quarterly* 61 (3): 458–67.

Heaney, Michael T. 2012. "Bridging the Gap between Political Parties and Interest Groups." In *Interest Group Politics,* ed. Alan Cigler and Burdett Loomis, 8th ed., 194–218. Washington, DC: CQ Press.

Helderman, Rosalind S. 2008. "Edwards's Campaign Builds Steam as She Outraises Wynn." *Washington Post,* February 3.

Hernandez, Raymond. 2002. "Pushed to the Margins, She Stood Her Ground." *New York Times,* January 6.

Herring, Pendleton. 1965. *The Politics of Democracy.* New York: W. W. Norton.

Herrnson, Paul S. 2009. "The Roles of Party Organizations, Party-Connected Committees, and Party Allies in Elections." *Journal of Politics* 71 (3): 1207–1224.

Herrnson, Paul S., and James G. Gimpel. 1995. "District Conditions and Primary Divisiveness in Congressional Elections." *Political Research Quarterly* 48 (1): 117–34.

Hibbing, John R. 1991. *Congressional Careers: Life in the U.S. House of Representatives.* Chapel Hill: University of North Carolina Press.

Hirano, Shigeo, James M. Snyder, Stephen Ansolabehere, and John Mark Hansen. 2008.

"Primary Competition and Partisan Polarization in the U.S. Senate." Unpublished manuscript, Columbia University.

Hoover, Kent. 2002. "Poll: Most Employees Still Trust Employers." *Business Journals,* July 8. http://www.bizjournals.com/extraedge/washingtonbureau/archive/2002/07/08/bureau3.html.

Horowitz, Jason. 2010. "In Alaska's Expanses, Who Looms Larger?" *Washington Post,* July 30.

Isenstadt, Alex, and Byron Tau. 2011. "Barney Frank Will Not Seek Reelection in 2012." *Politico,* November 28.

Jacobson, Gary C. 1989. "Strategic Politicians and the Dynamics of U.S. House Elections, 1946–86." *American Political Science Review* 83 (3): 773–93.

Jacobson, Gary C. 2004. *The Politics of Congressional Elections.* 6th ed. New York: Longman.

Jacobson, Gary C. 2006. "Why Other Sources of Polarization Matter More." In *Red and Blue Nation?,* ed. Pietro S. Nivola and David W. Brady, 1:284–89. Washington, DC: Brookings Institution.

Jacobson, Gary C. 2007. "Explaining the Ideological Polarization of the Congressional Parties since the 1970s." In *Party, Process, and Political Change in Congress,* ed. David W. Brady and Matthew D. McCubbins, 2:91–101. Stanford, CA: Stanford University Press.

Jacobson, Gary C., and Michael Dimock. 1994. "Checking Out: The Effects of Bank Overdrafts on the 1992 House Elections." *American Journal of Political Science* 38 (3): 601–24.

Jacobson, Gary C., and Samuel Kernell. 1986. "Interpreting the 1974 Congressional Election." *American Political Science Review* 80 (3): 591–93.

Johnson, Donald Bruce, and James R. Gibson. 1974. "The Divisive Primary Revisited: Party Activists in Iowa." *American Political Science Review* 68 (1): 67–77.

Kamarck, Elaine C. 2009. *Primary Politics: How Presidential Candidates Have Shaped the Modern Nominating System.* Washington, DC: Brookings Institution.

Kanthak, Kristin, and Rebecca Morton. 2001. "The Effects of Electoral Rules on Congressional Primaries." In *Congressional Primaries and the Politics of Representation,* ed. Peter F. Galderisi, Marni Ezra, and Michael Lyons, 116–31. Lanham, MD: Rowman and Littlefield.

Karol, David. 2009. *Party Position Change in American Politics.* New York: Cambridge University Press.

Katz, Richard S., and Peter Mair. 1995. "Changing Models of Party Organization and Party Democracy: The Emergence of the Cartel Party." *Party Politics* 1 (1): 5–28.

Kazee, Thomas A., ed. 1994. *Who Runs for Congress? Ambition, Context, and Candidate Emergence.* Washington, DC: CQ Press.

Kenney, Patrick J. 1988. "Sorting Out the Effects of Primary Divisiveness in Congressional and Senatorial Elections." *Western Political Quarterly* 41 (4): 765–777.

Kenney, Patrick J., and Tom W. Rice. 1984. "The Effect of Primary Divisiveness in Gubernatorial and Senatorial Elections." *Journal of Politics* 46 (3): 904–15.

Kenney, Patrick J., and Tom W. Rice. 1987. "The Relationship between Divisive Primaries and General Election Outcomes." *American Journal of Political Science* 31 (1): 31–44.

Key, V. O. 1949. *Southern Politics in State and Nation.* Knoxville: University of Tennessee Press.

Key, V. O. 1958. *Politics, Parties, and Pressure Groups*. New York: Thomas Y. Crowell.

Kiely, Kathy. 2010. "Conservative Insurgents Shake Up Utah Incumbent." *USA Today*, May 6.

King, Aaron, Frank J. Orlando, and David B. Sparks. 2011. "Ideological Extremity and Primary Success: A Social Networks Approach." Paper presented at the Annual Meeting of the Midwest Political Science Association, Chicago.

King, David. 2001. "Congress, Polarization, and Fidelity to the Median Voter." Unpublished manuscript, Kennedy School of Government, Harvard University.

Klinkner, Philip A. 1995. *The Losing Parties: Out-Party National Committees, 1956–1993*. New Haven: Yale University Press.

Koger, Gregory, Seth Masket, and Hans Noel. 2009. "Partisan Webs: Information Exchange and Party Networks." *British Journal of Political Science* 39 (3): 633–53.

Krasno, Jonathan S. 1994. *Challengers, Competition, and Reelection: Comparing Senate and House Elections*. New Haven: Yale University Press.

Kraushaar, Josh. 2008. "Party Activists Bring Down Maryland Duo." *Politico*, February 14.

Kraushaar, Josh. 2011. "Growth Industry." *National Journal*, September 17, 28–33.

Laffey, Steve. 2007. *Primary Mistake: How the Washington Republican Establishment Lost Everything in 2006 (and Sabotaged My Senatorial Campaign)*. New York: Penguin.

La Raja, Raymond J. 2008. *Small Change: Money, Political Parties, and Campaign Finance Reform*. Ann Arbor: University of Michigan Press.

Layzell, Anne C., and L. Marvin Overby. 2004. "Biding Their Time in the Illinois 9th." In *Who Runs for Congress? Ambition, Context, and Candidate Emergence*, ed. Thomas A. Kazee, 150–64. Washington, DC: CQ Press.

Lebo, Matthew J., Adam J. McGlynn, and Gregory Koger. 2007. "Strategic Party Government: Party Influence in Congress, 1789–2000." *American Journal of Political Science* 51 (3): 464–81.

Leibovich, Mark. 2010. "Lincoln in Lonely Race in Arkansas." *New York Times*, October 16.

Levendusky, Mathew. 2009. *The Partisan Sort: How Liberals Became Democrats and Conservatives Became Republicans*. Chicago: University of Chicago Press.

Loomis, Burdett. 1988. *The New American Politician: Ambition, Entrepreneurship, and the Changing Face of Political Life*. New York: Basic Books.

Luo, Michael. 2010. "Money Talks Louder Than Ever in Midterms." *New York Times*, October 7.

Maisel, L. Sandy. 1986. *From Obscurity to Oblivion: Running in the Congressional Primary*. Knoxville: University of Tennessee Press.

Maisel, L. Sandy, Cary T. Gibson, and Elizabeth J. Ivry. 1998. "The Continuing Importance of the Rules of the Game: Subpresidential Nominations in 1994 and 1996." In *The Parties Respond*, ed. L. Sandy Maisel, 3rd ed., 147–69. Boulder, CO: Westview.

Mann, Thomas. 2006. "Polarizing the House of Representatives: How Much Does Gerrymandering Matter?" In *Red and Blue Nation?*, ed. Pietro S. Nivola and David W. Brady, 1:263–83. Washington, DC: Brookings Institution.

Masket, Seth E. 2009. *No Middle Ground: How Informal Party Organizations Control Nominations and Polarize Legislatures*. Ann Arbor: University of Michigan Press.

Mayer, William G. 2009. "Superdelegates: Reforming the Reforms Revisited." In *Reforming the Presidential Nomination Process*, ed. Steven S. Smith and Melanie J. Springer, 85–108. Washington, DC: Brookings Institution.

Mayhew, David. 1974. *Congress: The Electoral Connection.* New Haven: Yale University Press.

Mayhew, David. 1986. *Placing Parties in American Politics.* Princeton: Princeton University Press.

McCarty, Nolan, Keith T. Poole, and Howard Rosenthal. 2006. *Polarized America: The Dance of Ideology and Unequal Riches.* Cambridge, MA: MIT Press.

McDonald, Michael. 2006. "Redistricting and Competitive Districts." In *The Marketplace of Democracy: Electoral Competition and American Politics,* ed. Michael P. McDonald and John Samples, 222–44. Washington, DC: Brookings Institution and Cato Institute.

McGhee, Eric, Seth Masket, Boris Shor, Steve Rogers, and Nolan McCarty. 2011. "A Primary Cause of Partisanship? Nomination Systems and Legislator Ideology." Unpublished manuscript, Princeton University.

Menefee-Libey, David. 2000. *The Triumph of Campaign-Centered Politics.* New York: Chatham House.

Merriam, Charles E. 1908. *Primary Elections: A Study of the History and Tendencies of Primary Election Legislation.* Chicago: University of Chicago Press.

Merriam, Charles E., and Louise Overacker. 1928. *Primary Elections.* Chicago: University of Chicago Press.

Miller, Sean. 2010. "Rep. Lynch Survives; Challenged on Health Care 'No' Vote." *Hill,* September 14.

Moore, Stephen. 2003. "Franco-Republicans? Voinovich and Snowe Act More Like Daschle Than Like Reagan." *National Review Online,* April 22. http://www.national review.com/articles/206669/franco-republicans/stephen-moore.

MoveOn.org. 2008. "People-Powered Action: MoveOn.org Political Action Post-Election Report." Washington, DC: MoveOn.org. http://s3.moveon.org/pdfs/moveon_postelectionreport_ah14.pdf.

Naymik, Mark. 2008. "Kucinich Drops Presidential Bid." *Plain Dealer,* January 24.

Nichols, John. 2006. "No to Pro-War Democrats." *Nation,* May 8.

Noah, Timothy. 2004. "Who's Afraid of the Club for Growth?: The Most Fearsome 527 Has a Bark Much Worse Than Its Bite." *Slate,* November 16.

Olson, Bradley, and Matthew Hay Brown. 2008. "Incumbents Wynn, Gilchrest Ousted: Change-Minded Electorate Sides with Challengers in Congressional Districts." *Baltimore Sun,* February 13.

Olson, Mancur. 1971. *The Logic of Collective Action.* Cambridge, MA: Harvard University Press.

Patterson, James T. 1967. *Congressional Conservatism and the New Deal.* Lexington: University of Kentucky Press.

Pearson, Kathryn, and Jennifer L. Lawless. 2008. "Primary Competition and Polarization in the U.S. House of Representatives." Paper presented at the Annual Meeting of the Midwest Political Science Association, Chicago.

Perlstein, Rick. 2008. *Nixonland.* New York: Scribner.

Peters, John G., and Susan Welch. 1980. "The Effects of Charges of Corruption on Voting Behavior in Congressional Elections." *American Political Science Review* 74 (3): 697–708.

Pierson, James E., and Terry B. Smith. 1975. "Primary Divisiveness and General Election Success: A Re-Examination." *Journal of Politics* 37 (2): 555–62.

Politics in America. 1979–2011. Washington, DC: CQ Press.

Polsby, Nelson W. 1983. *Consequences of Party Reform.* New York: Oxford University Press.

Porter, Michael E. 1985. *Competitive Advantage.* New York: Free Press.

Praino, Rodrigo, Daniel Stockemer, and Vincent G. Moscardelli. 2011. "The Lingering Effect of Scandal in Congressional Elections: Incumbents, Challengers, and Voters." Paper presented at the Annual Meeting of the Northeastern Political Science Association, Philadelphia.

Raju, Manu. 2010. "Shaken Senators Start Prep for 2012." *Politico,* November 18.

Ranney, Austin. 1975. *Curing the Mischiefs of Faction: Party Reform in America.* Berkeley: University of California Press.

Reichley, James A. 2000. *The Life of the Parties.* Lanham, MD: Rowman and Littlefield.

Rothenberg, Lawrence. 2010. "Environmental Groups: What Political Science Has to Offer." In *Good Cop/Bad Cop: Environmental NGOs and Their Strategies Toward Business,* ed. Thomas P. Lyon. Washington, DC: Resources for the Future.

Rozell, Mark J., Clyde Wilcox, and David Madland. 2005. *Interest Groups in American Campaigns: The New Face of Electioneering.* 2nd ed. Washington, DC: CQ Press.

Ruben, Adam. 2008. "Victory! Progressives Defeat a Right-Wing Dem in Congress." E-mail message to MoveOn.org membership, February 13.

Ruben, Adam. 2010. "Bill Halter vs. Blanche Lincoln." E-mail message to MoveOn.org membership, March 30.

Rucker, Philip, and Peter Slevin. 2010. "Despite Arkansas Loss, Progressives Say Lincoln Runoff Sent Warning to Incumbent Democrats." *Washington Post,* June 9.

Rutenberg, Jim. 2009. "Bloggers Create PAC to Recruit Liberal Candidates." *New York Times,* February 26.

Sabato, Larry J. 1984. *PAC Power: Inside the World of Political Action Committees.* New York: W. W. Norton.

Salisbury, Robert. 1969. "An Exchange Theory of Interest Groups." *Midwest Journal of Political Science* 13 (1): 1–32.

Schantz, Harvey. 1980. "Contested and Uncontested Primaries for the U.S. House." *Legislative Studies Quarterly* 5 (4): 545–62.

Schlesinger, Joseph A. 1966. *Ambition and Politics: Political Careers in the United States.* Chicago: Rand McNally.

Schlesinger, Joseph A. 1994. *Political Parties and the Winning of Office.* Ann Arbor: University of Michigan Press.

Sherrard, Michael. 2010. "Important Update from Little Rock." E-mail message to MoveOn.org membership, May 19.

Simon, Adam. 2002. *The Winning Message: Candidate Behavior, Campaign Discourse, and Democracy.* New York: Cambridge University Press.

Skinner, Richard, Seth Masket, and David Dulio. 2012. "527 Committees and the Political Party Network." *American Politics Research* 40 (1): 60–84.

Sobieraj, Sarah, and Jeffrey M. Berry. 2011. "From Incivility to Outrage: Political Discourse in Blogs, Talk Radio, and Cable News." *Political Communication* 28 (1): 19–41.

Sorauf, Frank. 1992. *Inside Campaign Finance: Myths and Realities.* New Haven: Yale University Press.

Steen, Jennifer A. 2006. *Self-Financed Candidates in Congressional Elections.* Ann Arbor: University of Michigan Press.

Steinhauer, Jennifer. 2010. "McCain Is Now Running Just to Stay in Place." *New York Times,* June 21.

Stewart, Charles. 1994. "Let's Go Fly a Kite: Correlates of Involvement in the House Bank Scandal." *Legislative Studies Quarterly* 19 (4): 521–35.

Stone, Walter J., and L. Sandy Maisel. 2003. "The Not-So Simple Calculus of Winning: Potential U.S. House Candidates' Nomination and General Election Chances." *Journal of Politics* 65 (4): 951–77.

Sulkin, Tracy. 2011. *The Legislative Legacy of Congressional Campaigns.* New York: Cambridge University Press.

Taylor, Andrew J., and Robert G. Boatright. 2005. "Can I Win Next Time? Strategic Repeat Challengers in House Races." *Political Research Quarterly* 58 (4): 609–17.

Teachout, Zephyr. 2006. "Powering Up Internet Campaigns." In *Get This Party Started: How Progressives Can Fight Back and Win,* ed. Matthew R. Kerbel, 151–64. Lanham, MD: Rowman and Littlefield.

Theriault, Sean. 2006. "Party Polarization in the U.S. Congress: Member Replacement and Member Adaptation." *Party Politics* 12 (2): 483–503.

Theriault, Sean. 2008. *Party Polarization in Congress.* New York: Cambridge University Press.

Toeplitz, Shira. 2010. "GOP Senators See Threat on Right." *Politico,* November 10.

Travis, Shannon. 2011. "Tea Party Activist Calls Sen. Snowe 'Almost as Bad as Obama,' Announces Primary Challenge." *CNN Political Ticker,* February 11. http://political ticker.blogs.cnn.com/2011/02/11/tea-party-activist-calls-sen-snowe-almost-as-bad -as-obama-announces-primary-challenge/.

Tumulty, Karen, and Philip Rucker. 2010. "How Joe Miller Caught Lisa Murkowski by Surprise." *Washington Post,* August 25.

Turner, Julius. 1953. "Primary Elections as the Alternative to Party Competition in 'Safe' Districts." *Journal of Politics* 15 (2): 197–210.

Uslaner, Eric. 1997. *The Decline of Comity in Congress.* Ann Arbor: University of Michigan Press.

Uslaner, Eric, and M. Margaret Conway. 1985. "The Responsible Electorate: Watergate, the Economy, and Vote Choice in 1974." *American Political Science Review* 79 (3): 788–803.

Viser, Matt. 2010. "Brown Answers McCain's Call for Help." *Boston Globe,* March 5.

Von Drehle, David. 2010. "Stuck in the Middle: Can Blanche Lincoln Survive a Democratic Challenge?" *Time,* May 14.

Walker, Jack L. 1983. "The Origins and Maintenance of Interest Groups in the United States." *American Political Science Review* 77 (2): 390–406.

Ware, Alan. 2002. *The American Direct Primary: Party Institutionalization and Transformation in the North.* New York: Cambridge University Press.

Weissman, Stephen R., and Ruth Hassan. 2006. "527 Groups and BCRA." In *The Election after Reform: Money, Politics, and the Bipartisan Campaign Reform Act,* ed. Michael J. Malbin, 79–111. Lanham, MD: Rowman and Littlefield.

Weissman Stephen R., and Kara D. Ryan. 2006. *Nonprofit Interest Groups' Election Activities and Federal Campaign Finance Policy.* Washington, DC: Campaign Finance Institute.

Weissman, Stephen R., and Kara D. Ryan. 2007. *Soft Money in the 2006 Election and the Outlook for 2008: The Changing Nonprofits Landscape.* Washington, DC: Campaign Finance Institute.

Welch, Susan, and John R. Hibbing. 1997. "The Effects of Charges of Corruption on Vot-ing Behavior in Congressional Elections, 1982–1990." *Journal of Politics* 59 (1): 226–39.

Wilson, James Q. 1973. *Political Organizations.* New York: Basic Books.

Wright, John R. 1996. *Interest Groups and Congress: Lobbying, Contributions, and Influ-ence.* New York: MacMillan.

Yardley, William. 2010. "Feud with Palin in Background of Alaska Upset." *New York Times,* September 1.

Zeleny, Jeff, and Carl Hulse. 2010. "Specter Defeat Signals a Wave against Incumbents." *New York Times,* May 18.

Index

Note: In this index, an italic *t* following a page number denotes a table; an italic *f* following a page number denotes a figure.

Printed and bound by CPI Group (UK) Ltd, Croydon, CR0 4YY

09/06/2025

14685670-0003